How to Be a Better Birder

How to Be a Better Birder

Derek Lovitch

Princeton University Press
Princeton & Oxford

Copyright © 2012 by Princeton University Press

Published by Princeton University Press, 41 William Street, Princeton, New Jersey 08540

In the United Kingdom: Princeton University Press, 6 Oxford Street, Woodstock, Oxfordshire OX20 1TW

press.princeton.edu

All Rights Reserved

ISBN 978-0-691-14448-1

LIBRARY OF CONGRESS CATALOGING-IN-PUBLICATION DATA
Lovitch, Derek, 1977–
How to be a better birder / Derek Lovitch.
    p. cm.
  Includes bibliographical references and index.
    ISBN 978-0-691-14448-1 (cloth : acid-free paper) 1. Bird watching. I. Title.
  QL677.5.L68 2012
  598.07234–dc23   2011037128

British Library Cataloging-in-Publication Data is available

This book has been composed in Garamond Pro

Printed on acid-free paper.∞

Printed in the United States of America

10 9 8 7 6 5 4 3 2 1

To my Father, Alan,
whose fostering of my crazy interest in birds while I was growing up
helped lead to my lifelong passion for birds, birding, and ultimately,
this book.

Contents

Acknowledgments

First and foremost, I want to thank my wife, Jeannette, for everything that she does. She's not only my primary editor, but she's also the sounding board for all of my ideas, concerns, and questions. I am also much appreciative of all of the extra hours she put in at the store in order to allow me the time to complete this and all other projects.

Helpful and often inspiring discussions with many individuals regarding ideas about this book and the specifics therein were of the utmost help. Special thanks go to Cameron Cox, Richard Crossley, Ed Hess, Steve Howell, John Jensenius, Jr., David LaPuma, Paul Lehman, Dan Nickerson, Michael O'Brien, Evan Obercian, Will Russell, and many others for the thought-provoking discussions and encouragement while working on this project. I thank Luke Seitz for assisting with the illustrations and Richard for sorting through his photo library in the midst of his own book tour.

Individual chapters were greatly augmented by comments from Pete Bacinski, Scott Barnes, Cameron Cox, Rich Eakin, David LaPuma, Paul Lehman, Ian McLaren, Eric Mills, and Michael O'Brien. Without their feedback, the substance and utility of each chapter would not have been where I—or you, for that matter—wanted or needed it to be. They also offered plenty of editorial comments that helped me avoid embarrassing errors. Many others answered questions from one to many, offered inputs and ideas, sifted through their photo libraries, or otherwise contributed in some way, shape, or form to the project, for which I am also most grateful: Moez Ali, Ken Behrens, Louis Bevier, Gavin Bieber, Nick Bonomo, Chris Borg, Lysle Brinker, Jim Danzenbaker, Andrew Farnsworth, Rich Eakin, Mike Greenfelder, Steve Kolbe, Tony Leukering, Bill Maynard, Brad Murphy, Dan Nickerson, Forrest Rowland, Rick Radis, Luke Seitz, Deborah Shearwater, Jeremiah Trimble, Rick Wright, and Louise

Zemaitas. (I hope I included everyone!) Of course, every birder I have birded with, learned from, worked for and so on, throughout my birding life have influenced me and for that I am most grateful and forever indebted to you all.

And last, but certainly not least, a huge thank you to Robert Kirk and everyone at Princeton University Press for believing in the concept and helping guide me to its fruition.

How to Be a Better Birder

Introduction

It's early November here in Maine, and I'm in sitting in a coffee shop with my laptop open, busily typing away at a draft of this book. Although the overall bulk of autumn bird migration is winding down, we're entering one of my favorite times of year: rarity season. Therefore, I need to know what the weather is like—will these southwest winds that are so good at guiding vagrants our way continue, or will this front that is approaching from the west produce a fallout of late-season migrants? Also, I want to make sure that if a "good" bird is located, I find out about it as soon as possible; there's no point in writing a book on birding if I'm not able to get out and go birding, especially when my state list requires it. So there are a cluster of minimized windows at the bottom of my screen—weather forecast, email, and the listserve archives. And the cell phone is nearby.

The next weekend will be our fifth annual Rarity Roundup. On the first or second Sunday in November, a group of us get together to scour the southern Maine coast for rarities. Now I readily admit that I stole this idea from the great birders down in the mid–Atlantic Coast, but for each of the past five years (and counting), I've organized a roundup here in Maine.

Granted, many of the people simply participate as an excuse to get together at the end of the day to enjoy good food, great beer, and engaging conversation as we compile our cumulative list and wait in anticipation to hear what we might have to chase first thing the next morning. But the impetus for the event is that Maine is a relatively large state, with a myriad of peninsulas, islands, and other places where birds may concentrate, but very, very few birders to check them all.

For at least one Sunday, at the peak of the rarity season, a dozen or more of us get together to scour the south coast in the hopes of finding the next mega-rarity, or simply, "mega." Of course, we can't check every nook and cranny, even in this more limited geographic area, so we focus on the best places. Using geography and habitat to refine our effort to thoroughly check the places that are most likely to produce good birds, we head out to improve the collective Rarity Roundup list, and perhaps find that mega that will cause each of us to abandon our routes and rendezvous at some local hotspot to exchange high fives over someone's great discovery (such as the first state record Gray Kingbird discovered during Rarity Roundup VII in 2010).

Whereas the Christmas Bird Count attempts to count every bird in every section of the circle, a Rarity Roundup attempts to find only the cream of the crop. We all but snub our nose at the usual cast of characters as we look for the golden needle in a haystack. It's not a practice that I usually preach, but for one full day out of the birding year, it's all about finding the buried treasure.

But why November? And why along the coast? And where do we go? The simple answers will be found in chapters 2, 3, and 4. A combination of weather, geography, and habitat variables focuses our search for the good birds. Although these are some of the topics that we apply to finding rare birds on the Rarity Roundup, we can also apply many of them to our daily birding—for both the rare and the common—throughout the year.

In nothing more than coincidence, seven months have passed, and I'm putting the final touches on the first draft in early June—at the same coffee shop, looking out the same window. It's now spring rarity season (or, really, early-summer rarity season), so once again I am left to daydream about what's out there. Well, let's find out! And by applying a few new tools, we can make that search more efficient and more effective, and at the same time, help to make ourselves better birders.

Although the title *How to Be a Better Birder* seems fairly straightforward, I have decided to not explicitly attempt to offer a definition of it, because it means something a little different for just about everyone. For some, it's about building a bigger list. For others, it's simply about identifying more birds more of the time. And yet others may feel that becoming better birders will allow them to share the joy of this hobby/sport/passion/sickness with others. I don't like labels, whether it's "beginner," "intermediate," or "advanced." No matter what level of birder you are, or think you are, there is always more to learn—and more challenges to confront. That being said, I will make a few assumptions that by picking up a book entitled *How to be a Better Birder*, you already consider yourself a birder. Therefore, you have already acquired a basic knowledge of many birding terms, from feather groups to the most frequently used vernacular and birding slang. I'm hoping you have already devoured the myriad of resources targeted at "beginning" birders and are now ready to take the next step.

So while I hesitate to define just what being a "better birder" really is, my goal with this book is to give some helpful hints, spur additional study, and simply provide some information that we can apply to our own birding in pursuit of becoming better birders, whatever that means to you. You'll find some chapters more inspiring than others, and you'll want to learn more about some topics. But, I do believe that birders of all levels can use these tools to make themselves better birders.

By no means are the topics presented here the only issues related to becoming a better birder, and by no means are any of these an exhaustive treatment of the topic. They are most definitely not the end-all, say-all definitive treatments of any of these topics. Instead, my goal is to simply introduce you to other ways of thinking, other methodologies, and other disciplines that we can use to apply to our own growth as a birder. Hopefully, some of these topics will excite you enough to dig deeper, beginning with some of the resources that I have outlined in each chapter.

Many of the chapters are peppered with personal opinions, personal preferred methodologies, and so on. Your own interests and opinions and the opinions of other birders will probably vary considerably, but the tools can be applied to suit your needs. There's an explosion of new technologies and new advances in the collective knowledge bank and toolbox of the birding community, and I want you to be part of this excitement.

Advanced Field Identification

The "Whole Bird and More" Approach

Before your eyes glaze over in apprehension of a long discourse on the finer points of the lower mandible color of *Empidonax* flycatchers, let me assure you, I'm not going to go there! The goal of this chapter will not be to rehash what other, much more qualified authors have written—and written much better than I could have. Instead, I want to suggest how we can use specific resources and techniques to further refine and develop our skills and how we can modify our approach and our mindsets to become better birders.

Quite possibly the biggest step to becoming a better birder is learning how to identify more birds. No one can identify *every* bird *at all* times—at least if you're honest!—but we do want to strive to identify *most* of the birds *most* of the time. And I don't mean only when the bird is sitting still for 15 minutes on a feeder 25 feet from your window. I'm also talking about identifying that flitting warbler in a tangle, the sparrow flushing from the grass, that soaring raptor spotted out of the corner of your eye while you're driving 75 miles an hour on the interstate. Yes, it can be done, and yes, *you* can do it!

How? Practice. Practice. And then: more practice. And a little good old fashioned studying liberally sprinkled in between.

Here's an example. A couple of years ago, my wife and I visited the beautiful country of Norway. During the course of our birding, we ran into a number of Norwegian birders and befriended a few new colleagues. In the course of our conversations, we learned of a somewhat controversial American Black Duck record from the country. It's quite the rarity there, as you might imagine, so it received much attention and much scrutiny. A few people thought that at least one of the recent birds suggested a Mallard × American Black Duck hybrid (fig. 1-1), something that is becoming increasingly common as Mallards (fig. 1-2) increase their range and number within the breeding range of black ducks in Eastern North America.

Being from Maine, where black ducks are one of the most common species of waterfowl, I was asked a few simple questions. One was, Can otherwise "pure-looking" black ducks ever show a hint of green in the head?" It seemed like a simple question, but despite encountering American Black

FIGURE 1-1.
The green stripe through the top of the head (which can be hard to see in poor light), which is reminiscent of a drake American Wigeon, coupled with the orangey-rust chest and white-bordered speculum are classic signs of a male American Black Duck × Mallard hybrid. But what about females? Backcrosses? What is the extent of green on the head, gray on the back, or white along the speculum in these individuals? When was the last time you looked close enough at your most common birds to really understand their variation? *American Black Duck × Mallard hybrid, Westbrook, Maine, 3/11* © Jeannette Lovitch.

Ducks (fig. 1-3) on the majority of my birding outings throughout the year in Maine, I couldn't completely answer it.

I was also asked to comment on two recent black duck records, and when I returned home, I received a series of photos. A few of the questions that had arisen during the Norwegians' review of these records included not only the one about the green flecking but also one on how extensive the dark in the underwings should be. Simple enough, but to be honest, I couldn't answer them. Although I have *seen* countless black ducks in Eastern North America, I couldn't recall when the last time was that I had really *looked* at an American Black Duck! When was the last time I scrutinized a flock of black ducks to see how many birds showed some, if any, trace of green in the head?

As is often the case with vagrants, the level of scrutiny they receive far surpasses the time birders spend studying the birds where they're "supposed" to be. Clearly, I had plenty to learn about American Black Ducks, so a few days later, my wife and I spent some hours at a few local urban parks. (Urban parks, with their breadfed, obliging ducks, are superb locations for studying common species up close—although you do need to be careful about the genetic influence of domestic species, feral sorts, and other "trash" birds.)

We photographed as many black ducks as we could and looked at every one as carefully as possible. I probably learned more about black ducks that day than I had in my previous 20-plus years of birding! (A good birder never stops learning.) I returned home, composed an extensive blog entry analyzing the photos and describing my observations, and consulted a number of references and colleagues. All of this was the result of a casual inquiry from a new acquaintance about a bird I should have known as well as the back of my hand. Lesson learned: it is important to closely study our most common birds, because such detailed and careful attention will help when such questions arise. Before you endeavor to become a better birder, you really should get to know your most common birds very well. Start with your backyard feeder birds, then the denizens of your local woodlot, and keep moving out—and growing—from there. Then, when you are faced with a novel species, you can reference your familiar friends as a basis for beginning the project of identification. "Size of a robin," "shape of a

Figure 1-2.
Mallards are common and ubiquitous, but they still have plenty to teach us. *Mallard, Westbrook, Maine, 3/11* © Jeannette Lovitch.

Figure 1-3.
How often do you look at, and I mean really *look* at, the most common species in your area? Do you know how often you see green flecks in the head of otherwise pure-looking American Black Ducks? *American Black Duck, South Portland, Maine, 9/08* © Jeannette Lovitch.

chickadee," and so on are very useful references as long as you actually know what the size of a robin or shape of a chickadee is.

But before we dive into identification minutia and in-depth study, many of us are still struggling with identifying more birds, more of the time. And despite my earlier claim that we do not always look hard enough at birds, in many cases, I think we may actually be looking *too* hard at birds—at least for basic identification of most species—most of the time. Central breast spots on sparrows? Counting tail bands on flying raptors? Tertial fringes on juvenile peeps? Do we really need to look for the color of individual feathers in the crown of an American Black Duck in order to identify it in most cases?

Some of these "field marks" may, indeed, be very important when it comes to identifying rarities or unfamiliar species, as with such instances as the Norwegian American Black Duck quandry. However, most of the time, we don't need to look so closely—so specifically—at such obscure details. In fact, I think we're spending too much time looking too hard at birds when a more holistic approach will identify a greater percentage of our observations in much less time—and then save the detailed analysis for when we have the time, opportunity, and interest to do so.

So what do we do to correct this problem? Well, how about going birding! No book will substitute for time in the field—lots of time in the field. Looking, listening, studying, and watching. First, don't just identify birds, *watch* them. *Look* at them. I firmly believe that we need to put the "watching" back in "birdwatching." Too often, too many of us see a bird, identify it, list it, and move on. But each and every bird has a lot more to offer. If you take nothing else from this chapter, remember this—you need to watch birds! How does the bird move? What is it shaped like? What is it doing? What is it feeding on? Where is it feeding? Size? Shape? In other words, "What does it look like?" is only one question that should be answered.

Classic birding, which uses the field mark system, focuses almost exclusively on appearance: wingbars, eye rings, color patterns, and so on. However, the "holistic"—or as I prefer, "the whole bird and more"—approach takes *everything* into consideration. It goes beyond GISS (general impression of size and shape, or gestalt) and combines that with field marks and the how, what, where, and when's. Look at the whole bird, what it's doing, and where it is doing it. This is what I mean by the "whole bird and more."

I often hear birders argue that the field mark system is "easier." While I'll respectfully disagree, I will certainly agree that it is the method we are most used to seeing and hearing about (until recently), and what we are used to is what we often consider easier just because it is more familiar. But the "whole bird and more" concept is not about forgetting everything you know and learning something new. It is, however, about applying something we already know to our bird identification.

Don't believe me? Well, how do you identify your significant other? Do you need to see your spouse's eye color to identify her or him? No, then why do you need to see the red eye of a Red-eyed Vireo? Hair color? Then why do you need to see the black cap of a Black-capped Chickadee to identify it?

Each and every day we recognize people, places, and things by a suite of characteristics. Psychologists call this ability cognitive fluency—essentially, how easy it is to recognize something. The more regularly we see something, for example, our significant other, the easier they are to recognize. We don't have to go through a long, detailed analysis of minute details in order to make an identification of our loved ones, so why do we go through a long, detailed analysis of minute, obscure, and sometimes even misleading field marks in order to identify so many birds? Certainly we will need to do that with species that we are unfamiliar with, such as when we travel to a new continent where we may not even be familiar with the bird families, but for most birds, we can, with practice, identify the bird by looking at the whole picture.

While we don't want to ignore a bright, red tail on a soaring raptor, we can readily identify a Red-tailed Hawk at a distance beyond where we can see its red tail, not to mention immatures that don't have red tails, by using a combination of shape and size (including proportions) and sometimes even the bird's behavior (figs. 1-4 and 1-5). Red-tails have big, broad, muscular wings that are nearly as broad at the tip as they are at the base, with a bulge in the middle. They have a moderate-length tail and a relatively large head (as compared with other buteos), and they usually soar with their wings showing a slight dihedral. They're rather steady in flight in most wind conditions, and in full soar, they make large, broad circles with infrequent flapping, and often these flaps are nothing more than a slight movement of one wing. They sometimes hover, and they are one of the few raptors that can truly "kite" (remain motionless in the air).

This is all subjective and can only be learned through comparative experience, and yes, a lot of practice. A first-time hawkwatcher visiting a popular watch site will marvel at a veteran's ability to identify a Red-tailed Hawk at three miles—"How can you see a red tail or its belly band from here?" But that's exactly it—we can't. I like to joke that if you can see the bird's red tail you should have identified it an hour ago. But all kidding aside, at an extreme distance, the tail color is definitely not visible, but the general impression of the birds shape and size is, as is the behavior. How it's flying, when it's flying, and what it's doing are all part of the identification puzzle that when put together makes a Red-tailed Hawk. But keep in mind that before we can identify a Red-tailed Hawk a mile away, we first need to learn the basics of hawk identification by being able to identify the distant speck to family first. Once you can reliably tell an accipiter from a buteo from a falcon, then it's time to identify Sharp-shinned Hawks, Red-tailed Hawks, and Merlins, respectively.

I think that hawkwatching, and our Red-tailed Hawk case study here, is a perfect example of the type of birding that can be both incredibly challenging and incredibly rewarding to a birder who wants to be better. Too many of us rely on the field mark system and don't look at the whole bird and more. Hawkwatching forces us to take a different approach. Although many folks have recognized this over the years, we often fail to apply this practice to the rest of our birding. Hawkwatching and hawk identification isn't some sort of voodoo birding. It's nothing special; it's just birding! But seasoned hawkwatchers have long since moved beyond just field marks and have considered the whole bird and more every time that they make an identification.

Another example is "seawatching" or "lake-watching." You're not seeing the yellow-orange knob on a drake Black Scoter in a massive flock a mile out to sea while scanning from your local jetty. You're not seeing the colorful bill and white head spots of a drake Surf Scoter, either. However, with comparative experience, a veteran seawatcher will see a distance flock of "dark-winged" scoters and note subtle differences in bill and head and body shape in order to separate these birds. It isn't magic; it's just experience!

FIGURE 1-4.
At a hawkwatch, or anywhere else, you certainly don't ignore the bright red tail when we can see it on an adult Red-tailed Hawk. However, don't stop there—look at the shape of the wings, proportions, and how it flies. *Adult Red-tailed Hawk, Bradbury Mountain Hawkwatch, Pownal, Maine, 3/10* © Luke Seitz.

Once you are making most of your identifications most of the time, then you can go back to making those careful, detailed observations that I first began to pontificate about. After identifying an American Black Duck by its dark chocolate-brown body, which contrasts with the cool gray-brown head, that is dabbling in the muck in the middle of a mudflat, then when you have the chance to study it at close range, do it. Get to know the bird better, its plumage details, and its behavior. Then apply your newfound notes to your complete toolbox of duck identification. You don't need to see the color of the speculum or the bill to identify most black ducks from most Mallards. But once you are identifying them at a distance, make sure to get to know them in detail—for such times as when your Norwegian friends ask you to help them out with the identification of a vagrant. Do all black ducks in all parts of their range, as well as vagrants, show a slight greenish sheen on their crowns or a few green feathers mixed within?

FIGURE 1-5.
The additional features you learned about while studying the easy-to-identify adult Red-tailed Hawk with the bright red tail can be applied to immature birds. As a result, you'll soon find out how easily you can identify all Red-tailed Hawks at surprising distances, even when the classic field marks are not visible. *Immature Red-tailed Hawk* © Richard Crossley.

In order to grow as a birder, make sure to always seek out challenges. How about pelagic species? Even the experts are still learning as this rapidly advancing birding frontier develops. Get out on a boat—perhaps even a local whale-watch outing, a fishing charter (many charters will take birders aboard for a reduced fee), or a dedicated, expertly led, organized pelagic birding excursion. I'm sure there is at least one group of birds that each and every reader of this book can use more experience with.

Do you think you really know your warblers? Challenge yourself to identify them via silhouettes and flight calls at a morning flight location (more on that in chapter 4). Your first visit—actually probably your first hundred visits—to observe warblers reorienting at dawn will be a most humbling experience and also a completely new opportunity to and master a new set of birding skills.

I think morning flight-watching is another good example of how we don't always *look* at the birds we *see*. When that spiffy male Yellow Warbler is singing from a streamside shrub in early spring, we shouldn't just see a yellow bird with chestnut streaks on the breast but should note the whole bird—the length and shape of its tail, the color of the undertail coverts, the shape of the body, etc. Then, when that bird streaks overhead in subdued fall plumage, and with color barely recognizable with the sun still breaking the horizon, we will have an intimate knowledge of Yellow Warblers that can be applied—again, with practice—to a novel situation.

By getting to know the whole bird, you will have a much wider suite of characteristics, both subjective and qualitative, that can be called upon when needed. With experience, you don't need to see everything on every bird every time in order to come to a conclusion. Taking the time to study Red-tails from your local hawkwatching promontory, you'll really get to know the bird, so when you glimpse a raptor flying over the highway as you're racing to chase a first state record, your mind will synthesize what you have seen—and what you have not seen—and that will often lead to the correct identification.

Upcoming chapters of this book will look into some of those *where*'s and *when*'s, but for now, let's think about what really is difficult in the world of bird identification. "I don't do sparrows" or "I don't do gulls" is not an acceptable answer! However, "I don't have a lot of experience with sparrows" is a perfectly reasonable statement. You simply need to get out and do something about it. We all need to get out of our comfort zones and find challenges so that we can continue to develop our skills. No (honest) birder will ever be able to stop learning, and each and every bird has something to teach us.

Each part of the country will feature different challenges. Silent "empids," especially ones out of range, are always a challenge and probably always will be a challenge, although you'll be surprised by how a suite of characteristics from habitat type to behavior to overall color can be quite helpful in identifying these "little greenish-brownish-grayish jobs."

So when it comes down to it, there are very few families of birds that are inherently difficult to identify. There's no doubt that there are a few species groupings that can be extremely tough, however. The first goal then needs to be to break down our challenge into a smaller set of choices. How do we do this? You guessed it: the "whole bird and more" approach.

I think that sparrows are a perfect example. Just about every corner of our continent features a variety of sparrows. In most cases, they're not the most colorful, the most obvious, or the most confiding of birds, but they present excellent challenges and excellent opportunities to excel and impress our friends. Of all the commonly observed families of birds in where I live here in Maine, this is the group that I most often hear from backyard feeder-watchers and birdwalk participants as being "hard."

Getting a good look at some species can be challenging, but you'll be surprised about how much you can actually see in a fleeting glimpse of a fleeing sparrow. With experience, tail length and shape, overall size, overall color, habitat, and behavior can all be judged from a quick look. Did the bird look short-tailed, small, and slim and flutter just above the grass before dropping back down (as if it has just been shot) and never being seen again, like an *Ammodramus* sparrow? Or was it a more robust, rounder bird with a long, round tail, a moderate-sized bill, a darker brown color, and its flight took it up toward an exposed perch, like a *Melospiza* sparrow? By learning the stereotypic gestalt and behavior of each family of sparrows (often called the family, or generic—as in which genus the bird is in—approach), we can quickly narrow our choices from 49-plus species of birds in the family *Emberizidae* to between 1 and 5, a much more manageable number of choices!

When seeing a sparrow makes you immediately bury your face in a field guide and flip though tens of pages of species, the bird will be fully digested by a Sharp-shinned Hawk by the time you look up again. However, by looking at the whole bird—thinking about the habitat, looking at the behavior, and identifying it to genus first, you'll probably narrow things down to a single page or two in a field guide and be surprised by how manageable the task becomes.

So the next time that a robust, long-tailed, relatively dark sparrow flies out of a grassy edge and up into a bush, we should begin to think of a *Melospiza* sparrow. Like many sparrows, melospizas have streaking, but taking a closer look, we'll learn that all streaking is not created equal.

There are three members of the genus *Melospiza*. Once we've narrowed the choices down to these 3, we can then study some of the finer points, because 3 is a much more manageable number than 49, right? I'm not going to get too detailed here (that is what some of the resources listed below are for), but Song, Swamp, and Lincoln's Sparrows are actually readily identifiable. I like to use an art analogy.

A Song Sparrow is an oil painting, with thick, dark, heavy streaking and bold, contrasty markings. Lincoln's, with their fine, distinct streaking is akin to a pen-and-ink drawing, while the washed-out, blurry streaking and more subtle contrasts of the Swamp Sparrow are like a watercolor. Of course, this imagery is oversimplified, both in terms of my descriptions of the bird and in the general stereotyping of each style of painting, but you get the idea. But just don't focus only on the minute details of appearance, such as a central breast spot, a commonly cited but often misleading field mark; beside, 13 species of sparrows show some sort of a central breast spot at some time in their lives!

Each genus has a different shape—no doubt some are more different than others—and coupled with behavior, and in some cases habitat, identifying the birds to genus is the first step in making our sparrow identification quick and easy. Here are the general outlines of the genera of sparrow that occur in North America (fig. 1-6). Note the differences in head shape and size, the shape and length of the bill, the length of the tail, the robustness of the chest, and other features. See figures 1-7 and 1-8 for a couple of examples.

I'll admit that I am partial to sparrows. I find their (mostly) subtle colors and delicate markings to be quite beautiful. I enjoy the challenges that they can present, and I like finding them out of their range. I also firmly believe that they are not nearly as hard to identify as many birders make them out to be. We've simply been going at it the wrong way.

So now we've seen a few examples, from distant Red-tailed Hawks to sometimes skulking Song Sparrows, that I hope show you how looking beyond field marks and at the whole bird, as well as everything around it (the "and more"), can aid us in identifying more birds more of the time.

I've already mentioned the *P* word: practice (repeatedly!), but we also need to maximize time in the field. And such practice can be augmented by two additional habits. First of all, I believe that we would benefit from rediscovering the seemingly lost art of note-taking. I believe too few birders take notes these days, and even fewer take copious notes. When faced with a novel bird, instead of reaching for a field guide, reach instead for your notebook. Write down *everything* you see, from habitat to behavior to a detailed description of every single thing that you can see. I find that when we birders force ourselves to describe each and every part of a bird and its environment, it helps us notice and absorb more details, which will aid in identification at a later time.

Plus, good notes about items like weather, species lists, counts, etc., are wonderful references for future use. Whether it's looking up some obscure sightings for a new breeding-bird atlas or for a state-records committee re-search project or simply for your own use, good records of your sightings— whether in notebooks or in a online database such as eBird (see chapter 6)—can be called upon for later use.

What *I* like to do is regularly reference past sightings to compare them to what I am seeing at this time. We often find ourselves misremembering things, such as how "birdy" a local patch should be at a given time of year, or thinking about timelines. I know each of us has made a remark along the lines of "Boy, warblers seem late this year."

Instead of guessing, referencing our past notes can shed light on those issues and indicate whether we remember correctly or not. I keep my field notebook from the previous year on my bedstand, and each night I quickly skim my notes from that day of the last year. That allows me to regularly reference comparable birding outings and seasonal sightings. For example, early one spring while walking in a local patch, I found myself thinking that there weren't many Eastern Wood–Pewees around here that year. I counted four singing birds on my walk that day. Referencing my notes from last year, I see that I visited Hedgehog Mountain Park on exactly the same date the previous year and also recorded four singing Eastern Wood-Pewees. My fears of a wood-pewee population crash were quickly alleviated. I also no-ticed that there was a really good wave of warblers at a small local park at this time last year, and so I was reminded to pay this spot a visit. I will also occasionally scribble a novel observation or a small plumage detail that might end up being a useful addition to my toolbox for identification of that particular species in some later instance, and it always pays to be re-minded of such notes.

FIGURE 1-6.
Sparrow genus shapes ©Luke Seitz.

Ammodramus

Passerculus

Passerella

Melospiza

Zonotrichia

Junco

Calcarius

Plectophenax

FIGURE 1-7.
The (currently) monotypic genus *Passerculus* has a short, notched tail, a moderately flat head, a slim build, and a relatively long and slender bill. Combine these features, along with habitat and behavior, and you'll soon find that you don't have to struggle to see a central breast spot or a little yellow in the supercilium (which, as you can see here, is only noticeable in one of these three individuals. If you relied on this "classic field mark" as your only way to identify Savannah Sparrows, you'd have a tough time with two of these three birds! *Savannah Sparrows* ©Richard Crossley.

FIGURE 1-8.
The chunky, chesty body coupled with the round head and relatively small bill of the moderately large sparrows in the genus *Zonotrichia* is much different from the shape of those in the genus *Passerculus*. So just because the obvious and distinctive black and white crown stripes of the adult are not present on immatures, you'll soon be well on your way to identifying all ages. *White-crowned Sparrow, Yarmouth, Maine, 10/09* ©Jeannette Lovitch.

Second, we should have a well-stocked library to reference before and after birding excursions. We'll want to take advantage of online resources as well, and we definitely want to take advantage of the knowledge of others. Although birding is a social activity for some, silent solitude in the field will teach us a lot as well. However, birding with a group, especially with more experienced birders, whether informally or as part of organized outings, is also very helpful. I wholeheartedly recommend a mix of both.

An ever-increasing myriad of great resources are available, and I'm sure by the time you read this, many other options will be available. The sections on identification in National Geographic's *Birding Essentials* are excellent, and I think *Sibley's Birding Basics*, by David Sibley, is indispensable—

although many folks agree that it is slightly beyond the "basics" of birding. In fact, I firmly believe that page for page this is one of the absolute best birding books ever produced! There's a mass of invaluable information tucked within its pages. Another often underappreciated tome offering a wealth of knowledge on the big picture of how birds look, are shaped, and how they behave and so on is *Pete Dunne's Essential Field Guide Companion.* There's a lot of text to sift through, but try reviewing the entry for a given species after spending some time in the field with that bird. Dunne definitely has a way with words, and here he attempts to put the intangible, unquantifiable aspects of the "whole bird and more" approach into words.

Moving on to the next level, there is now a plethora of "family guides" available—entire books on a single family of birds. These books work well as references for specific identification quandaries, but they are also valuable to study before, and after, general birding excursions. The wealth of information contained between the covers of some of these treatises is unbelievable, and they are a great source of information for advancing our own birding skills.

One of the best is *The Shorebird Guide,* by Michael O'Brien, Richard Crossley, and Kevin Karlson. It is particularly remarkable and valuable in a number of ways. At the time I write this, I believe this is hands down the best family guide and advanced birding text available, and it's a must-have for every birder's library. The text is well written and approachable, and the photography is exceptional, but there are a few specific features in the book that make it so useful and helpful. First, there are a lot of photos for each bird, including a few sprinkled in that are clearly meant simply for enjoyment and appreciation (please don't ever forget that we're in this for the enjoyment of our hobby/passion/sport first and foremost). Second, there are many photos showing multiple species. Shorebirding, like hawkwatching and sparrowing, is quite subjective, and comparative experience is critical. It's hard to realize the value of photos of multiple species together until you get into the field and realize that multiple species are often together! Plus, quizzes are scattered throughout the book, keeping you on your toes but also providing immediate examples to test and reinforce what you have just learned.

One peep, or one yellowlegs, all by its lonesome self can be a real challenge. But when you have something to compare its size, color, shape, behavior, etc. with, identification becomes a lot clearer. I've always been perplexed as to why more guides don't show multiple species together for direct comparison, so hopefully the success and utility of *The Shorebird Guide* will start a trend.

Thinking back to my remarks about a distant Red-tailed Hawk from a hawkwatch, I can't forget to add the hawkwatcher's "bible," *Hawks in Flight,* by Pete Dunne, David Sibley, and Clay Sutton to our burgeoning library. This may be the first book that clearly articulated the concept of gestalt, and as we learned from the Red-tail example, general impression of size and shape, plus behavior, is everything at a hawkwatch. I've often heard the complaint that the birds in the photos of this book are small, distant, out-of-focus, black-and-white specks. Well, guess what they look like from a hawkwatch?

Jerry Ligouri's *Hawks from Every Angle,* and especially his newer book, *Hawks at a Distance,* are other helpful resources and include most of the western species (which *Hawks in Flight* unfortunately does not) and work as excellent complements to the latter. Try having one of these books open to the corresponding species that you are reading about in *Hawks in Flight* and glance back and forth between the text and the photos before your next hawkwatching sojourn.

Some of my other favorite references include *Flight Identification of European Seabirds,* by Anders Blomdahl, Bertil Breife, and Niklas Holmstrom, which is particularly applicable to the East Coast of our continent; *Gulls of the Americas* (in the Peterson's Field Guide series) by Steve N.G. Howell and Jon Dunn; *Warblers* (also in the Peterson Field Guide series), by Jon Dunn and Kimball Garrett; and *Hummingbirds of North America: The Photographic Guide,* by Steve Howell. All four of these books not only offer a wealth of information on cutting-edge field marks but also emphasize identification criteria, such as gestalt, that go above and beyond classic field marks.

Another suggestion is the under-appreciated *Shorebirds of the Pacific Northwest,* by Dennis Paulson. Although it is targeted to the title geographic area, the vast majority of the book is directly applicable to those species everywhere else they occur. I appreciate the thorough text and discussion, comments on habitat and behavior, and excellent photographs of this book.

Also, consider a copy of Peter Pyle's *Identification Guide to North American Birds, Part 1*, and the recently released *Part 2*—it isn't just for banders! There's a wealth of information on identification above and beyond what any other text covers, and the descriptions of minute details and especially molt strategies can be most helpful when researching an unusual bird or when dissecting a photograph of an unfamiliar vagrant. OK, so it's not the book you'll want to curl up with on the couch in front of the fireplace on a cold winter's night, but this resource is invaluable! (Note that Pyle himself qualifies some of the information in the new *Part 2* as unproven).

Molt is one of those topics that seems overwhelming to many birders, primarily because so far it has been limited to technical manuals, such as the Pyle guide, and therefore relegated to the shelves of only the serious ornithologist or bander. I think this is a mistake, because a lot can be learned from an understanding of molt, and not just its use as an aid to identification. The more we understand about birds, the more we know about how they "work" and how they relate, and the more we can appreciate, care about, and yes, identify birds.

It is with this in mind that Steve N. G. Howell, one of North America's most prolific birding and ornithological authors, developed the Peterson Reference Guide *Molt in North American Birds*. This book is a mostly nontechnical, popularly digestible, and "short and sweet" description of the molt strategies of each of North America's bird families. It relates these molt strategies to the life histories, basic ecology, migration, and feeding strategies of each family, all of which not only can be helpful in assisting with identification but also are important for fully understanding and appreciating each species of bird.

Perhaps one of the most relevant books to the current conversation is Richard Crossley's *The Crossley ID Guide: Eastern Birds*, which was published in the early spring of 2011. Shortly after its release, Richard visited our store in Freeport, Maine, for a book-signing appearance. Prior to his presentation, Richard and I spent the day birding around the area, catching up on life, gossip (we're friends from my days of visiting and working in Cape May), and all things birds and birding.

Quite a bit of our conversation revolved around his new book, my book (the one you're reading now), and some of their many similarities with each other—at least in regard to this chapter. If you haven't done so recently, read the introduction to *The Crossley ID Guide*. Without in any way disparaging the rest of his book, perhaps my favorite part of his epic and innovative work is the introduction.

There was plenty of friendly joshing that day—"Ask Robert. My draft was submitted before your book came out"—and returned by Richard with comments such as "It's only because you learned it from me!" But all kidding aside, there are a number of similarities—even down to a human recognition analogy, and I highly recommend reading it to reinforce what I have been discussing here. I wish either of us could claim that these are completely novel ideas, but when it comes down to it, we are both part of the school of birding that looks beyond classic field marks to what I call the "whole bird and more" approach.

During the course of our outing we applied geography, habitat, and the day's weather (all of these will be discussed shortly) to direct our birding, especially when it came to looking for opportunities for a few birds that Richard wanted to photograph. But we also had some good discussions about identification. I took Richard to a local park (Westbrook's Riverbank Park) to look for an Iceland Gull that I had been pondering for a while. In this case, we applied all of the identification tools: the classic field marks (the "old school," as Richard likes to say) and the general impression of size and shape, along with behavior and any other clues that happened to become apparent.

We started wide (shape, size, overall impression) and worked toward the minute (the color of inner verses outer primary webs, undertail coverts, and the retention of what appeared to be-juvenile feathers on the back). We also remarked on how this exercise was a perfect lesson about how to approach a challenging identification. We compared the bird's size and shape to nearby Herring and Ring-billed Gulls, and we scrutinized every feather on the bird's body. In the end, we both agreed that one of the most important lessons was that sometimes you have to walk away and say "I don't know," but we did throw around a few hypotheses, from an unusually large Iceland Gull of the nominate subspecies *glaucoides* to the more expected Kumlien's Gull (subspecies *kumlieni*), which had a leucistic second generation (cycle) of feathers (figures 1-9 and 1-10).

Kaufman's New *Field Guide to Advanced Birding*

It seems that birding books are being introduced as quickly as new smart phone applications or digital camera models these days. Quite a few new books were released in the time it took to prepare various drafts of this book, so some could not be included in full here. However, just arriving in time for a thorough read was the much-anticipated update to Ken Kaufman's *Field Guide to Advanced Birding*, which was first published in 1990. Although the classic edition is still full of valuable information, the new addition takes a completely different approach— an approach that considers "the whole bird and more" and not just the minutiae. Perhaps less "advanced" than the first edition, the second version has fewer pages devoted to the details of the hardest identification quandries, and instead, as the subtitle suggests, has many more that teach you how to "understand what you hear and see." If nothing else, read through the new edition and compare it with the classic one and see how our collective school of thought about how to approach bird identification has rapidly evolved in the past ten years.

In addition to books, there are a few magazines and periodicals that offer a wealth of information on field identification. First, there's *Birding* magazine, the membership magazine of the American Birding Association (ABA), which usually features at least one article on bird identification, often on cutting-edge identification techniques and hypotheses. These articles are usually worthwhile, and the magazine as a whole is a good tool for improving your birding skills. Personally, I have been longing for identification articles that are more advanced, and in some cases, more applicable to more people in more places. (Note of full disclosure: I am a former product

FIGURE 1-9.
This spiffy gull was identified by some as a Glaucous Gull due to its nearly all-white plumage and bicolored bill. However, the overall shape and size, head and bill shape, and wing length show that this is indeed an Iceland Gull. The two-toned bill along with the pale eye suggest the bird is in its second winter (second-cycle plumage). Along with the very white plumage, this bird is suggestive of an individual of the subspecies *glaucoides,* the nominate subspecies that is probably rare in the Northeast. Comparison with other individuals did not suggest the small, dainty "cuteness" expected from textbook individuals of this subspecies. *Iceland Gull, Riverbank Park, Westbrook, Maine, 3/11* ©Derek Lovitch.

reviewer/department editor for this magazine). The ABA also publishes the journal *North American Birds* (which I will talk more about later), which occasionally includes articles on identification of rarities, especially subspecific and other types of cryptic challenges.

Also, *Birding World* (www.birdingworld.co.uk), from England, is an excellent resource. It covers more advanced field identification topics than *Birding,* and it regularly feature articles directly applicable to North America,

FIGURE 1-10.
A different view of the gull in figure 1-9 shows the fairly well marked (if rather worn) underwings and undertail coverts, which suggest that this bird is not nearly as white as it appears to be. Feather wear on the upper parts could be at play, but a second-cycle Iceland Gull should have at least some gray feathers in the mantle (at least) by this time of its life. Also, despite how pale the bird is, the feathers don't look overly worn and ragged. Therefore, we postulated that perhaps the whiteness of the bird was due to new feathers on the upperparts being leucistic, making the bird look unusually white as the new feathers grew in, without the expected gray color. *Iceland Gull, Riverbank Park, Westbrook, Maine, 3/11* ©Derek Lovitch.

whether they are about vagrants from Europe or about North American birds that can occur in Europe (like the black duck discussed above, it is often the vagrants that get the most thorough analysis). I think North American birders will benefit greatly from a subscription to this journal.

Meanwhile, an incredible resource for learning bird songs (especially about how to critically listen to them) is Donald Kroodsma's remarkable *The Singing Life of Birds,* which is one of those rare works that is both a pleasure to read and remarkably educational. You'll never listen to birdsong the same way again, and your birding-by-ear skills will improve considerably. And on the topic of birdsong, which is such an indispensible part of bird identification, be sure to check out the *Birding by Ear* CDs (Peterson Field Guides) if you have not done so already. They aren't just reference recordings, they're instructional tools that really teach you *how to learn* bird sounds.

In addition to classic, printed material, the online world offers a whole host of resources. A simple Google search for a species (especially using Google Images) in question will yield hundreds of photos—some more helpful and more correctly identified than others!—and links to various texts on the various species.

There are countless websites dedicated to identification, photo galleries, and other helpful tools that you can take advantage of. Also, have a look at the "Frontiers of Identification" listserve (often referred to simply as "ID-Frontiers") created by Will Russell. You can view the most recent posts via Jack Siler's Birdingonthe.net at www.birdingonthe.net/mailinglists/FRID. html, or view the complete archives at http://listserv.arizona.edu/archives/ birdwg01.html. There are often numerous threads discussing the identification of unusual, difficult, and out-of-range birds. I often bookmark links to photographs for future reference, and occasionally I'll find a juicy tidbit of information or tasty tip that is worth remembering and jotting down. But be warned: just like everywhere else on the Internet, you want to be careful what you accept as fact. (I know, I know, not everything on the internet is true. Shocking, isn't it?) It won't be long before you figure out whose posts are to be read with caution!

Numerous other resources on advanced birding are available both in print and online, and I cannot possibly mention them all here, but hopefully I have given you a few new suggestions for augmenting your identification toolbox. I've only scratched the surface here, but it's a place to start. No one book, including this one, will single-handedly make you a better birder, but each additional resource provides you with more information.

The short version of all of this is that there are no longer any excuses not to "do" sparrows or any other group of birds. With a wide range of resources at your disposal and with a whole new outlook on how to look at birds, you can take the fear out of identifying difficult birds. In fact, before you know it, you'll be seeking out new challenges to push the envelope of your birding skills. From distant flocks of soaring raptors to the identification of pre-dawn silhouettes of passerines at a morning reorientation flight (which we will learn about in chapter 5), we all benefit from getting out of our comfort zone and taking on the most difficult identification scenarios.

But, for the rest of this book, I want to spend our time thinking beyond "simply" identification. Part of the "whole bird and more" approach is to also look beyond the bird, at habitat, geography, and so on. One reason for this is to help us identify birds. However, what I want to focus on is taking our birding to a higher level. Many of us also want more from our birding. Even if you are one of the lucky few who can bird all day, every day, we all can maximize our time in the field by taking other disciplines into consideration, such as meteorology, geography, and even technology.

While we all have different ideas as to what "becoming a better birder" means, we can call upon a wide range of tools to reach our respective goals, whether it be a bigger life, state, or patch list; to add to our collective knowledge of bird distribution by finding a first county breeding record; or simply to bask in the thrill of discovery.

A few identification sites worth visiting:
- David Sibley's blog and website at www.sibleyguides.com
- IDArticles on Surfbirds.com at www.surfbirds.com/ID%20Articles/idindex.html
- Mike Freiberg's *Birding to the Edg* blog at http://blog.nikonbirding.com/
- A library of photos, songs, and identification tips can also be found at the USGS Patuxent National Wildlife Center's website at http.mbr-pwrc.usgs.gov/bbs/ident.html

Birding by Habitat

When was the last time you saw a Palm Warbler in a palm tree, or a Prairie Warbler out in the prairie? Could you identify a Palm Warbler in a Black Spruce on its breeding grounds? Likewise, could you find a Prairie Warbler without needing to plan a trip to the prairie (or what's left of it) of the Midwest? OK, so there is a limitation to how exact of a science birding-by-habitat truly is, but you'll be surprised by how much the habitat that a bird is in can aid identification. Furthermore, bird finding can be made easier when we take habitat into consideration, as we will learn shortly. But in order to do so, we need to have a basic knowledge of plants.

Furthermore, I personally want to be a well-rounded naturalist, and therefore it is not just the names of birds I want to know. I like knowing the difference between a Red and White Oak, or a Longleaf versus Loblolly Pine. At the very least, it gives you something to point out and talk about when leading a birding outing in which the birds are not "cooperating"!

A basic knowledge of plants' identities will also help us recognize the diversity of trees, flowers, and everything else around us, further augmenting our appreciation of biodiversity, which simply makes being out in nature more enjoyable. And appreciating biodiversity leads to a development of the ethic of conservation, a first step toward developing a desire—if you don't have it already—to protect birds, which in the end, really is in our self-interest as birders, isn't it? (And you thought it was just about finding Pine Warblers in pine trees!)

How do we go about enhancing our knowledge of plants? Simple: the same way we advance our knowledge about birds—time in the field and time buried in the books. There are a number of resources for plant identification, although the quantity, quality, and diversity of field guides available are not quite at the level of our bird selections, at least not yet. However, at least for trees, that situation has changed with the recent publication of *The Sibley Guide to Trees*, by David Allen Sibley. Compared with its respective predecessors, this book might be even more revolutionary than his birding guide!

Using a field-guide approach that will be very familiar to birders and easily accessible to the amateur botanist who lacks experience with dichotomous keys and technical terms and methods, this book will do wonders for the ability of anyone to identify more trees more often. And perhaps, as David has promoted, "tree listing" will be the next new fad—at least chasing a rarity will almost always be successful!

I also recommend a pair of books by George W. D. Symonds: *The Tree Identification Book* and *The Shrub Identification Book*, both of which cover the majority of the United States east of the Rockies (unfortunately, I am not aware of a similar western alternative). These books focus on what the author calls practical identification, which is exactly what a nonbotanist like myself would want.

In fact, the author's methodology is strikingly similar to the "whole bird and more" approach to bird identification, which I discussed in chapter 1. Here's how he begins the introduction of the book: "The aim of this book is to present, visually, details of trees essential for practical identification, which in turns leads to tree recognition. The distinction between tree identification and tree recognition should be clearly understood at the outset. Identification is based on observation of details. Recognition means knowing trees at a glance, just as one recognizes one's friends."

Sound familiar? I'm guessing that this gestalt-like approach is what makes these books appeal to me. The next paragraph is amusing to me, because the author directly addresses the similarities and differences between tree and bird identification: "Birds conform to a pattern—two legs, two wings, definite markings (usually!)—but not so trees. There are certain advantages in tree identification, however, which the bird watcher doesn't have. A tree does not become alarmed and fly away. A tree has parts which can be touched at will, and all the details pictured in the keys of this book, with the exception of the bark, can easily be collected and carried away. It is not necessary to take the book into the field to identify most trees, and if a second look is necessary, the tree can usually be revisited, with or without the book."

The reason for this little tangent is obvious—no more excuses about not going out and learning your trees!

Since I have spent much of my life and birding/naturalist career in the Northeast, I have a distinctly regional bias to my own resource list. Therefore, to provide a more complete list of resources, I contacted a number of friends and colleagues around the country and asked for their recommendations. These suggestions, combined with my own experience, yielded the following list. Unfortunately, charismatic wildflowers are the most well covered but are often of slightly less importance to identifying habitat as a whole, at least compared with trees and shrubs. However, a few species can be important indicators of habitat, and at the very least, we should probably learn a few anyway to point out while leading our next walk. The classic tome is *Newcomb's Wildflower Guide*, by Lawrence Newcomb, which covers a wide area but relies on a dichotomous key that may be a bit cumbersome to those unfamiliar with the process and the terminology.

Here are some of the recommendations that I compiled, which have varying degrees of technicality and widespread utility.

East
- *Wildflowers in the Field and Forest: A Field Guide to the Northeastern United States*, by Steven Clemants and Carol Gracie
- *Flora of West Virginia,* by P.D. Strausbaugh (good for all of southern Appalachia and nearby habitats)
- *Flora of Maine,* by Arthur Haines and Thomas Vining (good for most of northern New England, but very technical)
- *Atlantic Coastal Plain Wildflowers: A Guide to Common Wildflowers of the Coastal Regions of Virginia, North Carolina, South Carolina, Georgia, and Northeastern Florida,* by Gil Nelson
- *East Gulf Coastal Plain Wildflowers: A Field Guide to the Wildflowers*

of the East Gulf Coastal Plain, Including Southwest Georgia, Northwest Florida, Southern Alabama, Southern Mississippi, and Parts of Southeastern Louisiana, by Gil Nelson
- *Wildflowers of Tennessee, the Ohio Valley and the Southern Appalachians*, by Dennis Horn, Tavia Cathcart, Thomas Hemmerly, and David Duhl

Midwest
- *Field Guide to the Trees, Shrubs, Woody Vines, Grasses, Sedges, and Rushes: Fontenelle Forest & Neale Woods Nature Center* (Nebraska), by Neal Ratzlaff and Roland Barth
- *Field Guide to Wildflowers: Fontenelle Forest & Neale Woods Nature Center* (Nebraska), by Roland Barth and Neal Ratzlaff

Mountains/Interior West
- *A Field Guide to the Plants of Arizona*, by Anne Orth Epple (good for Arizona, New Mexico, and Utah)
- *Manual of the Plants of Colorado*, by H.D. Harrington

West Coast
- *The Jepson Manual: Higher Plants of California*, edited by James C. Hickman
- *Plants of the Pacific Northwest Coast: Washington, Oregon, British Columbia, and Alaska*, by Jim Pojar and Andy MacKinnon
- *Plants of Southern Interior British Columbia and the Inland Northwest*, by Robert Parish, Ray Coupe, and Dennis Lloyd
- *Wildflowers of the Pacific Northwest*, by Mark Turner and Phyllis Gustafson

---

Many of the best plant identification books are produced on the state level. Forest services, or similar agencies, of a number of states publish very valuable tree identification guides. Often aimed at the woodlot owner, and therefore targeted at species of commercial value, the more local focus is often very useful for beginning tree identification.

A great way to learn plant identification is to take advantage of the knowledge of local experts. Local Audubon chapters, land trusts, agricultural extension services, garden clubs, and so on often lead walks or workshops on various plant identification topics. Also, consider a course or two at a local community college, continuing education center, or similar institution.

In other words, there is a myriad of resources available to help teach us about plant identification. It's just a matter of realizing the value and importance of knowing what plants are around and then making the effort to learn them. Then, we can put that information together to identify specific groups of plants—in other words, habitats for birds. Once we do that, we can apply that knowledge to our birding endeavors as we strive to become better birders. Also, when you call out a bird in a group (either as a leader or a participant), identifying the particular plant the bird is in—for example, with, "in the broad-leafed Sugar Maple"—is much more useful than a vague statement such as, "in the tree . . . uh, the one with the leaves . . . and some branches."

There are two main tenets of birding by habitat: bird identification and bird finding, and those are what I want to focus on with you. Just like some of the advanced identification topics that I talked about in the introduction, I'll leave the details of plant identification to the experts!

Bird Identification by Habitat

Even before you read this chapter, you already had a basic, but very important, knowledge of using habitat to aid your identification. Whether you realize it or not, you're birding by habitat all of the time!

If you are in the middle of the woods, are you thinking about ducks and wetland birds? If you're standing on a sandy barrier beach in the summer, are boreal warblers the first thing on your mind? If you're looking up in a tree at a small, active bird, do you think along the lines of warbler, vireo, or flycatcher, or do you consider a Least Sandpiper? If a large chunky bird is walking down a city street, do you first think Spruce Grouse, or Rock Pigeon (aka Roof Grouse!)? A few extreme examples, perhaps, but I think they get the point across. Almost every single identification that we have learned to make in our birding careers has in some way, shape, or form used habitat as a very early starting point in putting the identification puzzle together.

But I want to focus on here is using more specific habitat clues to aid in our identification challenges. There are countless examples from around the country where specific birds prefer specific habitats. Knowledge of these preferences can help us to detect and identify birds, and knowledge of how to identify those habitats can only make this task much easier. As usual, I'm not going to give an exhaustive treatment of the topic; an entire book could be written on the habitat preferences of birds. For more specific species relationships, the best resource is probably the species profiles in the seminal *Birds of North America* (see http://bna.birds.cornell.edu/bna/ for more information on this exceptionally valuable resource). But for now, let us take a look at a few examples of how habitat can aid in our bird-identification challenges.

In chapter 1, I said I was going to avoid discussing the finer points of *Empidonax* flycatcher identification. Well, I lied. Although I'm still going to leave the discussion of lower mandible and tertial fringe edges to other, more qualified persons, a few of our empids can nicely illustrate the birding-by-habitat method.

So, one early February morning, you have found yourself in the birding mecca of Patagonia Lake State Park in Southeast Arizona (if you haven't found yourself there yet, you probably will—and probably should—some day). You've just walked up the river from the campground, searching for that charismatic and rare Elegant Trogon that you are after for your life list, when you spot a drab, grayish empid perched silently in bushes along the edge of a dry draw.

Of course, the trogon is on your mind—and so is that Northern Beardless-Tyrannulet (with a name that sounds much more exotic than it looks) and Painted Redstart (looking just as exotic as it sounds) recently reported from here—but this is your first visit to the Desert Southwest in winter, and this little gray job may be a hole on your ABA-area list as well. (The ABA area comprises the United States—except for Hawai'i and U.S. territories—and Canada). Without looking any further and without having to dive into the field guide, you note your surroundings: tall cottonwoods growing along the river are shading thick, dense mesquite bushes/small trees (fig. 2-1). This is the preferred habitat of the Gray Flycatcher. Other empids that might be in the region usually prefer other habitats: the Dusky Flycatcher is found primarily in riparian vegetation such as willows, for example.

Oh, yeah, it's probably slowly dipping its tail, a diagnostic behavior of the Gray Flycatcher, which is great for helping to seal the identification that we suspected by just looking around to see where we were. Of course, birding by habitat, especially during migration season is not completely conclusive, but at the very least, it will rapidly narrow our choices and key us in to very specific characteristics, such as how it moves its tail (or not). The overgeneralizations presented here for Gray versus Dusky Flycatcher are just that—overgeneralizations. But it does give us a clue, and a rather big clue at that.

And in the breeding season, the habitat preferences of these species are even more pronounced where the species overlap. Grays will be in dry pine or piñon-juniper habitat, duskies will be found in open woodlands and mountainside brush, while Hammond's Flycatchers prefer coniferous woods and therefore will often be found at higher elevations as well. Although Cordilleran Flycatchers also breed in coniferous woods, as well as canyons, habitat alone quickly narrowed our choices from six species of rather similarly drab flycatchers to only two likely candidates, which at the very least will decrease the number of the field marks we then need to look for. And of course, hearing the bird sing or call is always nice!

While a magician never reveals his or her tricks, I'm about to reveal one of the tricks of the successful bird tour guide—know when and where to look for what! You can spend weeks in winter in southeast Arizona without ever seeing a Gray Flycatcher—unless, of course, you head into a dry draw dominated by mesquite.

Back in the East, where their ranges overlap, you'll be surprised to see how well named the Alder and Willow Flycatchers are in the breeding season. All bets are off during migration, but in Maine, for example, Alder Flycatchers really do prefer wetlands dominated by Speckled Alder, and

Willow Flycatchers really do prefer willow-dominated areas. In fact, one local patch that I visit regularly with clients and birdwalk participants has Alder Flycatchers singing from an alder swamp on one side of the road and Willow Flycatchers singing from a willow-dominated gully on the opposite side! Of course, we want to hear it or see it well (yes, these two birds are often separable visually given really good views at certain seasons, even when silent) to confirm, but at least we have a suggestion of what we need to be concentrating on. But this is all moot if you can't tell an alder from a willow (but no demerits for not being able to identify the specific willow; I certainly can't!).

And let us momentarily consider the importance of habitat and, more specifically, the identification of individual trees in the case of Red Cross-bills. Recent research suggests that as many as *nine species* of "Red" Cross-bills may occur in North America, with the "South Hills" Crossbill of Idaho perhaps achieving full species status by the time you read this! Although there are subtle differences with call notes, the speciation in "Red" Cross-bills (but interestingly, not in the homogenous White-winged Crossbills) may be directly linked to specialization in food sources, and their bill adaptations evolved to handle those specific foods. The "Red" Crossbills that feed on hemlocks, for example, may have a slightly thinner bill than the "Red" Crossbills that feed on pines (fig. 2-2). While range is important in identification, it stands to reason that identifying the food source may be a

FIGURE 2-1. *(opposite page)*
Often silent in winter, identifying *Empidonax* flycatchers can be a real challenge when you see them for the first time. Instead of immediately struggling to see the color of the lower mandible, perhaps you should start by looking around. If you're in a dry wash in the winter in the southwestern United States, such as at Patagonia Lake State Park, chances are you are seeing a Dusky Flycatcher. With that as a starting point, you can then begin to look at things like overall color and behavior (and jot it into your notebook!) before you attempt to look for the minutia. Chances are you'll identify and confirm the bird long before you see the color at the base of the lower mandible! *The Habitat at Patagonia Lake State Park* ©Richard Crossley.

helpful hint in separating these potential species, at least when the bird has a choice of foodstuffs.

Bird Finding by Habitat

Knowledge of habitats is critical for finding local species and extremely helpful in finding rarities. At the very least, targeting one's birding to valuable and interesting habitats can improve a birder's chance of success. You truly can become a better birder simply by using a knowledge—even just a rudimentary knowledge—of birds' habitats.

The examples presented above in "Bird Identification by Habitat" are all directly relevant to bird finding. You haven't seen a Gray Flycatcher? Head to a mesquite-dominated draw or creekside. You're missing Alder Flycatcher on your state list? Look for a wetland full of alders within its range. Need to add "Type 3" Red Crossbill to your subspecies/"identifiable form" life list? Guess you'll have to search for some hemlocks. How about some of those target species that you want to see, or perhaps, show to others? When friends or clients visited me when I lived in the Upper Peninsula of Michigan and Yellow Rail was on their want list, I didn't go out into just any wetland. Instead, I would focus my effort on wide, open bogs of Wiregrass Sedge, the preferred habitat. (Or I took them on one of the Yellow Rail tours given by the biologists of Seney National Wildlife Refuge, which I recommend for a higher success rate.)

Have you decided to bear the snow and frigid temperatures of the UP or Northern Minnesota in winter in the hopes of adding a few irruptive frugivores to your list? Well then, you'll want to keep an eye on large, open wetlands dominated by the deciduous holly known as Winterberry, and you'll definitely want to make a note of any mountain-ash trees loaded with berries. Both of these are the primary food sources for wintering Pine Grosbeaks and Bohemian Waxwings.

In chapter 8 we'll be discussing some tips for finding vagrants. Habitat identification, and even the identification of specific plants, will be directly relevant to that discussion. But before we get to that, in the next chapter, we'll be discussing what is known from a geographical perspective as the "island effect," but there's also an island effect that pertains to habitats. We

FIGURE 2-2.
If and when the Red Crossbill species is split into eight or nine species, the type of tree (here, Ponderosa Pine) may be key to an accurate identification. If a future "Ponderosa Pine Crossbill" is split into its own species, it will be helpful to know exactly what a Ponderosa Pine looks like. *Red Crossbill on Ponderosa Pine, Colorado, 11/04* ©Tony Leukering.

can use this habitat effect to help us find birds, whether it be a hole on your life list, or finding rarities, or simply seeing something different while taking a stroll through your local patch.

In most areas, habitat is not homogenous. With the exception of large stretches of open ocean without undersea topography of note or massive acreages of intensively farmed fields of monoculture, there's always some diversity, even subtlety so, to the areas we find ourselves in. These variations in habitats, and often the edges of these habitats in particular, are important for bird finding.

When looking for migrants in a heavily wooded region, aimless wandering through the mature forest is not much different from searching for a needle in a haystack. Instead of hoping to rendezvous with a mixed-species flock here or there, seek an edge—maybe the edge of a pond, a field, or even a yard. The edges between habitats, especially when one habitat is wooded and the other is open, are important concentration points for birds, and focusing our birding efforts in these spots can be most rewarding. If these edges happen to feature early morning sunshine, then activity, both of insects and the birds that feast upon them, can get underway earlier in the morning and in greater amounts than in the center of the woods.

In the Midwest and Desert Southwest, the key to locating migrants—both numbers of expected species and, especially, rarities—is to find "islands" of quality habitat. In the breadbasket of our nation, isolated woodlots, old farmsteads surrounded by tall trees and ornamental plantings, and waterways both natural and manmade—with a little vegetation around them are the places to focus one's attention. In the arid Southwest, the "oases" that have become legendary for birding are not always the natural springs and native plants of movie mirages but instead are man-made features, such as sewage treatment plants, farm ponds, and interstate rest areas dotted with nonnative plantings.

Some of the places that we find ourselves are less than aesthetically pleasing, but sometimes those are just the places we need to look for birds! Paul Lehman, often cited as North America's leading expert on bird distribution, is famous for discovering great birds in unexpected places. Recently, while co-leading a Deserts in Winter birding tour with him for WINGS Birding Tours, the group and I were treated to some great birds and a tour of some unexpected locations, such as the cooling ponds of power plants, ornamental landscaping in recreational-vehicle resorts, and dilapidated trailer parks, as we drove the interstate between the Salton Sea and Tucson. Normally birders whiz by this stretch of interstate monotony as quickly as possibly as they travel between these two birding ultra-hotspots, but not Paul! And his—and many other birders'—state and life lists are more the better for it!

On the other hand, when searching for migrants, vagrants, and other fun birds in heavily wooded regions—say, the Upper Peninsula of Michigan or Northern Maine—we take the opposite approach. We don't look for trees but rather for places *without* trees, such as small towns, isolated natural and man-made clearings, and other edges as described above.

Even known migratory hotspots from Point Reyes, California, to Cape May, New Jersey, do not uniformly have great birds. Even within these geographic concentration points, birders focus on specific habitats to find what they are looking for and possibly to encounter something unexpected. But even without such geographic concentration points, different habitats and their edges nevertheless provide concentration points for birds, both the common and the rare.

In fact, this concept brings up one of the current controversies among the birders who are interested in the occurrence of rarities, as I am. Conventional wisdom suggests that rarities concentrate along coastlines (a point I will discuss in chapter 3). However, we also know that birders also concentrate along the coast, both traveling birders, seeking a wide variety of species, and resident birders, who are concentrated along coasts simply because our population is concentrated along our coasts. What is going undetected in between?

As I write this particular chapter, I am on a plane, at a cruising altitude of about 37,000 feet. I'm crossing the continent, traveling between Portland, Maine, and Portland, Oregon. At the moment, I'm gazing out the window at a green-and-brown checkerboard of farm fields as far as the eye can see. Then, just below, there's an isolated island of trees. In any one direction, thousands of acres of monoculture—inhospitable, mechanically manipulated, chemically treated acres of vegetation planted in neat little rows. Then there's this island of trees, set well back from the nearest visible road. Hmm, I wonder what's down there. Has any birder ever set foot there? A migrant bird, let's say a Gray-cheeked Thrush, might be flying over the interior of the continent one night (see chapter 4) and as dawn approaches starts looking for any "port in a storm." That woodlot is a lot more inviting than the cornfield. And why wouldn't a vagrant think the same? What potential first-county or first-state record has called that woodlot home for a day or two but departed undetected? (If a vagrant lands in the woods and no one is around, has it been there?)

Heading farther west, I see an isolated town. Hmm, I ask myself what birds have found this little town. What's hanging out at a feeder, garden, or nicely landscaped ornamental pond? Then, as we cross the Rockies into the dry Great Basin, I notice a green gulch nicely contrasting with the brown hillsides. I wonder what trees are present. What birds are calling those trees home. How many places such as Colorado's migrant and vagrant trap, the Chico Basin Ranch, are out there to be discovered?

Coastal areas often harbor a greater variety of habitats than inland areas, more edges, and definitive concentrations of many migrants, such as shorebirds, passerines, and raptors (and of course, waterfowl). But the question is, are vagrants—for example, an overshooting Fork-tailed Flycatcher from South America, a mirror-migrant Chaffinch from Europe, or a misdirected wayward Western Tanager from the interior west of the United States that happens to move more east than south in the fall—really all that more likely at the coast than in the interior? Is it simply an issue of detection? Fewer birders, fewer regularly checked locations (we'll talk about that in chapter 9, which covers patch listing), and fewer concentration points would be just as likely, and perhaps more so, to impact detection rather than strictly impacting occurrence. If more of us focus on identifying and combing unique habitats away from coasts and other significant concentration points, what could we find? How many rarities are simply moving by undetected? What does the distribution of the occurrence of vagrants and extralimital migrants really look like? It's time to get out there and find out! But more on that later.

Not long before we began our descent on that recent cross-country flight, we were crossing ridge after ridge of mountains as we traversed Oregon. In the easternmost mountains (and mountains east of Oregon), the rain-shadow effect limits precipitation, and the slopes are relatively arid. Here, forests of Ponderosa Pine are home to Cordilleran Flycatchers.

However, as we pass into the wet coastal ranges, on the windward side of the tallest mountains, which are soaked by the cool, wet maritime air from the Pacific, we find the damp home of the Pacific-slope Flycatcher, which is dominated by Douglas Fir and Engelmann's Spruce. Here are two species that were once considered as one—the Western Flycatcher—that now find themselves separated, and separable by birders, by very different habitats created by geography. It should be noted that this is an extreme generalization offered here for sake of discussion. The exact dividing line is not yet well defined, in part due to the lack of birders in the interior region and also to the challenges of identification. However, if you're in the Coast Ranges in the summer, it's a safe bet that that little yellowish empid is a Pacific-slope Flycatcher, and if you're in mountains in far eastern Oregon in the summer, the Cordilleran Flycatcher is the one you should place your money on.

Now let's look at two examples of birding by habitat on a much smaller scale. In southern Maine's Scarborough Marsh, Nelson's and Saltmarsh Sparrows overlap in breeding season (fig. 2-3). Hybridization occurs as well, and research in this marsh was one of the reasons these species were "lumped" together, whereas subsequent research here helped to "split" them again. Birders from far and wide travel to this marsh, which is the epicenter of the species' overlap, for the opportunity to study these birds side by side.

I spend a lot of time in this marsh. For reasons that I cannot explain, on some days, one of the two species is far easier to find than the other. On some tours I really struggle to get my client a good look at the other one. So what do I do? Scarborough Marsh is 3,100 acres, and most of that is not accessible without miles of slogging through mud and marsh. How do I focus my attention on the target species, especially without damaging the habitat by trudging aimlessly through the marsh?

In my experience, Nelson's Sparrows prefer the margins of the marsh with the taller *Spartina alterniflora* and the other incrementally higher (in elevation, sometimes with a matter of millimeters making all of the difference) areas where the stems are taller and wider apart. Saltmarsh Sparrows, on the other hand, usually prefer the areas with *Spartina patens*, or salt hay, the thin, wiry, often-matted, and shortest spartina of the marsh (fig. 2-4). If I am looking for one sparrow or the other, I focus my attention on the patches with more of the desired plant species.

Similarly, at a local patch in Portland, which is referred to by birders as Dragon Field because it is adjacent to the Dragon Cement Company, an abandoned municipal landfill that is mowed once a year provides excellent habitat for migrant sparrows. This "sparrow-rific" patch has become well known by local birders for the volume of regular sparrow migrants, as well as for the regularity of rare-but-regular species, especially Dickcissel. Being a big fan of sparrows, I spend a lot of time in this weedy patch in late September and October.

Over the years, I have noticed a slight difference in the preferred micro-habitat of the various species of common migrants. Although in such a small area (only about 30 acres) most species can be found in all corners on

Figure 2-3.
Maine's Scarborough Marsh is 3,100 acres of habitat for the Saltmarsh and Nelson's Sparrows. However, not all acres are created equal, and each species does seem to show slight preferences in microhabitat. *Scarborough Marsh, Scarborough, Maine, 6/10* ©Derek Lovitch.

a regular basis, in certain parts of the park, particular sparrows tend to dominate. Although this observation is interesting in its own right, I have found it to be helpful when looking to add a specific species to a day's list, such as on my annual Sparrow Big Day.

Song Sparrows are the most widespread here, but they are usually found in the thicker, weedier, and somewhat brushy slopes and margins. Savannah Sparrows prefer the summit of "Mount Trashmore," where the grass is the shortest and the thicker-stemmed perennials are the fewest. Swamp Sparrows, appropriately enough, tend to prefer the cattail marsh at the base of the hill's western slope, as well as the wetter seeps scattered about. Meanwhile, most of the more uncommon Lincoln's Sparrows that I detect here are usually found along the northern edge of the park, where the woods meet a wet, brushy edge of the downslope. So, as you can see, even within

FIGURE 2-4.
When seeking specific species of "sharp-tailed" sparrows, it is helpful to focus on an apparent microhabitat preference. Nelson's Sparrows seem to prefer the taller, thicker stems of *Spartina alterniflora* (background), whereas Saltmarsh Sparrows can often be found in areas dominated by the shorter *Spartina patens* (foreground). *Scarborough, Maine, 6/10* ©Luke Seitz.

the small scale of a 30-acre park, slight differences in habitat can impact where birds can be found.

How about the much sought-after Smith's Longspur? Their high-tundra breeding habitat is hard to visit, so many birders seek them in winter. Their wintering range, which is one of the smallest of any North American endemic, is found in a small region of the lower Great Plains, including parts of southeastern Kansas, eastern Oklahoma, northeastern Texas, northwestern Louisiana, and western Arkansas. Even within this small area, the birds are very hard to find, but we have come to learn that Smith's Longspurs favor heavily grazed or otherwise disturbed (such as roadsides and airport runways) tallgrass prairie habitats that are dominated by three-awned grasses of the genus *Aristida*. In fact, if you can find large patches of *Aristida* grasses, you can often find your Smith's Longspur. In other words, it's time to learn to identify *Aristida* grasses.

Birders in urban areas in particular are becoming increasingly aware of the concentration of food resources that are provided by proliferating fruit-producing invasive plants (fig. 2-5). By seeking out patches of these plants, we are finding vagrants more regularly. By learning which patches are most productive, checking them frequently can yield some exciting surprises. A few years ago, I wondered how our knowledge of invasive plants is impacting our detection rate of vagrants, and I began to synthesize the idea of an article for the Changing Seasons column in *North American Birds*. After diving in way over my head in avian physiology and plant ecology topics, I found that all may not meet the eye. In fact, I began to wonder if our detection of the vagrants was less about the birds seeking out these food sources because they were good sources of nutrition and fuel, and more about the birds getting "stuck" in these patches because they were the only food source around, even though they weren't providing the nutrition the birds required. If the birds could not leave, but had enough food to simply survive, perhaps we're only able to find these birds because they are forced to stay put. (For the complete discussion, see the article "The Changing Seasons: Food for Thought" [Iliff and Lovitch 2007] that I cowrote). Regardless of the explanation, it is impossible to argue that checking dense concentrations of fruit resources—especially during "rarity seasons"—is not fruitful (pun intended).

Examples of microhabitat differences could run on for pages. Just think about seabirds: deep water verses shallow water, and rip currents, or tidelines (and even man-made microhabitats such as sewer outflows) in a bay or estuary can concentrate food sources and attract concentrations of waterbirds (fig. 2-6). Temperature breaks, an area of upwelling, and even the sea-bottom substrate can make a huge difference in where birds can be seen.

FIGURE 2-5.
Dense concentrations of food sources, such as invasive plants in urban areas otherwise devoid of food sources could attract unusual species, especially in late fall when most other food sources have been diminished. *Asiatic Bittersweet, Portland, Maine, 1/09* ©Derek Lovitch.

And tides, let us not forget tides. If you live along the coast, a tide chart is as important as your map, your field guide, and your notebook. High tide is when most shorebirds roost. Low tide is when most shorebirds feed. Midtide may be the best time at some locations to see shorebirds, because they concentrate at what is left of feeding areas before leaving for often-secluded roosting areas.

Each and every shorebirding location (and this is also true for the locations of roosting gulls, terns, and wading birds) has its own daily dynamics, which are closely associated with the ebb and flow of the water. A mudflat inundated by multiple feet of water is not a good habitat for short-legged peeps to feed; however, in shallow bays, extensive mudflats at low tide can

FIGURE 2-6.
Some microhabitats are less "natural" than others. A malfunctioning sewage out-flow pipe provided a dense concentration of nutrient-rich effluent. This attracted a mass congregation of Iceland, Herring, and Black-headed Gulls, Mallards, American Black Ducks, and American Wigeons in Halifax Harbor. This was a hotspot for a birding trip to the area that featured a count of well over 300 Iceland Gulls, including numerous probable individuals of the nominate *glaucoides* subspecies. *Gulls and ducks at sewage outflow, Halifax, Nova Scotia, 3/10* ©Jeannette Lovitch.

FIGURE 2-7. *(opposite page)*
Knowing when and where mudflats are exposed by receding tides will go a long way in finding shorebirds. A tide chart is a critical component of the coastal birder's tool box. *Mudflats at low tide, Yarmouth, Maine, 9/09* ©Jeannette Lovitch.

produce challenging conditions, such as distance, heat shimmer, and dispersed birds (fig. 2-7).

And let's not forget that not all feeding areas or all roosting areas are created equal. In many places, the long-legged shorebirds roost in taller grasses, while rock-pipers (i.e., turnstones, Surfbird, Rock Sandpiper, Purple Sandpiper, etc.) prefer to roost on bare rock above the high-tide line. Meanwhile, when it comes to feeding, rock–pipers can be found on rocks along the shore, most of the peeps on mudflats, and species such as Sanderlings and Red Knots usually on sandy beaches and sandbars. On a finer level, Semipalmated Sandpipers are often out in the more open and exposed stretches of mudflats, whereas Least Sandpipers often stay closer to vegetation (e.g., the edges of the flats and marshes).

The challenge, then, is to get to know your local shorebirding locale. Follow birds as they travel between roosting and feeding areas. Where do the peeps feed and roost? At what point in the tide cycle are viewing conditions optimal? And so on. Once we have spent the time to do the research (time in the field), we can easily learn to focus our attention on the best places for the best birds at the best times.

But, thinking back to the earlier, broader-scale examples, we have learned that habitat and geography are inseparably linked. And, therefore, just as birds can sometimes be found and/or identified by their habitat, birds can often be identified and discovered with the aid of geography.

Birding with Geography

Here are a few highlights from my day list for February 19, 2010:

6 Baltimore Orioles
1 Orange-crowned Warbler
1 Pine Warbler

Any guesses as to where I might have been? Somewhere on the Gulf Coast? Florida? Georgia? Maybe even the Outer Banks of North Carolina. All good guesses, but what if I added the following species to my day list?

358 Iceland Gulls in one place
20+ Black-headed Gulls together
Along with Boreal Chickadee, Gray Jay, Glaucous Gull, American
    Tree Sparrow

Give up? Confused? Well, this was a sample from a day list for a recent trip to Halifax, Nova Scotia! "Nova Scotia!? 6 orioles...in February...in Nova Scotia? Really?" See figure 3-1 if you don't believe me! And check back to figure 2-6 as well.

Although our tally of Iceland Gulls and Black-headed Gulls was quite impressive (thanks in large part to a malfunctioning sewage outflow), it is certainly our passerine highlights that were more noteworthy. The six orioles were actually all together, coming to an extensive feeding station featuring mealworms, suet, and fresh fruit in a Halifax backyard that had been hosting a dozen Baltimore Orioles in December! The Orange-crowned

Warbler was being pampered in a Dartmouth yard, with twice-daily offerings of live mealworms and suet. The Pine Warbler was hanging out with a
band of Black-capped Chickadees that visited a seed feeder in Point Pleasant Park just south of downtown Halifax.

While all of these birds were probably surviving in the area because of
the supplemental food being offered by these feeding stations, which is
needed even in a relatively mild winter, the feat of tropical and "southern"
birds overwintering this far north was no less impressive. And it made for
an amazingly diverse day list for this latitude in the middle of the winter.

Building on chapter 2, which discussed birding by habitat, the microhabitat provided in these urban areas, supplemented by the handouts of
feeder enthusiasts, has allowed these birds to survive the winter. But, it is
geography that is really at play here.

The province of Nova Scotia (fig. 3-2) is surrounded by open water that
moderates its climate, providing less severe winters and cooler (and fog-
gier!) summers, despite the province's high latitude. Furthermore, Halifax
itself is located on a peninsula, further moderating the air temperature. The
dense "concrete jungle" of the greater Halifax area adds additional warmth
to the air, as the pavement, buildings, etc. absorb heat during the day and
slowly release it at night.

One of Merriam's Temperature Laws, which were proposed by the then
chief of the United States Biological Survey in the 1890s and became the
"life zone model" that is still used by ecologists, states that "the physiologi-
cal constant of a species must be the total quantity of heat or sum of positive temperatures required by that species to complete its cycle of
development and reproduction." In other words, a species can only tolerate
a given range of temperatures in order to survive and eventually reproduce.

FIGURE 3-1. *(opposite page)*
A combination of the geography, climate, and habitat of the urban areas in the
Greater Halifax area of Nova Scotia in winter yields a surprising wealth of overwin-
tering Neotropical migrants, such as these six (of nine) Baltimore Orioles in the
winter of 2009–10. *Baltimore Orioles in tree in Nova Scotia backyard, Halifax,
Nova Scotia, 2/10* ©Jeannette Lovitch.

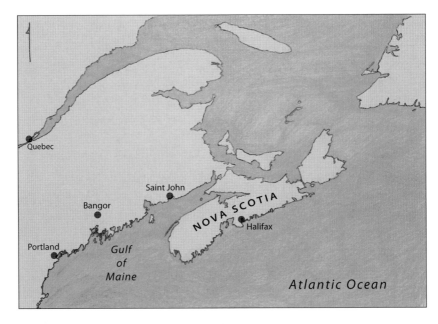

FIGURE 3-2.
Map of Nova Scotia ©Luke Seitz.

Therefore, it is a combination of regional and local geography that has moderated the climate enough to allow these wayward waifs to survive (with assistance anyway).

And geography plays another important role—getting the birds there in the first place. Let's consider the Pine Warbler, and look at a map of its range (figs. 3-3 and 3-4).

This bird, an immature, as is often the case, was not just "lingering" as many birders say. Instead, this bird was probably a mirror migrant, one that flew in the wrong direction (also known as 180° misorientation, which we'll learn more about in chapter 7) and because of various geographical characteristics, found itself funneled to the end of a small peninsula within the massive peninsula that is Nova Scotia. Perhaps it flew as far as it was programmed to do, but just in the opposite direction, and as the season progressed, its urge to migrate farther either withered away as certain hormones

FIGURE 3-3.
A familiar sight to many in the Eastern United States, the Pine Warbler (here an adult male) is a real treat to birders in the Maritimes of Canada. *Pine Warbler* ©Richard Crossley.

waned, or it simply lost the ability to build the fat reserves necessary for migration (which, theoretically, could have caused the bird to fly off in the wrong direction once again, likely spelling its doom over the vast expanse of water in the North Atlantic, or perhaps, making landfall in the Azores or United Kingdom, to the delight of thousands of dedicated "twitchers" (dedicated, and often obsessive-to-a-fault seekers of rarities!). And so it stayed.

Hypothetically, the Orange-crowned Warbler, on a long leg of its migration from, say, Alaska to Texas, either drifted eastward assisted by a massive storm that swept across the continent, or perhaps its internal compass was just a little less off the mark than our Pine Warbler's. It's hard to say, but once it found itself near the end of a small peninsula within a larger peninsula, it, too, stayed.

Since the number of Baltimore Orioles in this one yard is so impressive, it is possible that they arrived via a variety of mechanisms (which we will

FIGURE 3-4.
As you can see, Pine Warblers do not breed in Nova Scotia. Therefore, the Pine Warbler that overwintered in Halifax, Nova Scotia, in the winter of 2009–10 was obviously not simply "lingering." Map of Pine Warbler Distribution. From *Birds of North America.*

also be discussing in chapter 7), but these birds also found themselves at the end of a small peninsula within a larger one.

It's difficult to understand how these birds got to Nova Scotia and why they stopped going any farther, but at some point they "decided" to attempt to overwinter, and then the microclimate (provided by geography and a sprawling city) and microhabitat factors came into play.

And while we're on the subject, we can also thank geography for that impressive count of Iceland and Black-headed Gulls: Nova Scotia is much closer to where these birds breed. If I wanted to see these birds for the first time, Nova Scotia or Newfoundland should come to mind before, say, Arizona or New Mexico.

Do you own, or have you ever used, an "eastern" or "western" field guide? Perhaps Peterson's, Sibley, or National Geographic? If so, then you've begun to bird with geography! On a continental scale, one side of our country has a very different avifauna from the other. Iceland Gulls are most common in Nova Scotia, and Western Gulls are most common on the West Coast. But let us take a look at geography on a slightly smaller scale.

By now you have probably heard of such places as Point Reyes, Point Pelee, and Cape May. Although far apart geographically, all share a couple of similarities. No doubt that first one that comes to mind is that they are all great for birding! In fact, these are some of the most famous birding locations in North America. What do these three locales have in common? They're all peninsulas. Surrounded on three sides by water, they all offer food, cover, and a refuge from the vast stretches of inhospitable wetness. Just like Halifax, Nova Scotia.

What about southeast Arizona, the Lower Rio Grande Valley of Texas, and St. Paul and Gambell in Alaska? Although not all of these places are islands or peninsulas, why do birders spend so much time in these places? Location, location, location! (No, it's just not a mantra for investing in real estate!)

In chapter 2 we discussed how habitat can be used as an aid in both bird finding and bird identification. Geography and habitat are intrinsically linked, and just as birding is intrinsically linked to habitat, so too is birding linked to geography.

In addition to a pair of binoculars, a spotting scope, a field guide, and a notebook, the advancing birder is not fully equipped without a good map. There are plenty of bird-finding guides out there, but many birders want to find new locations on their own. Finding new and unique hotspots or seeking out personal patches is greatly impacted by geography. A map is the first place to start.

I think maps are an undervalued tool in the birder's toolbox. Sure the bird-finding guide and/or GPS unit will get us to a place (hopefully), but there's so much more to be learned by looking at a good map. Beside, we don't want to be dependent on bird-finding guides, especially in places with little, or no, good references, so learning habitat and geography is critical to finding good places to bird on your own.

In addition to aiding with identification and discovery, a broader understanding of geography is of great value to a birder. Being familiar with bird

FIGURE 3-5.
The species formerly known as the Western Flycatcher was split into two—the Cordilleran Flycatcher and the Pacific-slope Flycatcher. Your location goes a long way to identifying this species, especially during the breeding season. Notice that the Cordilleran Flycatcher is sitting in a locust tree, probably New Mexico Locust, a common species of that area (although from the photos, it could be a Black Locust, a widely planted nonnative). *Cordilleran Flycatcher, Manitou Lake, Colorado, 6/06* ©Bill Maynard.

distribution and its seasonal status on local, regional, and continental scales simply makes you a better birder by augmenting your identification toolbox—where you are is a very important clue as to what you might be looking at. Also, knowing bird distribution will help you pursue a variety of birding interests, such as state and county listings, by providing you with background knowledge to help you focus your effort in pursuit of specific additions to your lists.

All of us benefit when a birder's knowledge of local and regional bird distribution is called upon to update range maps in a field guide. Paul

Lehman calls upon state and regional "experts" to comment and contribute to each round of map updates he makes. That's why his maps, which are found in just about all of the major field guides these days, are so accurate.

Bird Identification with Geography

Not unlike birding by habitat, we have been using geography to assist our birding since day one. Have you ever looked at the range map in your field guide? Guess what? You were birding with geography! Returning to *Empidonax* flycatchers once again, we can narrow our choices by about 50% right off the bat by knowing if we are east or west of the Rockies.

Let us think back to the previous discussion of Cordilleran and Pacific-slope Flycatchers in Oregon (fig. 3-5). The habitat on one side of the state versus that on the other corresponds directly to geography. Foreshadowing chapter 4, Birding and Weather, it is weather—climate, to be exact—that is impacted by the geography of this area and that results in the habitat that these two morphologically similar birds call home. (I should mention that Pacific-slope Flycatchers *do* nest locally on the east side, but for sake of discussion, we'll ignore the isolated exceptions to the rule).

As cool, moist air over the Pacific Ocean moves over land, it is pushed up against the tall mountains of the Coast Ranges. As the air rises up and over the mountains, it cools even more. Cooler air holds less moisture, and therefore, it rains. This precipitation on the windward side of the mountains results in the damp, water-rich habitat that Pacific-slope Flycatchers (who even have geography in their name!) prefer (fig. 3-6).

Then because the air is "wrung dry," the leeward slopes receive much less precipitation, which further diminishes as one heads farther east. This results in the rain shadow effect, which first produces the Ponderosa Pine–dominated habitat of the Cordilleran Flycatcher, and where it is even drier, such as in the Great Basin, the result is the Gray Flycatchers' pine and piñon-juniper breeding habitat.

Looking at a chickadee in Georgia? Think "Carolina Chickadee" first. Need to add Northwestern Crow to your life list? Yes, you have to head to the Northwest, but more specifically you need to head to a narrow coastal band that runs from north of Seattle through south-central Alaska. This

FIGURE 3-6.
You won't find the Cordilleran Flycatcher in the moist forests of the coastal ranges along the Pacific Coast. Instead, the spruce and firs here are the haunts of the Pacific-slope Flycatcher. *Pacific-slope Flycatcher habitat, Larch Mountain, Oregon, 6/09* ©Derek Lovitch.

species (at least it is currently thought to be a separate species, although barely so!) is generally considered to be distinguishable from the very similar American Crow only by its range—bird identification with geography taken to its most extreme level.

We can find dozens upon dozens of examples of how valuable range (and good range maps) is to aiding bird identification. Especially as beginners, we regularly reference maps to find out what birds are possible, or at least, what we are most likely to see. As travelers, we often prepare—or at least we should!—for an upcoming trip by browsing the range maps in field guides to get an idea of some of the possibilities, especially when we visit an area for the first time. In preparation for an upcoming trip, skim your favorite field guide to get an idea of what species to expect, and what identification quandaries may arise with unfamiliar species. Take some time to go through your library of identification references to prepare yourself for these challenges in advance.

Bird Finding with Geography

Early in the morning on the day that I wrote this, I was birding the famous Biddeford Pool area in Maine. There are some nice sandbars and mudflats at low tide, but there are nice sandbars and mudflats elsewhere in southern Maine. There are plenty of brushy, scrubby edges, some manicured (and some not-so-manicured) yards and gardens, but it doesn't look much different from other shore towns in York County.

So, what's so special about this place? Why did I drive an hour to get here? Why do so many birders, both from Maine, and visiting "from away," come here? Well, take a look at figure 3-7.

It is a very narrow (as little as a few hundred yards at its narrowest point) peninsula sticking out into the ocean. While the whole geographical entity is really two parallel peninsulas, most people (birders and non) refer to the southern peninsula as Biddeford Pool with the north peninsula being called Hill's Beach, and the body of water is actually labeled on maps as simply the Pool. When birders refer to Biddeford Pool, they almost always mean birding locations on the southern peninsula. Although the habitats on this peninsula are not all that special, their location—on a narrow peninsula surrounded by miles of water—makes them quite special indeed. One morning, I was seawatching from East Point, the very tip of the peninsula. It was late May, and overnight the winds had shifted suddenly to the northwest as a cold front passed through. That shift to an offshore wind caused migrant passerines to drift out over the open waters of the Gulf of Maine. Come dawn, a tired songbird needs to get to land before a jaeger, gull, or exhaustion catches up with it.

The warblers, orioles, and flycatchers had turned west and made a beeline for the nearest place of safety—the first cover, the first bite to eat to replenish depleted reserves. In a mere hour at the point, I tallied six species

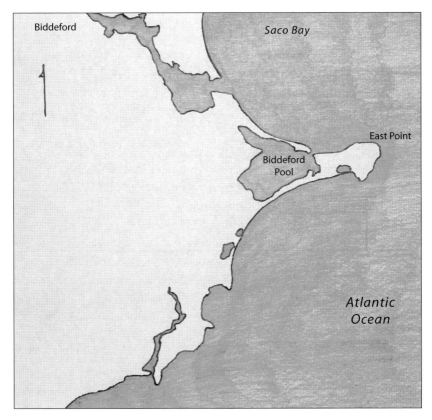

FIGURE 3-7.
Map of Biddeford Pool ©Luke Seitz.

of warblers, a Hermit Thrush, and a Baltimore Oriole making landfall. The six Yellow-bellied Flycatchers that arrived was the second-highest total of Yellow-bellies that I have seen in Maine at any one location during migration.

The only place that has beaten that count for me was Cape Neddick on a similar morning a couple of years earlier. In a half-mile stretch of brush and woods there were eight Yellow-bellied Flycatchers! I'm betting you can guess what Cape Neddick looks like.

Yup, another skinny peninsula sticking out in the ocean (fig. 3.8)!

Now, here's a map of the entire southern Maine coastline (fig. 3.9). What other peninsulas do you see? Guess what? These are some of the other best places to bird in southern Maine during migration.

How about Point Pelee (fig. 3-10)?

Point Reyes (fig. 3-11)?

Cape May (fig. 3-12)?

And what about on a much larger scale (fig. 3-13)?

Although it goes without saying that on a peninsula that big, some areas (coasts, habitat islands, urban parks, etc.) will be more favorable for birds than others (for example, inland orange groves) and therefore more likely to concentrate them—so that they can be enjoyed by birders.

Well, I think you get the idea. Peninsulas concentrate migrants. Although some migrants desperately seek out peninsulas, islands, and other "ports in a storm" when caught offshore, many, many other migrants simply funnel down peninsulas—such as Point Pelee and Cape May in the fall, or Whitefish Point, Michigan, and Sandy Hook, New Jersey, in the spring—in an attempt to avoid open-water crossings. Magee Marsh along Lake Erie on Ohio's north shore is not a true peninsula (it's actually more of an island if you consider the marsh to the south and the lake to the north), but in spring, astounding numbers of migrants congregate as they await favorable conditions for a nighttime departure for points north across a huge lake that might as well be an ocean to a small songbird.

Raptors are a perfect example of the funneling effect of geography. Buteos and vultures in particular rely on rising columns of warm air (thermals) to efficiently fuel extensive legs of their long-distance migrations. I'll touch on the development of thermals in chapter 5, but for now, all we need to know is that thermals develop over land and not over water. Therefore, it is in a migrant Broad-winged Hawk's best interest to avoid crossing large bodies of water.

Many hawkwatches strategically take place at such concentration points, including peninsulas and other coastal sites, and they record the largest counts of Broad-wings. The two southernmost hawkwatches in the United States—Corpus Christi and Smith Point, on the Texas Gulf Coast—tally hundreds of thousands of Broad-wings in a fall season, due to their lower

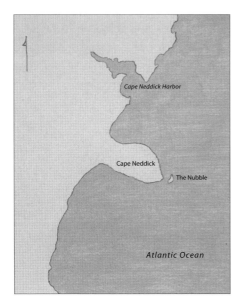

Figure 3-8.
Map of Cape Neddick ©Luke Seitz.

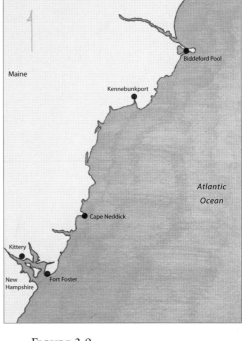

Figure 3-9.
Map of south coastal Maine
©Luke Seitz.

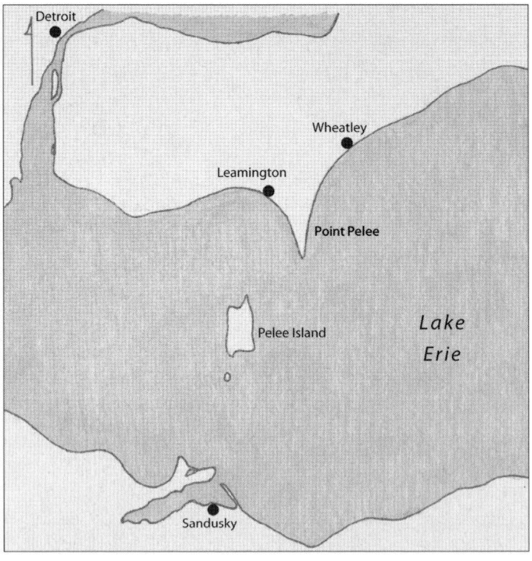

Figure 3-10.
Map of Point Pelee ©Luke Seitz.

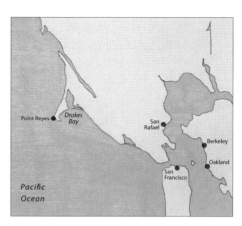

FIGURE 3-11.
Map of Point Reyes
©Luke Seitz.

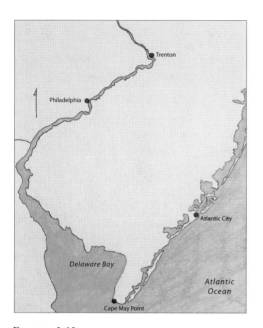

FIGURE 3-12.
Map of Cape May
©Luke Seitz.

FIGURE 3-13.
Map of Florida ©Luke Seitz.

latitudes (birds funneling from all points north) and shoreline concentration mechanisms.

Of course, these tallies pale in comparison to the counts in Veracruz, Mexico; Kekoldi, Costa Rica; and at the Panama Canal, because almost all of North America's Broad-winged Hawks are concentrated here as they pass through an ever-narrowing isthmus on their way to and from their South American wintering grounds (with the exception of a relatively small number that head to Florida, perhaps getting "stuck" there to spend the winter, as well as of an even smaller number at the Mississippi River delta in Louisiana and a few in south Texas).

Islands take these examples a step further. Distant islands, such as Hawai'i, have their own avifauna, as a result of evolution and biogeography, but in nearshore waters, islands provide sanctuary for a host of species of regular passage migrants. Once again considering Maine, Monhegan Island, which is about 12 miles off of the middle coast of the state, is arguably the best location in the state for observing migration on any given day in the spring and fall. Of course, weather directly impacts the quality of the birding on any given day, but if I had to choose one place to be on any given day in spring or fall in the state of Maine and a weather forecast was not provided for my decision-making, I would undoubtedly choose Monhegan.

Monhegan is conveniently located (and conveniently accessible by regularly scheduled ferries) in the Gulf of Maine due south of the parallel peninsulas of the Mid-Coast region. In the fall, birds flying over these peninsulas during the night pass over Monhegan as they cut straight across the water toward Cape Cod and southern New England, or as in the case of many Blackpoll Warblers, straight offshore all of the way to the West Indies and South America! In the spring, the birds head north over the Gulf, where strong storms and even the lightest westerly winds can push the birds offshore.

Whatever the reason (many of which we will revisit in subsequent chapters), when the first light of an impending sunrise breaks the horizon, nocturnal migrants begin to look for shelter. Over open water, shelter and safety are nonexistent. Although many birds simply turn for the nearest part of the mainland, others need to stop sooner, and an island such as Monhegan is a perfect place to take a break.

On a night that is clear and calm or a night with light tailwinds of the favorable direction for a given season, many birds will stop flying well before dawn (which we'll see for ourselves later on when we talk about monitoring migration by radar) and settle down into favorable habitat. However, when weather conditions are less favorable, the birds use more energy trying to get to where they want to go and so must spend more time finding shelter and food once they arrive at a destination.

Imagine, if you will one spring night, when northbound migrants, including a petite Northern Parula, have been nicely cruising along with a southerly tailwind (in the warm sector of a low, between a cold front and a warm front) over southern New England. Then, in the middle of the night, they begin to interact with the cold front and encounter overcast conditions and veering winds, then moderate rain, and finally a sudden shift to a northwesterly headwind as they pass through the cold front, pushing them offshore. Now, working harder, the parula begins to struggle. Instinct tells it to keep pushing forward—nothing comes close to the drive of a migrant bird. But now there's a lot more work to do, and the parula is rapidly depleting its energy (fat) reserves. In fact, still over open water, the bird has used up all of its supply and actually begins to metabolize its muscles to fuel its flight.

This can only last so long, so the parula desperately searches for a place to land. Tired and hungry—and so far having evaded potential predators such as Herring Gulls and Parasitic Jaegers—the parula finally sees a speck of green. Monhegan Island is in its sights, and it turns towards it in a race against time and physiology.

A birder sitting on the rocks at Lobster Cove, on the island's southern tip, scans the skies. All morning long, little specks have appeared low over the surf as tiny passerines attempt to avoid offshore predators and exhaustion. The birder sights a very small, short-tailed bird struggling toward land. It's the parula, and it's in the home stretch. A Great Black-backed Gull—a truly remarkable and enviable predator when it wants to be—makes a run at our traveler, but the parula has enough power to escape. As it nears shore, a Merlin is hunting over the water, picking off the most tired of migrants. Luckily for the parula, the Merlin has just grabbed an unlucky Magnolia Warbler and returns to a shoreline spruce to enjoy its breakfast.

Finally reaching the island, the parula lands on the first solid ground it can find—the rocks at the feet of our well-positioned birder. The birder is deemed less of a threat than metabolism, and therefore the parula immediately begins to feast on Northern Seaweed Flies in a wrack line and on some unidentified midges of some sort or another. This is one of the famous "Monhegan rock warblers" of a spring fallout on this magical island.

With just enough calories to inhibit starvation, the parula makes the short flight of about a hundred yards or so and disappears into the woods to spend the next day, or perhaps three or more, for a full refueling stopover, foraging with other parulas, "maggies," and sometimes as many as two dozen other species of warblers (such as Blackburnian Warblers, which usually prefer the tallest conifers [fig. 3-14] or Canada Warblers, which usually seek out dense wooded swamps [fig. 3-15]), vireos, and the like.

Meanwhile, other parulas, perhaps ones who had a slightly thicker reserve of fat or maybe simply have not been flying as far this night, are passing over the birder's head and immediately disappear into the thick spruce woods. Individuals with remaining reserves decide it would be best to avoid the competition for the island's limited resources and the dense concentration of equally hungry Merlins and Sharp-shinned Hawks, and after a few moments, they launch off of the island's west coast. A ferry is steaming toward Monhegan, its bow full of birders who watched the weather forecast, predicted a fallout, and decided this was a great day to call in sick.

A Black-throated Green Warbler has misjudged the distance and its fuel reserves and lands on the boat, exhausted. Another one is snagged by a Herring Gull. Others are streaming overhead in a race for the safety and food resources of the mainland. The birders are getting excited. They called it right (and in chapter 4, we'll learn how to make such predictions), and an outstanding day awaits.

Good thing that Monhegan Island was there!

Entrained by the processes that provide these islands and peninsulas with concentrations of migrants are rarities. While rare birds are indeed rare, in some locations, rare birds are essentially expected. Cape May, Whitefish

FIGURE 3-14.
Exhausted and hungry, this Blackburnian Warbler found shelter *under* a birder on Monhegan Island, Maine, during a fallout. A Merlin is unlikely to hunt under people! *Blackburnian Warbler, Monhegan Island, Maine, 9/05* ©Lysle Brinker.

FIGURE 3-15.
Desperate to feed upon arriving on Monhegan Island in a fallout, a Canada Warbler seeks the first potential food source—insects, such as the Northern Seaweed Fly–in the wrack line along the rocky shoreline. *Canada Warbler, Monhegan Island, Maine, 9/05* ©Lysle Brinker.

Point, Point Reyes, etc. Looking for rarities? Then these are some of the places that you need to visit.

Birders also tend to concentrate at such areas, which often results in the discovery of yet more "good" birds, which is often referred to as the "Patagonia picnic table effect": when birders go somewhere to chase a specific rarity, occasionally other rarities are discovered. This phenomenon is named for the famous Patagonia Roadside Rest Area, near Patagonia, Arizona. The discovery of a Rose-throated Becard here led to dozens upon dozens of visiting birders. Some of these birders then turned up other exceptional finds, such as the Thick-billed Kingbird and then Black-capped Gnatcatchers and Five-striped Sparrows.

Even when taking water out of the equation, there are still many geographical influences on where we look for birds. In chapter 3, we learned to look for birds by identifying habitats, and geography directly influences which habitats are found where.

If you bird in North America, and especially if you keep an ABA-area list (a list of all of the birds that you have seen in the continental United States and Canada), there is no doubt that you have visited, or have hoped to visit, Western Alaska, southeastern Arizona, southern Florida, and the Lower Rio Grande Valley of Texas. Location, location, location!

Although I have discussed offshore islands extensively, we should also consider "sky" islands. Especially in southeastern Arizona and extreme southwestern New Mexico, the northern limits of some predominately Mexican or Central American species are reached atop some of the region's mountain ranges, which extend into the United States like rugged fingers. Greater Pewees, a variety of hummingbirds, Mexican Chickadees, Olive Warblers, and many others call the sky islands of the Chiricahuas, Huachucas, Santa Catalinas, etc., home. It is not simply because these birds like to spend the summer in the cooler mountains rather than the surrounding oppressive desert heat (not that you can blame them!), but it is the combination of temperature and precipitation that yields the habitats where these birds find the food resources that they depend on for survival and family rearing.

Latitude is another important geographical consideration. Latitude—and the related length of growing season—directly impacts habitat as well. South of the 25th parallel, the peninsula of Florida reaches into the subtropical Caribbean habitats, including mixed hardwood hammocks and mangrove forest wetlands. This means Black-whiskered Vireos, Antilean Nighthawks, Mangrove Cuckoos, and White-crowned Pigeons can make homes in the ABA area. Similarly, southernmost Texas extends into the Tamaulipan brushlands scrub habitat of Northern Mexico, which harbors White-tipped Doves, Ringed Kingfishers, Couch's Kingbirds, Green and Brown Jays, and numerous other "Texas specialties" and are therefore within reach of the domestic traveler.

St. Paul Island, Attu Island, and Adak Island in Alaska are all islands, and we've now learned how and why islands are valuable. Gambell, Alaska, is on a narrow peninsula at the northwestern end of St. Lawrence Island a little further north. But a more significant reason that these locations are such popular destinations is their proximity to the continent of Asia. In fact, Russia is visible from Gambell (the only year-round town in North America where someone can actually see Russia from their windows—despite recent references to the contrary in the world of politics—a mere 46 miles across the Bering Strait. This proximity to another continent provides a much greater chance of seeing Asian species to add to your ABA list, or, as birders in Western Alaska have been discovering, add to the collective North America and ABA-area list! If your goal is to see or find a first North American record, well, then one of your best, but by all means not your only, chance is to "Head (north)west young man!"

Although the prevailing winds and weather patterns are not as conducive to strays from the other side of the pond, European vagrants are much more likely to occur in Newfoundland than in Kansas. Is a Yellow-legged Gull, European Golden-Plover, or perhaps a Fieldfare on your ABA-area want list? Then you might want to consider planning a trip to St. John's, Newfoundland. Whether we're at the extreme western side or the easternmost side of our continent, longitude also strongly impacts birding.

Thinking Locally

So now that I've discussed all of these wonderful, famous birding destinations, we can also apply these lessons on a more local level wherever we live. When I move to a new area, and at regular intervals thereafter, I spread out a good, detailed map and take a long look. What geographic features are noteworthy? A large lake? A long peninsula? Rivers? An isolated hill or cluster of mountains? What looks different? Where might certain types of birds concentrate, or where might we find a different habitat from the surrounding area?

Where should you go birding tomorrow? How about one of these unique geographical features? Just because you don't live near Cape May, Point Reyes, Monhegan Island, or any other well-known birding mecca doesn't mean you can't find good birding or find "good" birds, and a detailed map will help!

Birding and Weather

If the forecast calls for rain, bring a rain jacket. It if supposed to be cold, wear a parka. That's all that we have to know about weather, correct? Well, not quite! Although being comfortable and well-prepared for the elements, especially when traveling, will probably result in a better birding experience, a basic understanding of how birds react and move according to specific weather patterns can greatly enhance our birding experiences and help to make ourselves better birders.

First, you'll want to have an understanding of some of the basic concepts in meteorology, such as fronts, low and high pressure systems, wind, and precipitation. All of these factors enter into where and when birds may or may not be present. For this reason, I recommend at least skimming, if not thoroughly studying, a decent introductory meteorology textbook. However, an even more convenient tool is available free of charge: the National Weather Service's "JetStream—Online School for Weather," which can be found at http.srh.noaa.gov/jetstream/. Arranged by subjects, including birding-relevant topics such as wind patterns, tropical storms, and Doppler radar, I find the material to be very accessible, well written, and very useful as a good place to start your schooling in meteorology.

Ask a birder what their favorite time of year is, and you'll invariably receive an answer of spring, fall, or a specific month therein. Plainly and simply, bird migration is fun! Large numbers of birds, the chance of seeing great diversity, and yes, the increased chance of finding rarities—all of these aspects increase in the months of peak migratory movements. The spectacle of tens of thousands of shorebirds wheeling over the mudflats of Gray's Harbor in Washington, or millions of Short-tailed Shearwaters streaming through the Bering Sea, or a blizzard of hundreds of thousands of Snow Geese taking flight in a corn field in Nebraska are simply wonderful to watch. You don't need to keep a life list; heck, you don't even need to be a birder to enjoy sites such as these!

It is a common misperception that weather actually *causes* migration. This is not technically accurate, at least it does not directly cause migration. Instead, migration is a deep-seated response to long-established seasonal and geographical variations in the availability of food. Of course, the availability of certain food sources is often linked to weather—but to weather on a broader scale: that is, to climate. For example, an insectivorous warbler will have a tough time finding food in northern Manitoba in February, but in the summer, as any visitor to the boreal forest knows, insects are plentiful.

It is currently thought that Neotropical migrants (birds that migrate to and from the New World tropics of Central and South America, such as most of our warblers, vireos, orioles, etc.) are actually birds that evolved in the tropics. As the last Ice Age ended, the glaciers slowly retreated, and summer occurred farther and farther north. The birds began to migrate with the summer to the forests of North America to take advantage of the bounty of nutritious insect life found there and then "return" to their tropical homes for the winter.

As we know, weather is quite variable even in one place. The weather on, say, October 11 in northern Quebec is likely to be very different from one year to the next. If an insectivorous Tennessee Warbler waited until it was forced to migrate south due to a lack of food, what would happen when a massive frost or early-season snowstorm blankets the area and kills every midge, mosquito, or caterpillar (or forces them into hibernation)? Well, there aren't too many bird feeders in the boreal, so the options are more than a little limited.

Birds are not big gamblers; their life and their potential reproductive success ("fitness") in coming years is on the line. Therefore, it makes much more sense (and evolution has slowly wired this in) to leave at a relatively consistent time each year. And what is constant each and every single year? No, not just paying taxes, but also the duration of daylight—each and every fall, the day length slowly decreases. As a result, hormonal changes begin to occur in the birds, triggering many of them first to molt—replacing old, worn feathers for fresh, efficient ones that allow for a long-distance flight—then to develop fat reserves, the fuel for these annual journeys. And finally—occasionally after a period of *zugunruhe*, or "migration restlessness," when birds may appear antsy—something tells the bird it is time to get going. Hopefully this occurs long before the first killing frost or major blizzard.

Luckily, humans haven't been able to tamper with the changes in day length and light, so these annual comings and goings continue on a fairly constant schedule. However, it is important to remember that the rapid shifts in temperatures, growing seasons, and food availability due to climate change is resulting in tens of thousands of years of evolution of timing being thrown out of whack, because long-distance migrants are unable to change as rapidly as the climate.

Although weather does not directly affect when and where birds will migrate to and from, it absolutely and unequivocally has an impact on the migration process itself. Weather can facilitate, it can hamper, it can kill, and it can push a bird the wrong way, and it certainly directly affects our observation of migrants when we are birding. But before we talk about this, let's step back for a second.

I just finished saying that weather does not directly cause migration. Well, to be honest, this is not entirely true. Yes, the ultimate cause of all movements of all birds is the pursuit of food, but for some, weather is a more important proximate cause of seasonal movements. Some long-distance migrants have little choice. They are programmed to come and go at a relatively constant time each year. To oversimplify things a bit, consider a Tennessee Warbler that breeds in northern Ontario. It has spent a warm and comfortable winter in the rain forests and shade-coffee plantations of Central America, but sometime around early April, it gets the urge to fly north.

The bird can't possibly know what conditions are like in northern Ontario, so even if it has been a very cold spring there and insect life has yet to hatch, the bird migrates regardless. The window of time it has to breed in the northern latitudes is very small, and it has to be ready to set up a territory, attract a mate, raise a family, molt, fatten up, and then migrate south—all before the weather makes a turn for the worse. That's a lot to do in a short period of time, so the bird needs to migrate at about the same time each year to make this happen. This type of bird is called an obligate migrant. It has little choice but to move when its body tells it that it is time to do so.

Facultative migrants, on the other hand, are more flexible. They don't fly as far and are more general in their dietary requirements, so their migration is more variable. Red-winged Blackbirds are a good example of this type of migrant. In some winters they can be found farther north than in other winters, or they are found later in the fall than in other years—all because they can vary how far they fly depending on weather and the conditions that make food easier or harder to find.

If an early snowstorm blankets their food resources, a flight of a mere couple of hundred miles (or even a lot less) could put them back onto bare ground. If a big high-pressure system moves in early in the spring (or technically, for blackbirds, late winter), causing a rapid warm-up and snowmelt, these birds begin to trickle north. Especially males. Why just males? Well, in the world of the Red-winged Blackbird, the home-field advantage is everything. It behooves a male Red-winged to get to its breeding territory as soon as possible, set up a territory, and begin to fight off intruders and competitors so it is in prime position when the females begin to arrive, often a month or more later. Now, if a Red-winged Blackbird arrives a little too early and a snowstorm hits, their flexibility allows for a quick retreat to fairer conditions.

Similarly, waterfowl tend to come and go as ice comes and goes. A mild winter allows waterfowl to winter farther north than usual. A colder winter can push birds farther south than usual. Birders who frequent the reservoirs of Arkansas or northern Georgia love it when hard freezes occur up north and push larger number of ducks into their areas. Birders on the Christmas Bird Count in New England and Minnesota hate heavy freezes (which used to occur much more frequently) that ice over all of the freshwater bodies and limit the chance of finding a lingering dabbling or diving duck to brighten a cold, gray winter's day.

Therefore, in the case of facultative migrants, weather does in fact have a significant impact on the movements of birds, but nevertheless, food—or lack thereof—is still the root, or ultimate, reason for migration.

The phenomenon of migration is truly stupendous and downright mind-blowing Since the days of Aristotle, when he proposed that swallows hibernated in the mud for the winter (don't laugh; frogs and turtles do it, so it's not that much of a stretch to have imagined that birds did too), humans have been fascinated and confounded by migration. And we still have so, so much to learn.

Recommended Reading on Migration

To learn more about migration, I highly recommend the following resources. These readings will give you a greater understanding of the wonders of bird migration.

- Scott Weidensaul's brilliant *Living on the Wind: Across the Hemisphere with Migratory Birds,* which so eloquently and entertainingly follows birds around our hemisphere as they make their annual sojourns. (Actually, this book is also a must-read for anyone who enjoys great natural-history writing.)
- Ian Newton's seminal *The Migration Ecology of Birds.*
- *Gatherings of Angels: Migrating Birds and Their Ecology,* by Kenneth P. Able, another extremely well written and well researched, enjoyable, and digestible tome.
- "Migration," by Ian Newton, in *Handbook of the Birds of the World,* provides an excellent overview.

But for now, we're going to move on. The task at hand is to discuss the *observation* of migration. Although migration is not usually *caused* by weather, as we have just learned, weather has everything to do with when we can observe migrants. With a basic understanding of meteorology and a little tutoring in what to look for in an upcoming weather forecast, we can focus our energies at the best time and place for general or specific migration observation.

As you flip through the pages of this book, especially in this chapter, you may notice more than a few references to the journal *North American Birds.*

This quarterly publication is of significant value to birders. There's a vast birding community's worth of insight and information within its pages. Most of the references contained within this chapter, and elsewhere in this book, are from the Changing Seasons column, which attempts to dissect, correlate, or postulate what is going on out there. The Changing Seasons column is archived online and is accessible at no charge on the American Birding Association's website at www.aba.org/nab/archives.html. (I highly recommend taking a look at some of the articles cited within here, as in the example below, as well as the articles listed in the references at the end of the book.)

The benefit of the journal is that it summarizes sightings from throughout the continent each season. This record allows observations to be compared and contrasted, patterns to be detected, and the big picture to be resolved. This is especially true when it comes to deciphering how birds respond to weather, both in the short term and the long term. For example, in a recent issue entitled "Spring Migration: March through May 2009" (vol. 63, no. 3; the issues are named based on the season that they synthesize, not when they are published), a rash of early migrants and southern overshoots (which will be discussed below) in the northeastern United States and Maritimes of Canada (especially) was correlated with a pair of unusual storms that led migrants traversing the Gulf of Mexico and Caribbean Sea to be displaced far over the Atlantic Ocean and then deposited (the lucky ones anyway) in New England and the Maritimes—far, far beyond their usual ranges—in numbers that had never been seen before.

It would be impossible to discuss every single way weather can impact birds and birding in each and every region of the continent. Therefore, we'll just take a look at a handful of case studies that exemplify how meteorology can be applied—often together with the discipline of geography (chapter 3)—to aid our bird finding and help to make ourselves better birders. Whether our goal is simply to observe and appreciate the wonders of migration or to discover a vagrant – or anywhere in between – we want to look at weather for information beyond just how to dress for our outing.

While we birders are beginning to think that vagrancy actually has less to do with weather (with the exception of displacement by massive, strong storms) than we once thought, we know that weather directly impacts the detection of said rarities. Historically, the conventional wisdom said that vagrants simply got blown to the wrong place, for example a strong storm moving west to east across the continent would simply push a Black-throated Gray Warbler to Virginia. But now we are thinking that other phenomena, such as reverse migration or mirror migration (when birds fly 180 degrees or so in the wrong direction), and other "simple" mistakes may have more to do with it (we'll revisit this issue in chapter 8). Other vagrants can be explained by the phenomena of overshooting (flying too far in the appropriate direction), prospecting (somewhat intentional wanderings to explore for new habitats and food sources), and other potential causes, some of which may not have even been discovered yet.

For now, however, let us take a look at a few examples of how weather directly impacts birding, both for the rare and the commonplace.

When migrant birds—both big and small—are on the move, changes in weather are not always welcome, no matter what the birds' size. Although the birds departed in favorable conditions, they are unable to know the weather forecast for hundreds of miles away—despite being able to sense variations in pressure, which is one of the first clues that a change, either for the better or for the worse, is in the air (pun intended!). But for many species, especially long-distance migrants, conditions are likely to change en route. When those conditions become worse, the birds need to end their migration for the time being. By knowing what conditions could cause birds to cease flying, we can put ourselves in the best place to observe unusual species, unusual concentrations, or birds in unusual places.

Grounded Shorebirds

Migrant shorebirds, which are some of our longest-distance fliers, cross long stretches of open water or wide swaths of shoreless land with ease. Well, at least they cross with ease when conditions are favorable. When conditions are not, such as when a strong storm system pushes through the birds' path, they need to put down. If a nice patch of species-specific favorable habitat is within sight, the birds will head for it. More often than not, however, less favorable habitat is all that can be found on short notice, and when it comes to bad weather, the option really is the clichéd "any port in a storm" (fig. 4-1).

Heavy rains can produce ephemeral wetlands in farm fields, playing fields, and even front lawns. These are prefect places to find something out of the ordinary, or just ordinary birds in less-than-ordinary locations. This is especially helpful to those of us who do not have a handy wetland, mud-flat, or other prime shorebirding patch nearby. In addition, such short grass environs provide excellent viewing opportunities, thanks to the lack of tall vegetation for the birds to hide within.

Especially at the peak of fall migration, large numbers of shorebirds can fall out when conditions change rapidly. When heavy rains soak the soil, causing puddling on fields and lawns, I take a short drive around a regular loop that passes by a number of low-lying hayfields (which are usually mowed, often for the second time, by early August here in Maine), cattle pastures, small wetlands, and manicured recreational fields to look for dis-placed shorebirds. In my area, it usually takes a couple of inches of rain, more or less, depending on how saturated the soil is, to cause ponding. If we receive two to three inches or more in a given August storm, I drive this loop and almost always turn up a smattering of Greater and perhaps Lesser Yellowlegs, Least Sandpipers, Solitary Sandpipers, and occasionally Pecto-ral Sandpipers and Wilson's Snipe.

However, once in a while, I'll find dozens upon dozens of shorebirds. Why? The fields that I check are only about 10–20 miles from the coast, with its extensive salt-marsh wetlands, mudflats, sandbars, etc., and Scar-borough Marsh, one of the premier shorebirding locales in the state of Maine, is only about 30–40 miles from these fields as the peep flies. It is not surprising then, that under normal conditions, few shorebirds drop into these puddles; much better habitat is a short flight away. But when shore-birds that have been flying hundreds of miles are faced with a switch to unfavorable conditions, such as a heavy thunderstorm or an advancing warm front that switches to a southerly headwind (during southbound flights in the fall), birds literally can drop from the sky. The farther you are inland, the farther you will be away from prime shorebird stopover habitat,

FIGURE 4-1.
Buff-breasted Sandpipers are one of the shorebirds we affectionately refer to as "grass-pipers," and especially after a storm, any grass will do. These two birds found the putting greens of the Pease Golf Course in Portsmouth, New Hampshire, to be good enough until they could refuel for the next leg of their journey. *Buff-breasted Sandpiper, Portsmouth, New Hampshire, 8/96* ©Steve Mirick.

and so the more likely you will be to see shorebirds seeking refuge in ephemeral habitats such as fields and lawns.

The same scenario—in-air migrants encountering unfavorable weather, especially precipitation, and ending up in unusual places—also occurs with waterfowl. Seaducks, such as scoters, often fly exceptionally high overhead as they cross over land, and only the largest bodies of water are likely to host such migrants. But, once again, any pond or lake of any size is a better place than the sky when exhaustion or other dangers are imminent.

Gulf Coast Fallout

The same scenarios that result in fallouts of shorebirds or waterfowl can also result in a fallout of songbirds. Think back to the discussion of warblers on Maine's Monhegan Island in the last chapter. Now, multiply that by the tens of thousands, perhaps even hundreds of thousands. That will give you an idea as to why birders flock to places like High Island in Texas, Peveto Woods in Louisiana, and Fort Morgan in Alabama.

One of the highlights of any birder's lifetime is witnessing a fallout of passerines. It is ironic, however, that what so many birders hope for is something that is actually so downright bad for birds. From a bird's perspective, fallouts are not good things.

Fallouts occur when tired and hungry migrants, often at or near the verge of exhaustion, have to seek immediate refuge, and literally fall out of the sky when the first potential shelter is spotted. Let us look at migrants over the Gulf of Mexico as an example (fig. 4-2).

On some late April evenings, shortly after dusk, tens of thousands of warblers, vireos, and flycatchers will launch themselves off the coast of Mexico's Yucatan Peninsula and make a beeline for somewhere on the shores of Texas, Louisiana, Alabama, Mississippi, or western Florida. These birds carefully "choose" favorable conditions in which to begin their journey (the exact mechanisms that instruct a bird when it is or is not a good time to go are still unknown).

The problem, however, is the Gulf of Mexico. There is about 500 miles of open water between Mexico's Yucatan Peninsula and one of the goals for many species, the southernmost land of the Mississippi River delta in southeastern Louisiana. A lot can happen in 500 miles. On most nights, though, not much happens at all, and the migrants flow inland, passing high over the barrier islands and scrubby coastal woods of southern Louisiana and heading for the food and shelter of the more expansive woodland habitats of the state's interior. Since a bird's fuel reserves are well stocked with enough energy to battle unfavorable conditions, favorable ones allow the migrants crossing over the Gulf to still have some energy left when they make it to land. They therefore can avoid the shoreline habitats that have more competition, less food, and more predators.

FIGURE 4-2.
Normally confided to the highest canopies in the woods, a tired and hungry Tennessee Warbler that encountered strong northerly winds as it flew nonstop across the Gulf of Mexico will seek food anywhere it can find it. *Tennessee Warbler* ©Richard Crossley.

But if these trans-Gulf migrants find themselves over the Gulf when a large, strong cold front sweeps down upon them from the Great Plains, things don't happen that way. When a Black-throated Blue Warbler that has been cruising along nicely reaches the front, the precipitation associated with it is the least of the bird's problems. At the moment that the bird reaches the front, it probably feels a change in the wind speed; however, as soon as it has crossed that narrow boundary, it is unlikely that the bird actually feels anything different (although it probably senses a change in pressure, and perhaps temperature).

The finely tuned machine that is a flying bird still beats its wings at a certain rate. In fact, with the possible exception of that initial change in wind direction as it encounters the front, the bird's *air* speed (how fast the bird is moving in comparison to the surrounding atmosphere) is not known to change even though it is now facing a direct headwind. However, its *ground* speed (the distance traveled between two points on land) most definitely does change. (And this is key, well, we think it's key, but some researchers are now looking into this.)

Therefore, as our Black-throated Blue Warbler is traversing the open Gulf, it is flying at a preprogrammed and physiologically very specific air speed, which, if all goes well, will get the bird to the coast before its energy reserves are depleted.

Faced with a headwind for the last hundred or so miles, the sun comes up, the fat stores are running low, but the bird finds itself still over open water; no land is in sight. Now, it has more work to do. Its fat reserves are rapidly depleted, and believe it or not, in the most desperate of situations, the birds begin to metabolize their own muscles! In effect, they digest themselves in the hope that just a few more miles will make the difference between a coastal mangrove hammock or a watery grave.

These are the conditions that result in fallouts. The birds don't have the option of flying overhead and looking around for preferred habitat. No, it's any port in a storm, and a small scrubby woodland on a barrier island, a forest of mangroves, even a few trees in an urban backyard can be a lifesaver.

Concentrated in small patches of coastal habitat, thousands of passerines compete for limited food sources, while predators such as Merlins and Sharp-shinned Hawks—needing to fuel their own long-distance journeys—are on the prowl. Combined with the development that has ravaged the vast majority of the most extensive coastal habitats, and what we have is an absolute nightmare for a tired migrant—they've reached land, finally, but there's no place to find food or shelter!

For all the birds that do make it to land, countless others fall short of their goal and die from exhaustion. Some land on oil platforms or boats, but since food is not to be found on these artificial islands, this is only a temporary place to rest, not to refuel. It's sad and tragic, and it's hard to fathom the loss of life in such a situation.

That said, obviously, more birds must survive than perish. If that weren't the case, natural selection would have long ago resulted in migratory paths that did not involve crossing the Gulf of Mexico. And since fallouts do happen, we might as well be in a place to take advantage of the spectacle. Of course, passerine fallouts are not limited to the Gulf Coast; they can happen anywhere on the continent, but in spring, a number of meteorological and geographical features combine to produce exceptional events.

In spring, the conversion of warm, humid air from the Gulf of Mexico collides with the cold, dry air dropping down from Canada. This interaction of air masses results in strong cold fronts with strong storms that sweep across the entire continent, and some of them will sweep down all the way into Mexico and often across a part of the Gulf. This is the change in weather—wind direction, in particular—that makes a good night for flying into a dangerous situation for a bird, such as for many of our warblers that weigh less than a nickel.

Narrow barrier islands separate the mainland from the seas. Sometimes, these barrier islands are multiple miles offshore, with more open water and salt marsh lying in between, neither of which are much help to migrant warblers. Therefore, hungry, tired, and desperate, passerines struggling to find land seek refuge in the limited vegetation, which is becoming rapidly more limited by development, sea-level rise, and hurricane damage and which itself struggles for survival in the nutrient-poor, sandy soils and wind-whipped, salt-sprayed air of these habitats. Some of the best known refuges, such as High and South Padre Islands in Texas, Peveto Woods Sanctuary in Louisiana, and Fort Morgan in Alabama, attract volumes of birders that can actually rival the volumes of birds in these coastal migrant traps.

By learning how to predict when and where weather systems could result in the conditions that lead to a fallout, we can get ourselves to the best place to observe these fallouts, and a fallout truly is stupefying! The trees are literally dripping with birds—warblers dangling from every twig and leaf, thrushes scratching and scraping in the undergrowth, and flycatchers sallying for insects from every exposed perch. Pull up a chair, lean back, and

enjoy the show! The take-home message is simple: if there is migration occurring at night (which I will talk about much more in chapter 5) and it
begins to rain (especially after midnight), get up early and go birding!

Overshoots

Just as weather conditions can cause a bird to fall short of its destination,
and perhaps land on an oil platform in the middle of the Gulf of Mexico,
much more favorable conditions, such as an increased tailwind, can greatly
aid a bird's progress. Each spring, birders get excited by birds that have traveled "too far" to the "north" (fig. 4-3). In the East, species such as Hooded
Warblers, Summer Tanagers, and Blue Grosbeaks regularly end up in places
farther north, such as Maine, Nova Scotia, and occasionally even Newfoundland, than the species usually breeds. Are these birds simply lost? Perhaps. But it seems more likely that for most of these birds something else is
at play.

Because it is spring and these migrants have already made one long-
distance journey (in the previous fall), it is unlikely that the birds were
"wired incorrectly," as we often say for simplicity's sake. If their internal
compass or whatever else was not working, it is likely that these birds would
have made their mistakes, probably with dire consequences, on their first
migration in the previous autumn.

Although some overshoots are probably simply birds that flew the "correct" distance in the spring but had wintered farther north than is typical
for the species, many more of the overshoots that we celebrate may be birds
that simply flew beyond their target destination. Sometimes overshooting
results in a species discovering new territory to occupy, an event that may
happen more often as climate change alters habitat more rapidly than it
does birds' migratory patterns, and other times it results in a need for a
short-distance flight in the other direction to get back to where they "want"
to be.

But whatever the consequences of such overshooting, we as birders can
often be rewarded with some exceptional rarities. Certain weather conditions, principally long-distant, broadscale southerly flows, can aid in the
arrival of overshoots. Nothing beats a Tropical Kingbird in Washington or

FIGURE 4-3.
Normally confined to the extreme southern and southeastern corners of the United States, Painted Buntings are one of the species that seems to have a particular propensity to end up quite a bit farther north than they are "supposed" to in the spring. Although the exact mechanism or cause for this is unclear, a bird this gorgeous is always a welcome treat! *Painted Bunting* ©Richard Crossley.

a Kentucky Warbler in New Brunswick to brighten a spring morning of birding!

In fact, we can often predict the arrival of spring overshoots by watching the weather and, especially, the winds. In the Northeast, deep southerly and southwesterly flows can result in the arrival of species such as Mississippi and Swallow-tailed Kites, White-winged Doves, White-eyed Vireos, and a variety of "southern" warblers, among others. Such promising wind conditions occur ahead of strong cold fronts and also on the west sides of large domes of high pressure. When I see a string of days of moderate to strong southwesterly winds in the spring here in Maine, I begin to think about a Hooded Warbler or a Summer Tanager in one of my local patches or perhaps finally a Mississippi Kite for the Bradbury Mountain Hawkwatch—and, hopefully, my state list!

Remember the mention of air speed in the discussion Gulf Coast fall-outs? Just as a headwind does not affect air speed but significantly reduces ground speed, a strong tailwind—such as a southerly wind behind a spring warm front crossing through New England—does not affect air speed but greatly increases ground speed. Therefore, if a Summer Tanager that is pro-grammed for flying at a specific air speed and/or perhaps a specific length of time is flying along one night with a southerly wind, it will cover more ground than it's "supposed" to and therefore end up quite a bit farther north than normal. Therefore, this overshoot didn't simply make a mistake and fly too far, but it did cover more ground than it is physiologically pro-grammed to, much to the delight of the birders on Maine's Monhegan Is-land who just added a Summer Tanager to their state lists.

Or perhaps not. The counterargument is that this explanation should yield far more overshoots—extended periods of southwesterly winds are far more common than southeastern species in northern New England, but there still seems to be some role for extended periods of tailwinds to play here. The *North American Birds* article that I referenced earlier hypothe-sizes that, at least in that particular spring, southern species were first blown out over the Atlantic, and then a strong southerly flow carried some of these birds much farther north. In this case, the southerly winds were the proxi-mate, not ultimate, cause of the vagrancy. The ultimate cause was the area of low pressure that steered the birds over the open water, but it was the south-erly winds that delivered these treats to birders in the Northeast and Maritimes.

Tropical Storms

True seabirds live most of their lives at sea, coming to land only for a short period of time to breed, and for most of these pelagic species, "land" is some distant offshore island. Thus, seeing seabirds usually entails a long and often tumultuous boat ride, unless, of course, you live near the coast and you spend hours scanning the seas when a cold and damp onshore wind is

FIGURE 4-4.
Tropical storm systems can displace seabirds far out of range, even well inland. Some birds, like this Sooty Tern discovered in Cape May, well north of its usual haunts, are not always in the best shape after such events. *Sooty Tern, Cape May, New Jersey* ©Richard Crossley.

blowing. But even then, many birds will not be spotted by landlubbers, and beside, what happens if you live hundreds of miles inland?

Whether you live near the coast and are hoping for a massive flight of seabirds close enough to enjoy, or you live far inland and are daydreaming of terns and tubenoses, then your best, and perhaps only, chance of seeing such things is immediately following the passage of a tropical storm system. From frigatebirds to pelicans, from Sooty Terns to Laughing Gulls, from Band-rumped Storm-Petrels to Sooty Shearwaters, being in the right place at the right time can yield some amazing discoveries and everlasting memories (fig. 4-4).

Reservoirs in Oklahoma have hosted Cory's Shearwaters, Magnificent Frigatebirds, Bridled and Sooty Terns, jaegers, Sabine's Gulls, and much more. Frigatebirds (presumably all, or at least mostly, Magnificent) have been transported to Nova Scotia, Minnesota, Michigan, and throughout the East. Royal Terns have been spotted in Arkansas, American Flamingos in Florida, flights of Sooty and Bridled Terns off of Virginia, and so on.

Hurricanes, and even the somewhat weaker tropical storms, are complex, vicious, and often very destructive weather systems. Leave it to birders to find the silver lining to such events! While there are, no doubt, many joys to be had by a seabird fallout inland or a first state record displaced half a continent away, let us not forget that these storms can cause billions of dollars in damage and cost people their lives. Please do no construe our interest in documenting—and yes, enjoying—the avian wonders resulting from such events to anyway dismiss the graveness of these storms. But, as birders, our quest for knowledge, for new birds, or for something different to look at once again puts us at odds with common sense. Just don't lose sight of the fact that these storms are dangerous during and afterward, and that despite our quest for rarities, we need to avoid putting ourselves in harm's way (e.g., flooded roads and downed live wires).

Those concerns aside for the time being, where should we go birding? We still have a lot to learn about when and where to look for storm-entrained birds immediately after the passage of strong tropical storms, and your area's birding community will have more details about where you should specifically be looking than I do. There are, however, a few basic concepts to keep in mind.

We believe that there are two main ways that birds get displaced by storms. One is by being entrained, or simply, "stuck," within the storm. The other is being pushed out of the way.

The northeast quadrant of an organized tropical storm is the most intense. Here the combination of the rotational winds of the storm (the counterclockwise spinning of a low pressure system) and the translational winds (the forward motion of the storm) combine to create the most powerful—

and most destructive—winds. This is also, therefore, the sector of the storm that is most likely to push birds out of the way or cause birds to flee.

It is usually where this northeastern quadrant first hits land that much of a storm's destruction occurs. It is also the quadrant that is the most likely to produce rarities. (Of course, I should add a disclaimer once again—no one is suggesting going out to bird, or do anything else for that matter, when a major storm is about to hit!) For weaker storms when safety is not a significant concern, or after the passage of a strong storm, one of the places that we want to focus our attention on is where the northeast sector passed over and through.

Presumably, most birds that get entrained by the storm are entrained within the eye. Here, they ride the benign weather surrounded by the violent eyewall. Especially well inland, where tropical lows rapidly weaken, birds that have been entrained in the storm will fall out as conditions permit.

Whether pushed out of the way or entrained by the eye, many of these birds will seek the nearest large body of water when the storm weakens. If you live near a large lake or reservoir, that would be a good place to check. It would be especially worth scanning any "bottlenecks" where birds milling in the lake would be concentrated as they move about, such as where a lake narrows or drains into a river. Peninsulas, open stretches of shoreline with nice vistas, or nearby hillsides might also be worth some time.

Since many of these displaced seabirds want to head back to sea, figure out which direction they came from (which way the winds were blowing) and which direction will take them back out to open ocean. (Time to get out that map that we came to know and love in chapter 3!) Try focusing your effort on that side, attempting to spot the birds as they depart. Likewise, many displaced seabirds will use rivers to find their way back to the sea, and therefore if a major river is nearby, scanning from its shores may pay dividends. And closer to the sea, the mouths of bays, estuaries, and sheltered coves are all places that might produce storm-tossed excitement.

Study the weather maps. Where is the storm going to make landfall? What path will it take? When will it weaken? When do the winds shift? Then, look at a map (see chapter 3), study it, strategically place yourself in the potential path of birds as described above, and wait. You really can expect the unexpected.

And let us not forget that it is not just the "big ones" that can displace birds far and wide. In fact, quite a few of the better birding storms in recent years have been relatively weak tropical storms. For a good overview of such a storm, see the article "Special Interregional Report: Tropical Storm Ernesto" (Davis et al. 2007) as an example.

Cave Swallows in the East

Once considered a mega-rarity outside of Florida and Texas, birders on the eastern half of the continent now fully expect to see Cave Swallows in the fall, especially in late October and early November (fig. 4-5). Triple-digit counts in Cape May, dozens around the Great Lakes, and even some as far afield as Newfoundland are now becoming the rule, not the exception. In fact, we now realize that Cliff Swallows are the rarer of the two *Petrochelidon* species in the East by November!

Although we're still not completely sure why this is happening, we do know that Cave Swallows are rapidly expanding their range. We also know that the vast majority, if not just about all, the carefully studied records of this species outside of Florida in the fall are of the southwestern subspecies, *pallida*, which breeds in Central America and Mexico north through New Mexico and Texas almost all of the way to the Oklahoma border, so we know roughly where these birds are coming from (i.e., *not* Florida or the West Indies, which is where the *fulva* group of subspecies breeds).

We also know which weather pattern facilitates the species' arrival in the East. While it may or may not be the "ultimate cause" for these prospecting, pioneering, or just plain lost swallows, we do know that prolonged periods of south-to-southwesterly winds that originate from Texas transport greater numbers of Cave Swallows farther afield.

So in late October, I get pretty excited when I take a look at the upper-level winds. I usually use the National Center for Atmospheric Research's "RAL Real-Time Weather Data" webpage at http.rap.ucar.edu/weather/.

FIGURE 4-5.
After being ushered east by late fall weather patterns and/or storm systems, these Cave Swallows in Cape May, New Jersey, where they are now expected annually in varying numbers, seek shelter and warmth by roosting together on the closest thing to a cliff or cave that Cape May can offer. *Cave Swallows, Cape May, New Jersey* ©Richard Crossley.

Clicking on the "Forecast" tab and looking under "Aloft plots," I check out the winds at 925 millibars of pressure (about 2,500 feet up), which is a good place to start. This is about the altitude where most birds are flying, and therefore it is more directly relevant to where birds might be blown to or from. However, I also like to keep an eye higher up, such as at 300 millibars (30,000 feet). Although this is far above the height of migrating birds, I do think that it offers a good, quick overview of which directions winds, storms, and overall weather patterns are originating from and heading to. I have found that with the 300-millibarimage as a guide, I am better able to interpret the graphics of the more directly relevant 925-millibar image.

FIGURE 4-6.
Strong westerly winds, especially southwesterly, escort exciting vagrants to the remote outposts of the western Alaskan islands. This Jack Snipe was an exceptional find after a late-spring/early summer storm that blew through St. Paul Island in the Pribilofs. *Jack Snipe, St. Paul Island, Alaska, 6/08* ©Gavin Bieber.

So after a lengthy period of southwesterly winds, I then hope for a nice, sweeping cold front to cross the continent, pushing wandering birds to the coast or other concentration points where I—and you—may find them.

The "Siberian Express"

When I was conducting the first ever fall avian survey on St. Paul Island in the middle of the Bering Sea, I chatted nightly with Paul Lehman, who was stationed—as he is in most recent autumns—at Gambell on St. Lawrence

Island, to my north We would compare sightings for the day, comment about how we were two of the few people in the world who got excited about first island records of things like Chipping Sparrows and who attempted to correlate occurrences of certain species. One such tidy correlation was after a few days of a good westerly blow. Shortly thereafter, Paul recorded a major flight of Red-throated Pipits at Gambell. And the next day on St. Paul? You guessed it! A major flight of Red-throated Pipits.

As in previous years, occurrences of large numbers of species such as Red-throated Pipits in the outposts of Alaska foreshadowed numbers of these birds along the Pacific Coast, especially in California and Baja California later in the season, much to the delight of that region's birders.

Back in those Bering Sea outposts, along with places like Attu and Adak, birders would spend countless hours (and often countless dollars) in the hopes of seeing Asiatic species gone astray. Whether it's for building your own list or for the thrill of discovering a first record for North America, one eye should be on the birds, while the other is glued to the weather maps on the computer.

On St. Paul, an extensive period of northeasterly winds resulted in the island's first records of Lincoln's Sparrow and Townsend's Warbler, but it is indeed a select few who get that excited about such things. But when the winds shift and the gales blow from the southwest, west, or northwest, then visions of Red-flanked Bluetails, Siberian Rubythroats, Hawfinches, Eyebrowed Thrushes *and* maybe even a mega like a Jack Snipe (fig. 4-6) dance in our heads and hopefully soon in front of our binoculars.

While some of the most astounding rarities that have occurred in St. Paul, such as the Chinese Pond-Heron and Brown Hawk-Owl, were reverse migrants (we'll talk more about such phenomena in chapter 7) for which the weather pattern at the time facilitated their deposit onto this 44.4-square-mile rock, there's little doubt that winds out of the west produce "good" birds, even if it's "only" flocks of Wood and Sharp-tailed Sandpipers.

When a parade of strong low pressure systems marches across the region, birds get displaced, birders get excited, and rarities get discovered. And when things are really hopping in the Bering Sea, observers on mainland

Alaska surely take note, as do serious rarity-seekers from British Columbia all the way down to Mexico. Once some of these birds get displaced to the "wrong" side of the sea, some will continue to migrate southward, and perhaps months after being blown across the Bering Sea, a Red-throated Pipit will greet a birder on a lawn in Cabo San Lucas.

The Bigger Picture

All of the previous examples have described relatively small, short-term effects of weather; however, we should also be thinking about broader-scale, longer-term effects of variations in climate. Drought can affect breeding success, can mean fewer insects for nestlings, and can affect even the wintering ranges of seedeaters by reducing seed production of plants. Likewise, cold wet weather over the course of a season can impact birds' breeding success. And then there are the increasingly obvious and increasingly serious effects of global climate change, which are significantly affecting bird distribution and weather patterns, as in the examples described above.

Almost every column of the Changing Seasons in *North American Birds* attempts to draw some conclusions about how the very real, and very perceptible, changes in our climate are affecting birds. Once again I'd like to mention that this journal is an indispensible resource for the student of bird distribution and its changes. At the same time, Christmas Bird Counts, North American Breeding Bird Surveys, and even eBird reports (all of which I will discuss in detail in chapter 6) are tracking these changes, and those data are accessible to all of us.

Paying Attention to the Weather Forecasts

So now that we've talked about how important it is to pay attention to the weather, we now actually have to pay attention to it. Personally, I like to use the text product of the National Weather Service, which describes the weather, variables, and possible forecasts before it is synthesized into a sun or cloud symbol on a TV weather report.

Especially when traveling, I find it easy and convenient to simply log on to Weather Underground (http.wunderground.com), at least for the

United States (in Canada, see the *Weather Network* at http.theweathernet-work.com or Environment Canada's *Weatheroffice* at http.weatheroffice. gc.ca/canada_e.html). After typing in a zip code to get to the area that you are interested in, scroll down the page to "Forecast," and at the very bottom of that section, you'll find a small-type hyperlink entitled "Scientific Forecaster Discussion," which will take you to the text from the National Weather Services' weather discussion. I prefer to use this forecast instead of the boiled-down ones, because it discusses some of the variables, uncertainties, and larger-scale atmospheric conditions that go into the making of a weather forecast. Sometimes the discussion is so technical that it's over my head, but more often than not, I can at least glean some tidbits of note.

My daily routine involves looking at the current and forecasted surface maps, followed by the winds, and then reading the "Scientific Forecaster Discussion" for my local area. Usually I begin with the current conditions and the conditions (especially winds and any precipitation) of the past 24 hours. For that, I visit the National Weather Service's Telecommunication Operations Center for my area. Go to weather.noaa.gov/index.html. Select the state in the drop-down menu, and then in the next menu, select the nearest location to you; the result will show you the current conditions and the 24-hour summary.

Next, I study the surface maps to see where fronts and storms are. On http.rap.ucar.edu/weather/model/ (this is a page that is most worthy of bookmarking, because it has a lot of birding-pertinent information a mere click or two away), I check the "Current Analysis," the "12-hr Forecast," and the "24-hr Forecast." Then I check the radar from overnight (which I will talk about at length in chapter 5), and finally I digest the "Scientific Forecaster Discussion."

Armed with a basic knowledge of meteorology, some background information on climate, and the forecast discussion for the next couple of days, birders can get themselves into the right place at the right time to take advantage of what surprises and wonders various weather patterns may have in store. By adding a little meteorology to a basic understanding of how birds react to certain weather conditions, we can better use our time in the field, find more birds, and become better birders.

For an excellent conversation on the myriad ways that weather events, from cold fronts to hurricanes, affect birds and birding, take a look at "The Changing Seasons: Weatherbirds" (Dinsmore and Farnsworth 2006). This article is also a good primer for the topics that we will cover in chapter 5, "Birding at Night."

Birding at Night

Perhaps it is to take advantage of a more stable atmosphere, or maybe it is to avoid predators, or maybe it's to avoid overheating in the sun, but whatever the reason, almost all of our Neotropical migrants (flycatchers, vireos, warblers, tanagers, orioles, etc.), most of our sparrows, rails, and many other groups of birds migrate at night. Meanwhile, some species, like geese and American Robins can move both day and night.

For most birders, the idea of birding at night conjures up images of creeping around in the darkness of the deep woods, trying to follow the deep, bellowing, and resonating hoots of owls emanating from its depths. If you're really lucky, you might even succeed in finding a nearly-three-foot-tall Great Horned Owl perched on an exposed tree limb. But what about a four-inch-long warbler flying hundreds, or perhaps even thousands, of feet above you? Not likely to happen, right?

Well, actually, it's much easier to "see" warblers at night than it is to see owls!—and we don't even have to grab a flashlight. In fact, we don't even have to leave the comforts of our living room. So, grab your laptop, kick off your shoes, curl up on the couch with a good beer or perhaps a steaming cup of hot chocolate (depending on season), and let's go birding!

I'm serious.

The majority of our passerines migrate at night high above, out of sight and out of mind to most people, even to most birders. But, not anymore! With the aid of weather radar, a little knowledge of the current weather conditions, and some basic understanding of bird ecology, you can not only see tens of thousands of birds migrating overhead, but you can use this information to plan your birding adventures the following day.

First, log onto your favorite weather website that you learned to love after reading chapter 4, "Birding and Weather," and check out the NEXRAD (NEXt generation RADar) Doppler radar image for your local area. For looking at birds, I prefer to use the National Center for Atmospheric Research's "Real-Time Weather Data" page. To access your nearest NEXRAD radar image, visit www.rap.ucar.edu/weather/radar/, click on the nearest radar site on the map, and take a look at the latest image. (We'll talk more about viewing the overnight images a little later.)

Doppler radar works by emitting bursts of waves outward. It then listens for energy that is reflected back, collects it, and measures it. The radar bounces off of rain, sleet, snow, dust, pollen, birds (figure 5-1a-c), and buildings; however, by analyzing both the reflectivity and velocity images together, we can often figure out exactly what is being shown on the radar.

Before we move on with the radar discussion, let me talk about a few things we can learn from the Doppler image in figure 5-2. In the upper left, we see the four-letter code of the radar station and its location. Portland, Maine's radar is actually located in the nearby town of Gray, hence "Portland, ME/Gray." "Base reflectivity 0.5 degrees" refers to the amount of reflected energy measured when the angle is 0.5 degrees above the ground (see figure 5-1 a-c). More important, for our purposes anyway, is whether the image is reading "clear-air mode" or "precip mode." Clear-air mode is much more sensitive because it is actually detecting dust particles and cloud droplets; therefore, birds—or big, fat raindrops for that matter—will appear to be in greater density in clear-air mode than in precip mode. There-

FIGURE 5-1. *(opposite page)*
(Top) Early in the night, as birds first begin to leave the trees, they are too low for the radar beams to detect. Here, for example, is a schematic interpretation of the radar beams emanating from the top of a tower, but the birds are below the angle at which the radar beams are emitted. (Middle) However, during the peak of the birds' nocturnal movements, birds are flying high enough that they are within the range of the radar. In this diagram, the birds are passing through the radar beams emanating from the top of the tower and therefore are reflected back to the radar, as seen in figures 5-1 to 5-7. (Bottom) As the birds' nocturnal movement comes to an end, the altitude of the flight rapidly diminishes, and in the predawn hours, most birds are flying lower than the radar can detect. ©Luke Seitz.

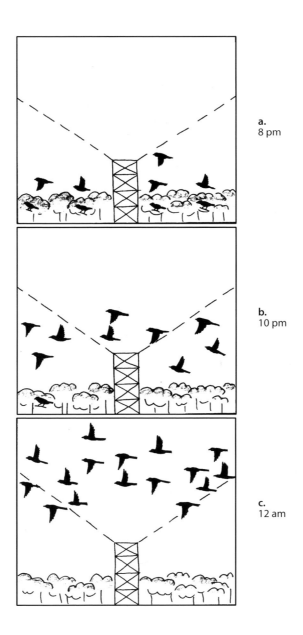

a.
8 pm

b.
10 pm

c.
12 am

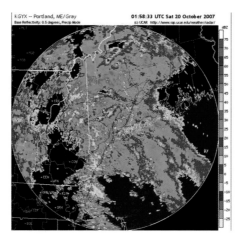

FIGURE 5-2.
We are all familiar with radar images from our local weather forecasts. Here, southern Maine is covered by rainfall of varying intensities.

fore, if what looks like a massive flight (as in fig. 5-6 below, for example) is being detected in clear-air mode, it's actually not quite as massive as if the same colors were appearing in precip mode.

We all know what rain looks like on the radar (fig. 5-2). When it's not raining, however, we can still see quite a bit on a radar image. Figure 5-3 shows what meteorologists often refer to as ground clutter. While meteorologists often refer to anything that is not precipitation as ground clutter, we know that birds, bats, and insects, along with dust, pollen, and smoke can all be detected by NEXRAD radar, and, obviously, those are not on the ground.

In the case of this image, we are in fact seeing ground clutter, or, more scientifically, anomalous propagation. Ground clutter appears on radar when dust or other small particulates in the atmosphere cause the radar beams to bend and intercept the ground and/or surrounding trees and buildings. However, unlike birds, anomalous propagation has no velocity associated with it, since the ground is never moving toward or away from the radar, so Doppler radar does not register a velocity.

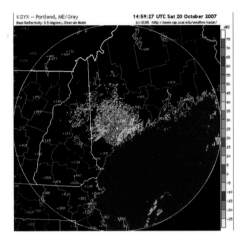

FIGURE 5-3.
Even on clear nights, NEXRAD radar registers images, which are often referred to as ground clutter.

During the months of migration, both spring and fall, we can actually watch migration in action across the United States thanks to the free, widely available tool of NEXRAD Doppler radar. While we are not yet quite sure as to *why* birds migrate at night (I'll leave that for another book), we know *that* they do. Especially on clear nights (we know that birds use the stars for navigation) with favorable winds, birds take to the skies.

Unfortunately, Canadian birders do not have a nationwide NEXRAD system, but the Canadian Weather Surveillance Radar (CWSR) shows promise in being as valuable a tool for both scientific and casual observation and documentation of nocturnal migration. For more information, see "A Comparison between Nocturnal Aural Counts of Passerines and Radar Reflectivity from a Canadian Weather Service Radar" (Gagnon et al. 2010).

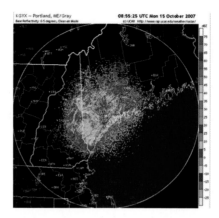

FIGURE 5-4.
However, in addition to precipitation and ground clutter, NEXRAD radar also detects bird migration, such as on this base reflectivity image.

With that established, let's go back to a radar image, say one in the month of September in Maine (fig. 5-4). Prior to looking at the Doppler image, I checked the current conditions. For that, I used the National Weather Service's Telecommunications Operation Center page. (Go to weather.noaa. gov/index.html. Select your state, and then nearest location.) In our case study here, I see that it is clear and calm. It's a good night for flying, and we can see all of this play out on the NEXRAD imagery.

Start by pointing your browser to http.rap.ucar.edu/weather/radar. Note that the times (in the drop-down menu under "End time") are listed in UTC (Coordinated Universal Time. To convert UTC to Eastern time, subtract four hours from the UTC during daylight savings time, or five hours during standard time. For example, 0200 UTC is 10:00 p.m. Eastern Daylight Time. As we head west, subtract one additional hour from the UTC to get your local time. Therefore, in the Pacific Time Zone, local time is minus 7 (during daylight savings time) or minus 8 (during standard time). The first thing to do is to check a pre-sunset image to see what the radar looks like when no migration is occurring. This is also a good way to determine whether or not you should expect to see ground clutter or other atmospheric noise such as dust or smoke come nightfall.

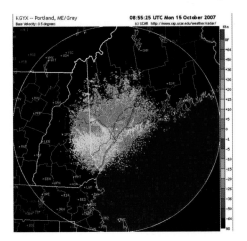

FIGURE 5-5.
The velocity image tells us how fast and in what direction the objects being detected by the radar, whether precipitation or birds, are moving.

To do this, set the end time to the time closest to sunset at the radar station in your area. Then click on the radar station on the map that you are interested in. Next, by changing the end time, you can cycle through different key times during the night to determine (1) whether migration is occurring, (2) the scale and magnitude of the event, (3) whether any atmospheric barriers to migration have presented themselves, and (4) where you should go birding in the morning!

I usually look at the 10 p.m., 1 a.m., and 4 a.m. (local time) images to get a feel for what was or was not happening on a given night. When I want to explore further, I then study the loop by setting the loop duration for the entire night and then once again clicking on the radar station of interest. This provides a continuous loop for the entire overnight period, demonstrating the ebbs and flows of the tide of passing migrants.

But, we don't want to jump to any conclusions just yet, so let's make sure that it is indeed birds that we are seeing on the radar. Click on "Velocity Image" (on this particular website, simply left click on the base reflectivity image to toggle between the two, or select "0.5 degree velocity" when you're at the radar home page, and we get a pretty picture like this one (fig. 5-5).

This product is called the radial velocity image because it displays the direction of targets moving to and from the radar's origin. If most of the targets are moving toward the radar from the northeast, as in our example here, and away from the radar to the southwest, then the resultant velocity image will show the greatest velocities in those directions. On this website, negative velocity values represent targets moving away from the radar and are shown in warm to hot colors (red, orange, yellow, etc.), and those moving toward the radar are coded in the cool (blue, green, purple, etc.) colors.

Likewise, when birds are passing tangentially to the radar, it results in a no-speed (or, null) reading (which on this website is presented as gray), because they are neither flying toward or away from the radar station. This null line is also helpful in determining the actual direction of migration, since the flight direction is at a right-angle to this null line. Direction is an important indicator of migration, because we also know that in fall birds generally fly north to south, whereas in spring that tendency is reversed. Be aware of winds, however, which may cause birds to migrate in mysterious ways!

By knowing the average ground speed of targets moving across the radar (thanks to the velocity image), the wind speed from the surface readings, and that, on average, birds fly 10–15 knots faster than the prevailing wind (their air speed is constant, as we learned in chapter 4), we can determine whether the signal we see on the base reflectivity images is indeed birds, and if so, we want to figure out where they are heading.

Looking back at the velocity image, we can see that whatever is being detected is moving NNE to SSW at approximately 10–15 knots. Earlier, I had mentioned that the wind speed on this particular evening was calm, which equates to 0 knots. So we can subtract the current wind speed (0) from the reading obtained from the velocity image to get the actual speed of the targets moving across the radar. Even without having to reach for a calculator, you can immediately see that whatever is moving across the radar is under its own power, and given the speed that we see here (10–15 knots), there is little else that this could be other than birds. Not just individual birds, though, but thousands and thousands of birds of a myriad of species captured briefly in a single snapshot that samples only what is actually extending across the land over the course of the entire night.

These velocity images can get messy at the toward the edges of the imagery, but in general as one gets farther from the radar, velocity levels rise because the radar is pointed upward at an angle (we'll skip the geometrical analysis of this for now; just take my word for it—as I did when it was explained to me by a National Weather Service Meteorologist!), not because birds are flying any faster. At the farthest reach of the radar beams, they are taking readings as high as 9,000 feet, which is well above the altitude of migrant passerines, and therefore an image of birds does not fill the entire screen, as did our image of widespread rainfall.

Now that we have determined that we're seeing birds, go back to the reflectivity images to get an idea of the spatial extent and overall density of the migration. And remember, you are not seeing individual birds, or even flocks of birds. Instead, you are seeing a snapshot of the overall density and extent of the night's flight.

It's just that easy. Or, I should say, it's just that easy with practice. NEXRAD radar analysis can greatly enhance our birding experience and knowledge. It's interesting in its own right, but it can also assist us in the field, which we will soon see.

We already know that some nights are better for migration than others. As a general rule of thumb, nights earlier in the migration season are less predictable than those during the peak. However, as the season progresses, birds are more inclined (or eventually desperate) to migrate in suboptimal conditions, especially in the spring season, when birds are making a bid to arrive first for the best breeding territories. Another rule of thumb is that successive migration events tend to decrease in density after each successive night of favorable conditions. This is probably due to a source-sink phenomenon, where there are only so many migration-ready individuals at a given time, and as new birds arrive, they require time to refuel before taking off again (perhaps about 3–7 days for many species). Therefore, after a few days of unfavorable winds and precipitation, for example, large numbers of birds are waiting to go.

In the following example from the fall, a cold front has just passed through, and behind it the skies clear quickly as night falls, but the wind has yet to pick up—perfect conditions for birds to get on the move. And indeed, birds have taken to the skies en masse. See all of the dark greens and blues in figure 5-6? In the regular radar image, the scale reflects the density of whatever the radar signals are bouncing off of. Dark blues and greens, in the "starburst" pattern surrounding the radar, means there are large numbers of birds in the air! And look at that pretty, symmetrical velocity image in figure 5-7: 10–15 knots NNE to SSW. A perfect image of birds on the move!

Now that we used the velocity image to confirm that what we are seeing are indeed birds, let's go back to that original radar image (fig. 5-5). Our understanding of geography (see chapter 3) and how birds react to it can help us further decipher this image. Do you see the long "tail" of green along Maine's southern coast from birds concentrating along the shoreline as they attempt to avoid wandering out over the open waters of the Gulf of Maine?

Also notice all of the greens and blues offshore—plenty of birds are indeed drifting offshore. Perhaps some of these are Blackpoll Warblers, for example, that launch straight off of Maine's coast and might not stop until they reach the West Indies. Others, however, are simply drifting offshore as a northwesterly wind develops behind the cold front (a common occurrence especially in the fall, when many inexperienced juvenile birds that make up the majority of the migratory population are undertaking their first southbound movement). This feature is very important to note for our morning's birding, but we're going to deal with that later, when the sun comes up.

Every minute of every day, all year long, NEXRAD radar is hard at work sending out signals, bouncing waves off of whatever is in the air at a given moment, and transmitting that information to a computer at the local National Weather Service office and then on to our laptop as we continue to sit curled up on the couch, birding vicariously through our computer screen. Recalling the radar image in figure 5.6, we see that there are a lot of birds along the coast. So now what?

~~~~~~

For a more scientific analysis of how weather radar can be used to document and analyze nocturnal bird migration and how it is affected by both weather and geography (use references in conjunction with chapters 3 and 4), see for example,

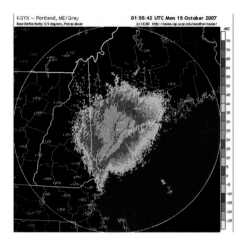

FIGURE 5-6.

Large, dense flights of nocturnal migrants yield a distinctive pattern on the base reflectivity image.

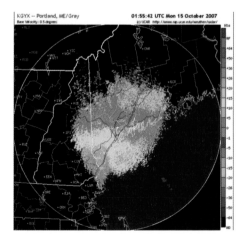

FIGURE 5-7.

The large, dense flights are confirmed as birds by noticing how fast (about 10–15 knots faster than the wind speed) the detected objects are moving. The pattern of the classic velocity image of a massive flight of birds looks a bit like a pinwheel.

- "Detection and Discrimination of Fauna in the Aerosphere Using Doppler Weather Surveillance Radar" (Gauthreaux et al. 2008).
- "Weather Effects on Autumnal Nocturnal Migration of Passerines on Opposite Shores of the St. Lawrence Estuary" (Gagnon et al. 2011).
- "Using a Network of WSR-88D Weather Surveillance Radars to Define Patterns of Bird Migration at Large Spatial Scales" (Gauthreaux, et al. 2003).
- "Radar Ornithology and Biological Conservation" (Gauthreaux and Belser 2003).

I would then highly recommend that those who want to learn more take a look through the reference sections of these articles for additional papers and resources worth reading.

~~~~~~

Well, now we wait for sunrise, and then we go birding! Using the radar as our bird-finding guide, we have just determined that birds have been pushed toward and over the coast and therefore will be reorienting themselves inland as the sun comes up.

The open water is not a hospitable place for passerines, so they begin to head for the nearest land when they find themselves over water come daybreak. Others have already arrived on islands, peninsulas, or along the immediate coastline where habitat is limited, competition may be fierce, and predators are more abundant. Furthermore, birds may also work their way inland to account for the drift during their night's flight. In all cases, though, the tendency is for birds at or near the coast to head inland at daybreak.

Therefore, our first couple of hours of birding on such a morning is directly related to birding at night. Essentially, beside having a lot of fun, it is important for "groundtruthing" our radar analysis from the previous night. Many of those migrants that drifted offshore over the course of the night's migration are now looking for a place to land in what is called the morning reorientation flight, or redetermined migration. While the exact biological mechanisms for these phenomena are still unclear—and the discussion of those mechanisms is once again beyond the scope of this book—what is very clear is that come dawn, a lot of nocturnal migrants either continue to

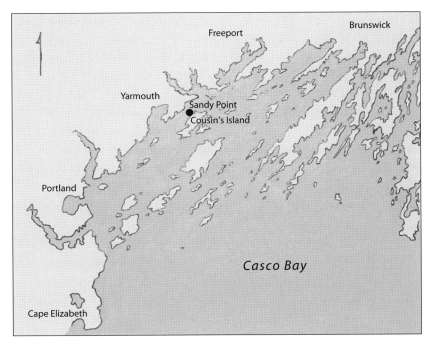

FIGURE 5-8.
Map of Casco Bay ©Luke Seitz.

fly or resume flying as they move in a very coordinated direction. (Even the direction they fly is open for debate, but at least in Cape May, which I will discuss in depth in chapter 8, the hypothesis is that the birds always reorient into the wind.) Some birds, however, do continue on in the direction that they were heading overnight—for example, heading south in the fall—even as the sun rises. This is known as onward migration, but this too is a portion of the morning flight, the more generic term that we use for all of the events that are happening as the sun rises.

Here in Maine, anytime there is a west or northwesterly wind during fall migration, I know that a lot of birds will be over Casco Bay at dawn (fig. 5-8), as suggested by the radar images from the last few hours of darkness. And on such a morning as that, I will inevitably find myself at what has become known as my office—the bridge to Cousin's Island at Sandy Point in Yarmouth. A cup of tea, hand clickers, notebook, pen, binoculars, and I am ready for the dawn (figs. 5-9 and 5-10).

Here at the base of the bridge on the island side, I have a great panoramic view of the narrowest point between the mainland and any of the large islands of Casco Bay. Birds funneling down the peninsulas of Brunswick and Harpswell, birds island hopping from Chebeague Island and beyond, and birds still high overhead make a turn for the mainland as the sun crests the horizon. From my vantage point on the bridge at the narrowest point, passerines make the jump from Cousin's Island to the safety and abundant foraging habitat of the mainland.

Many birds pass overhead, daring me to attempt to identify them by nothing more than silhouette. The cooperative ones give a call or two to announce their presence and aid in identification (sometimes). When the sun rises, color and contrast become more noticeable. When I'm really lucky, the birds will pause for a moment in one of the last two trees at the point, each conveniently located on each side of the road at the base of the bridge—an American Elm and a Paper Birch. I call these the "Magic Trees" because they seem to pull birds out of thin air. Other birds, especially Black-capped Chickadees and kinglets, which often make numerous false starts before finally completing their crossing to the mainland (it's stupefying to watch birds make it more than three-quarters of the way across only to suddenly panic and turn around!), seek out the shelter of these last trees as they seem to be gathering up the "courage" to make the crossing. Between birds pausing in these trees, passing below the bridge, and winging high overhead, I stand for hours, clickers and notebook in hand, simultaneously attempting (often futilely) to accurately identify and quantify the morning's flight while also finding myself mesmerized by the phenomena—enjoying it, but also at the same time confounded by it.

Here is a selected list of some of my high counts and rarer species that I have tallied in a morning at Sandy Point (through 8/15/11):

- 4,346 total birds, September 21, 2010.
- 3,069 total birds, October 7, 2008.
- 1,092 Northern Flickers, September 21, 2010.
- 471 Ruby-crowned Kinglets, October 6, 2008.

- 1,075 American Robins, October 17, 2010.
- 143 Northern Parulas, September 25, 2009.
- 731 Yellow-rumped Warblers, October 14, 2009.
- 200+ Black-throated Green Warblers, September 10, 2005.
- 444 Blackpoll Warblers, September 9, 2009.
- 304 American Redstarts, September 1, 2007.
- 20 Scarlet Tanagers, September 21, 2010.
- 250+ Dark-eyed Juncos, October 11, 2004.
- 20 Rusty Blackbirds, September 21, 2010.
- 232 Pine Siskins, October 7, 2008.
- 1 Prothonotary Warbler, September 23, 2004 (still the only one that I have seen in Maine).
- Dickcissels on seven different dates, including 3 on September 25, 2009.

FIGURE 5-9.
The author at his "office" on the bridge to Cousin's Island, Yarmouth, where he tallies the morning reorientation flight of nocturnal migrants moving inland after overnight winds blew them offshore. *Sandy Point Bridge, Yarmouth, Maine, 9/08* ©Stella Walsh.

Not too bad for a couple of hours of birding just 15 minutes away from home. Since this event usually only lasts for an hour or two after sunrise (three on the best days at this location), my birding day has just begun, and I have already seen more American Redstarts, for example, that most birders will see over the course of an entire season! And, I can see all of these birds and still get to work on time—if I so desire.

But you don't have to live in Maine or Cape May in order to enjoy and study the morning flight. Every morning of every day during every season of migration, morning reorientation flights are probably occurring all over the continent. It's just a matter of finding out where, and getting out of bed in order to observe it.

Using your newfound knowledge of birding by radar, coupled with some study of maps, there's no reason why you can't find a morning-flight observation point of your own. Lakeshores, ridgelines, peninsulas, even broad areas of unfavorable habitat, such as sprawling cities or miles of corn fields, should trigger some sort of morning reorientation flight that, given the time and energy to discover it, may be observable and quantifiable.

The fun part is that we see a lot of birds, and sometimes, we see a few rarities. It's hard to not be impressed by wave after wave of colorful warblers or chattering kinglets or noisy and gaudy Blue Jays. The observation and identification of passerines in flight is very difficult, but as we know, challenging ourselves is the way to grow as a birder. Even if you know what a Blackpoll Warbler looks like in the fall (no, they're really not all that "confusing"!), well, do you know what one looks like flying a couple of hundred feet overhead? Then why don't we find ourselves a morning-flight locale and find out!

There are other ways to detect nocturnal migration, as well. One is by sight, the other is by sound. Yes, it's night and its dark, so our usual sight-based birding is limited, but if the moon is out—especially a nice, big, fat, bright full moon—try focusing your spotting scope (preferably one with a wide-angled, bright fixed-power eyepiece) on its surface. See all of the craters and all of the ridges? Cool, right? Watch it for a few moments. "Hey, what was that?" you might exclaim as a dot passes through your field of view. And then another, and another . . .

FIGURE 5-10.
After flying hundreds of miles overnight, tired migrants find that they need to make one more jump to seek the shelter and food of the mainland. *View from Sandy Point, Yarmouth, Maine, 10/08* ©Derek Lovitch.

Although we may be interested in tallying the rate of passing migrants and perhaps identifying a few of the most obvious species, there really is only so much that we can do to qualify and quantify what we are seeing. While that may be frustrating to some, I think it is actually the biggest benefit of moonwatching—there's not much else to do but simply enjoy it!

"Birding by moonlight" is a great activity for a casual bird club, kids, and even nonbirders as well. There's no reason to make it technical—just look and watch . . . and marvel. I particularly enjoy hanging out on my back porch on a warm, clear migration night with a good local beer in one hand and my eye in a scope. I put the hand clickers, the notebook, and the field guide away, and I simply *watch* birds. (What a novel concept!)

For more information on moonwatching, see
- http.woodcreeper.com/moonwatching-2009/
- "Quantification of Nocturnal Bird Migration By Moonwatching: Comparison with Radar and Infrared Observation," (Liechti, Bruderer, and Paproth 1995).
- "A Continentwide View of Bird Migration on Four Nights in October" Lowery and Newman 1966).

Now, focus your ears skyward as well. Many, but apparently not all, nocturnal migrants give unique flight calls as they pass overhead. Currently, it is believed that these calls act as some sort of "air traffic control," perhaps minimizing the risk for collisions or disorientation. This would make sense, because we do seem to hear birds calling more often when there are more birds in the air, on cloudy or foggy nights where stars (critical for orientation) are invisible, and in areas with a significant amount of light pollution.

Since lights at night are known to confuse migrants, in some cases leading to massive death tolls at high communication towers, sky scrapers, and wind turbines (see the sidebar on bird strikes at lighted structures), it would only make sense that birds would call more often. For example, I once watched and listened to a Palm Warbler call repeatedly as it circled a stanchion of playing-field lights at a high school during a night game. In comparison, while listening overhead of my yard in my rural hometown I might hear a single call from that same Palm Warbler as it passed by.

For more on the issue of bird strikes at lighted structures, visit
- The Fatal Light Awareness Program at www.flap.org
- The American Bird Conservancy's page on the topic at www.abcbirds.org/conservationissues/
- www.towerkill.com

On a clear night, with stars plainly visible, with no bright lights or tall, lighted structures around, birds are passing overhead and have "little to talk about," as Michael O'Brien succinctly put it to me as we were cruising around Cape May one night, checking out his favorite listening posts.

In the fairly heavily developed shoretown of Cape May Point, some places are better for listening than others. In years of searching for the best listening locations, Michael looks for spots that have minimal noise pollution, such as quiet corners free of air conditioners and generators, and preferably with a few buildings, dunes, or other structures that block surf noise. Large trees were unwelcome in this case, because they limit the amount of available airspace overhead that one has to listen to. And he looks for light pollution, such as a brightly lit hotel or Victorian mansion for example.

These same factors apply everywhere. For optimal nocturnal listening, look for a spot without much noise (a pond teeming with frogs or a massive generator are just as unwelcomingly noisy for this particular purpose), a wide view of the sky, and if possible, free of people who might be tempted to call the police because someone is standing in the middle of the road at midnight staring straight up into the sky for prolonged periods of time. And light pollution is welcome, perhaps the only time when such a nuisance is, so brightly lit shopping centers, playing fields, or houses, and so on are places to check. Birds apparently call more often when disturbed and/or confused by bright lights, and we'll use that to our advantage. Furthermore, birds seem to call the most in the hours before dawn (for still unknown reasons), so a pre-breakfast listening session can be most rewarding.

For example, back home in Maine, my backyard is heavily wooded, with only a relatively small patch of sky visible overhead. I enjoy sitting out on my back porch, listening to the pair of Barred Owls, the neighborhood coyotes, and other sounds of the night while relaxing in a comfy chair with my ears and mind focused skyward, noting—and struggling to identify—calling passerines as they zoom overhead. But if I really want to fully experience the night flight's auditory performance, I would be better off getting in my car and driving four and a half miles to a shopping center parking lot. This is perhaps the only time I would be better off birding in a shopping center parking lot than in a heavily wooded rural yard, but in this case, the light pollution would be advantageous. (But admittedly, I almost always stick to the peace and quiet of my back porch and save the driving for the morning's birding adventure.)

Listening to migrants overhead is simple: 1. Go outside (preferably on a calm or nearly calm night). 2. Listen. That's it. Identification of said migrants? Well, that is a much different story! In short, it isn't easy—period. Even the experts are often unsure of what they are hearing. Our collective body of knowledge is just beginning to identify some of these calls, some of the time, at least those heard via the human ear. If you think recognizing warbler chip notes emanating from the brush is tough, then wait 'til you try to tackle warbler flight calls. However, some nocturnal flight calls, such those of thrushes, are very distinctive and easily learned. It's all about (you guessed it)—practice, and some studying.

At the moment, the primary reference for learning the identification of nocturnal flight calls is Bill Evans and Michael O'Brien's groundbreaking CD-ROM, *Flight Calls of Migratory Birds*. Recordings of (often) multiple examples of flight calls (sometimes, admittedly labeled only "presumed") are coupled with verbal descriptions and spectrograms. (The interpretation and understanding of sonograms is its own discipline that I will not cover here.) By beginning with the easier ones, like thrushes, you'll begin to ascend to the next level of birding by ear and be on the cutting edge of birding during migration.

If you really want to get into it, as more and more birders and ornithologists have, be warned: birding by radar and nocturnal listening is surprisingly addictive! We can take this discipline to the next level by setting up an acoustic monitoring station and automatically detect, record, and identify the night's migrants by linking a microphone to our computer.

Our collective knowledge of nocturnal flight calls and their identification is advancing with leaps and bounds. There's even a listserve dedicated to the subject. To see what's currently being talked about, visit www.birding-onthe.net/mailinglists/NFCL.html. Also be sure to visit www.oldbird.org for more information about acoustic monitoring, a catalogue of flight calls, and a very good bibliography of additional reading.

There is still much to learn about nocturnal flight calls. Warblers call, but vireos don't. Most usually secretive-by-day thrushes are vociferous at night but diurnally noisy mimic-thrushes are silent when flying at night. Why? What untold mechanisms are at work? Why do some birds communicate when airborne while others do not? Maybe some are flying too high for us to hear, or their calls are too high pitched or too soft for our ears to register. Do some species call only when confused by lights, or do birds call more often near the coast than inland? So many questions, and while the Sid Gauthreauxs, Michael O'Briens, David La Pumas, and Andrew Farnsworths (and others) of the world are trying to figure it out, why don't the rest of us get outside and learn what we can, or at the very least, just get out and listen and enjoy the phenomena.

As in most chapters of this book, I'm really only scratching the surface of the variety of the tools that we have at our disposal. I've hardly done justice to the complexity of birding by radar, but hopefully I have provided a place to start and have spurred your interest. So you can learn more, I will once again direct you to some persons and references who have quite a bit of knowledge of the subject.

One of the best and most accessible blogs about birding by radar is David La Puma's Woodcreeper website and blog (www.woodcreeper.com). As of this writing, David is a postdoctoral associate of Ecology, Behavior, and Conservation of Migratory Birds with the New Jersey Audubon Society. On his website he posts each night's radar images for New Jersey during both spring and fall migration and analyzes the flight to predict where birds will be come morning. Observers are asked to post their groundtruthing results to test his hypotheses. Furthermore, he has a multitude of links to tutorials, other radar blogs, and more resources that can be of help. Although this site is dedicated to New Jersey birding, the lessons learned can be applied wherever you are. David also wrote a great piece on using weather radar to predict birding conditions for *WildBird Magazine* (July/August 2007) that does an excellent job of getting you started with birding by radar, as well as some background information on radar ornithology.

Meanwhile, there's a great deal of great science being done right now with Doppler radar. Analysis of historical radar data is detecting noticeable decreases in trans-Gulf migrants, reflecting the observed and documented decline of many Neotropical migrants.

The Science of Studying Bird Migration with Weather Radar and
Acoustic Monitoring

Quite a few researchers are now looking into learning how we can scientifically quantify bird density using weather radar (beyond the terms
we use as birders, such as "none" and "crapload"). A few recent articles worth browsing include

- "A Comparison of Nocturnal Call Counts of Migrating Birds and
  Reflectivity Measurements on Doppler Radar" (Farnsworth,
  Gauthreaux, and Blaricom 2004).
- "Monitoring Flight Calls of Migrating Birds from an Oil Platform in
  the Northern Gulf of Mexico" (Farnsworth and Russell 2007).
- "Quantifying Bird Density During Migratory Stopover Using
  Weather Surveillance Radar" (Buler and Diehl 2009).
- "Acoustic Monitoring of Night-Migrating Birds: A Progress Report"
  (Evans and Rosenberg 1999).
- "Flight Calls and Their Value for Future Ornithological Studies and
  Conservation Research" (Farnsworth 2009).

"This is cool," you might be saying, "but so what? Although it is interesting
to know that birds are or are not on the move on any given night, what
good does this really do in making me a better birder?" Well, for one thing,
having a more complete understanding of the dynamics of birds and bird
migration (migration phenology) helps us appreciate and enjoy their wonders even more, but more directly, we can actually use what we learn from
the radar images and apply it directly to our birding the next morning.
Knowing whether or not birds were on the move the night before will help
us focus our energy on hitting the field on the most productive mornings,
and knowing whether or not birds were being affected by winds overnight
can be used to focus our attention and our efforts on the most potentially
rewarding locations. Furthermore, understanding what birds are migrating
based on flight calls and then seeing whether or not that composition is
reflected on the ground helps to deepen our understanding of the birds in
the field come sunrise.

6

Birding with a Purpose

Birding is fun. Period. And for most birders of any level of expertise, this is the first and foremost reason to go birding. However, as birders develops their skills, this wonderful hobby can be put to good use.

Birding can, and perhaps should, be about more than just putting a name on a bird and listing it. What about simply enjoying the wonders of avian life or the simple appreciation of the fascinating life of birds? And what about helping the birds that we enjoy so much, in whatever way we happen to be enjoying them? I have always been dumbfounded by the disconnect that exists between so many birders and the welfare of birds, especially at the population level. We might help them out with a birdfeeder or two, but it often does not go any further than that. If nothing else, bird conservation is self-serving: the more birds there are, the more birds we have to look at!

But it doesn't have to be a one-way street. On-the-ground field research—field ornithology: the study of birds in the field, as opposed to that in a laboratory—is one of the basic tools of bird conservation. Bird research can be anything from an outing on a Christmas Bird Count to a long-standing, intensive breeding-biology project, but in whatever way we support the collective pursuit of knowledge, we can add more purpose and motivation to our birding activities. Meanwhile, we can learn a whole lot to make ourselves better birders, all the while helping birds at the same time.

The pursuit of knowledge is one of the hallmarks of human society, and the birding society is no different. I strongly recommend getting involved with a project or two, whether it's a scientific study, a citizen science project, or perhaps a little independent study of your own. It will help you to become a better birder.

After graduating from Rutgers University, I set out on the life of an independent avian research consultant, aka a "bird bum." I wasn't sure what exactly I wanted to do with my career; I simply hopped from seasonal field job to seasonal field job, all of which focused on birds. Biological research, interpretative naturalist work, tour guiding, and often a combination of these and other projects greeted me as I took jobs in eight states over the course of the next five years.

Studying the breeding biology of the endangered finch-billed honeycreeper the Palila in Hawai'i, counting thousands of migrant Peregrine Falcons in the Florida Keys, working as a tour guide in Alaska's Pribilofs, breeding-bird atlasing in Michigan's Upper Peninsula, tallying raptors and assisting visitors at the famous Cape May Hawkwatch, etc. Each of these

FIGURE 6-1.
Moez Ali at work conducting nest searching/monitoring and point count surveys of montane forest birds in the "sky islands" (see chapters 2 and 3) of southeastern Arizona. This photo was taken at 8,500 feet in the Canadian Zone on Mount Lemmon in the Santa Catalina Mountains outside of Tucson ©Moez Ali.

projects and positions resulted in a wealth of new knowledge, experience, and, yes, life birds.

Although not everyone wants to live the life that I and many other birders have experienced for at least some period of time, being a bird bum can be very rewarding, but it can also relegate one to the poor house. The cliché "great when you were young" is also quite apropos for many.

There is a wide range of paid (barely!) field positions in basic avian research all over the world, which are great ways to spend a summer while in school, a season between "real" jobs, or a few months of retirement (fig. 6-1). There's nothing better for learning about birds than immersing yourself in the rigors of some good scientific research. Want to learn more about molt? How about working (or volunteering, of course) at a banding-station project? Holding a bird in the hand, taking detailed measurements, and studying each and every feather yields volumes of knowledge about the intricacies of plumage details that will help you with field identification and more. There are often opportunities available to spend months in exciting places such as South America by volunteering to assist researchers—and the experience that can be had will be second to none.

A surprising number of "bird jobs" are out there, and someone is always looking for assistance on a project. A couple of websites worth checking out are
- The "Ornjobs" listserve from the Ornithological Societies of North America (OSNA): www.osnabirds.org/jobs.aspx
- The "Job Board" from Texas A&M's Department of Wildlife and Fisheries Sciences: http://wfsc.tamu.edu/jobboard/

But let's face it, most of us are in the midst of careers, families, and so on, and a season-long commitment may just be impossible. Our life as "regular" people usually has to take priority. Enter the latest buzzwords in scientific research, *citizen science*.

Christmas Bird Counts (CBC), the Breeding Bird Survey (BBS), and breeding bird atlases are all great ways to apply one's knowledge to collect data that can be used for broadscale, long-term trend analysis. Such efforts are a great way to hone one's birding skills. Want to make your CBC route more productive? Then, use your new knowledge of birding by habitat (chapter 2) and geography (chapter 3) to find the choice patches. Habitat and geography can also be helpful in maximizing one's efforts while conducting surveys for breeding-bird-atlas projects. Reams of valuable data are gathered as we hone our own skills and put our knowledge to good use.

Christmas Bird Counts

Although the buzzword is fairly new, many of us have been participating in a "citizen-science" project for decades. Christmas Bird Counts are citizen science at its finest. Thousands of birders participating in hundreds of CBCs throughout the Americas cover vast amounts of land, count mass quantities of birds, and track population trends that can be used to help guide additional research and conservation action. To learn more, visit the CBC website at www.audubon.org/bird/cbc/. Make sure to take a look at the page "How the CBC Helps Birds."

Christmas Bird Counts give us the opportunity to bird with others, and birding with others is a great way to learn. I always enjoy how every bird counts on a CBC, and this is a good excuse to force us to pay attention to even our most common species. And finally, the thoroughness required of parties participating in the CBCs entices us to explore an area carefully, which may result in the discovery of new patches, new hotspots, and maybe even a rarity to add to our lists.

Breeding Bird Surveys

The venerable Breeding Bird Survey is a "cooperative effort between the U.S. Geological Survey's Patuxent Wildlife Research Center and Environment Canada's Canadian Wildlife Service to monitor the status and trends of North American Bird Populations" ("North American Breeding Bird Survey Home"; http://137.227.245.162/bbs/index.html). Unlike the more casual nature of CBCs, the BBS uses a more rigorous protocol. Volunteers conduct point counts (a methodology where all birds seen and heard within a certain distance from a single place during a set period of time are recorded) from roadsides along randomly established routes throughout much of the continent. Also unlike CBCs, Breeding Bird Surveys are more often done alone, or with a peer or two, but in this case, the potential for testing your skills is obvious: did you hear something that you are not familiar with? Better learn it!

To learn more, visit the BBS website at http.pwrc.usgs.gov/bbs/. See especially the "Vacant Routes" page to see if you can become involved in your area—there are plenty of routes available in almost every state and province.

Breeding Bird Atlases

Many states have, are, or it is hoped will be, conducting and compiling breeding bird atlases. These are comprehensive surveys of blocks of the entire state (or, in less-populated areas, sample blocks) where the goal is to find and confirm every breeding species in as many blocks as possible.

These projects enlist birders to thoroughly comb areas that are not regularly birded, and this often produces all sorts of fascinating finds: rarities, new county breeding records, etc. More importantly, perhaps, is that the birders are charged with not only seeing birds but also observing their behavior in hopes of confirming (not just suspecting) breeding status. This is a great way to learn about birds by seriously, carefully, and patiently watching them! I know that I gained considerable experience in *watching* birds when I first took part in New Jersey's Breeding Bird Atlas at the tender age of 15, when I covered my home block by bike and bummed rides from parents.

Knowledge of local habitat types (see chapter 2) can be used to find more birds within an assigned "block," and in the process of looking for birds, new habitat associations of local species may be discovered that could be applied to other places near and far. Moreover, bird behavior is simply fascinating, and observing it is its own reward. I'm willing to bet that after you participate in an atlas project, you'll find yourself *looking* at birds a lot more and a lot harder. As I mentioned earlier, I'm a big proponent of putting the *watching* back into *bird-watching*!

Check with your state Audubon chapter, fish and wildlife department, or other agencies that conduct biological surveys in your home state to see if there are any current or upcoming projects in your area. If not, perhaps your "birding with a purpose" is to start one!

Websites for Finding a Breeding Bird Atlas Near You
- U.S. Geological Survey's atlasing site: www.pwrc.usgs.gov/bba
- Cornell Laboratory of Ornithology's atlasing webpage: http://bird.atlasing.org
- Bird Studies Canada: http.bsc-eoc.org/volunteer/atlas/index.jsp

---

Both the BBS and participation in breeding bird atlases force us to observe bird behavior, which is something few of us do often enough. Observing birds carefully can teach us things that really do make ourselves into better birders.

And bird behavior is simply fascinating! Recently, I was birding a local park and I heard an odd call. When I found a Swamp Sparrow making this sound, I was intrigued, so I watched it for a few minutes. The bird making the call began to quiver, with its wings and tail vibrating rapidly. It was puffed out, looking much larger than usual. All of the sudden, a second "swampie" made *him*self known, with an interesting, muffled version of its typical song. He then made a few calls that were similar to the other bird's, presumably a female. The first bird, the female, then quivered even more rapidly and then began to mouse around on the ground, pausing in order to raise one wing, flashing the relatively bright-white underwing linings that contrasted with the bird's otherwise cryptic streaky brown plumage.

The male then moused its way toward the female, they disappeared behind a dense clump of rush, and she emerged, ruffling her feathers (we all know what that means!), and the male flew to a nearby bush to resume singing.

Jeannette and I and our Bradbury Mountain Hawkwatch counter for the season, Steve Kolbe (speaking of birding jobs, there's always a need for volunteer and paid hawkcounters all over the country), all looked at each other and agreed— that display was really cool! An otherwise slow morning of birding was highlighted by a fascinating behavioral observation. Despite Swamp Sparrows being such a common species, I have never seen such behavior from them, and if I had been compiling a breeding bird atlas, I would have just upgraded the breeding status of Swamp Sparrow for this area—and I learned something new in the process.

eBird

eBird is a tool in which every single bird that you see every single day can be easily and quickly entered into a database that can be accessed by researchers and the general public. It makes every sighting into a little data point in the big puzzle that is our attempt to understand bird distribution and populations. eBird is a recent and rapidly growing element of the Avian Knowledge Network (see http.avianknowledge.net for more information), which is an "international organization of government and non-governmental institutions focused on understanding the patterns and dynamics of bird populations across the Western Hemisphere . . . by organizing observation-based bird monitoring" efforts in order to "educate the public on the dynamics of bird populations, provide interactive decision-making tools for land managers, make available a data resource for scientific research, and advance new exploratory analysis techniques to study bird populations" ("About the AKN"; www.avianknowledge.net/content/about).

Launched in 2002 by the Cornell Lab of Ornithology and the National Audubon Society, eBird is the layman's tool, if you will, where every day every birder can enter every bird into the collective database. Vetted by a network of local experts, the data is pooled to create "rich data sources for basic information on bird abundance and distribution at a variety of spatial and temporal scales" ("About eBird"; http://ebird.org/content/ebird/about).

In exchange for this data set, eBird provides listing and checklist tools, including county, state, life, and year lists that are all automatically updated as you enter your data. You can then explore the data by creating maps, bar charts, summary tables, and other sorting criteria. For example, eBird states that "you can access your own bird records anytime you want, allowing you an easy way to look at your observations in new ways and to answer your personal questions about what birds you saw and when and where you saw them" ("Why Should I eBird"; http://ebird.org/content/ ebird/about/why-ebird). To learn more, visit www.ebird.org, and see especially the "About eBird" page.

We can even use eBird data to predict patterns of occurrence, such as irruptions or storm-driven rarities, which can be directly applied to aid our search for vagrants (see chapter 7). Looking through the data for neighboring states or counties, we may be alerted to species that deserve to be looked for in our local area. Many skilled birders understand that simply what can be expected is more than half the battle of finding good birds.

In the case of Christmas Bird Counts, breeding bird atlases, and so on, we do not need to justify our participation in these activities simply for the value of the data that we collect. Our rewards are just as important, especially in our pursuit to becoming better birders. Furthermore, leading bird walks—both formally and informally—is a great way to hone one's own skills while helping to advance the skills of other birders. Nothing is more helpful in remembering and developing techniques for advanced field identification than explaining and describing a bird to someone else.

In each and every one of these pursuits, our birding skills are being put to use. They're motivation to practice—and sometimes we need a little extra motivation to get out in the field, especially on a wretchedly cold, windy, or wet late December day. But anytime that we are out birding, we are learning, and that is the most important thing to remember from this chapter.

And don't forget what, for sake of conversation, we will call independent study. Take a walk sometime and think about your local avifauna. Why is one species in this park and not another? Why are you not seeing or hearing Whip-poor-wills anymore? In what trees or shrubs do Grace's Warblers like to build their nests in my area? Then, go find out! Again, we can't learn about birds or grow as birders if we're not out in the field, so sometimes we can motivate ourselves to hit the bush by pursuing the answer to a question. Who knows, we might even discover something new for the collective body of knowledge. If not, maybe we'll stumble into a rarity, discover a new park, or find a great new place for lunch! In any case, it will be more productive than sitting in front of the computer.

Perhaps we don't even need a birding motivation as an excuse to go into the field and find some great birds. One time when I worked as a guide on St. Paul Island, we would often complain about the summer doldrums. After the adrenaline-packed, sleep-deprived, mega-rarity fever of spring migration (which runs through early to mid-June in those latitudes), occasionally some of us guides needed an extra kick in the pants to get away from the TV in the middle of summer, a time with many fewer migrants and a much lower chance of finding rarities. However, some the most exceptional vagrants that have been found out there, for example, Chinese Pond-Heron, have been discovered in the middle of summer, when it's more tempting to sleep in or watch a movie.

Despite the island being only 44 square miles in size, plenty of birds can pass through undetected if no one is birding. So in the first year there, two goals were set by some of us guides as encouragement to get out. One was to summit all twenty or so hills on the island (OK, so the highest is only 665 feet, but the usually tussocky tundra can make some of these treks rather challenging). Another was to photograph all 120-plus species of flowering plants that occurred on the island.

I continued the pursuit of summiting all of the hills in each of my three summers out there and slowly built my plant photo library. (A worthwhile photo of Purple Mountain Saxifrage and Glaucous Gentian eluded me!) Meanwhile, we found the island's first breeding record(s) of the American Pipit, a couple of hybrid McKay's × Snow Bunting nests, and we stumbled upon quite a few rarities, including the island's first record of American Golden-Plover, which I discovered while trekking over the tundra in the middle of July of my third year there.

So, perhaps birding with a purpose is a bit selfish after all! But this is not a bad thing—collecting data while building our own skills is definitely a win-win situation. It's good for us as birders, and it's good for our birding and ornithology community as a whole.

And perhaps the single most important thing that you can do for the birding community is to take a child birding! Without the next generations of birders to follow in our footsteps, who will collect our data, find us rarities to twitch, become conservationists, and buy books like this one?

I don't know how I first got into birding. I didn't have any family members or friends who were birders, but somehow I developed the passion. I remember that I was 11 years old when I first wrote a date next to a lifer in my new National Geographic field guide, and I know I started looking at birds with a Peterson's First Guide (which, much to my surprise and excitement, I recently unearthed in a box hidden in an attic) before that. I recall climbing a big Russian Mulberry tree in my backyard in East Brunswick, New Jersey (before I understood that the tree was an invasive species!) and snacking on mulberries while surrounded by a horde of Cedar Waxwings. I remember having pet birds growing up, I remember my grandfather having a Purple Martin house (which may have been home only to House Sparrows), and my mother remembers a kindergarten unit on birds that I was particularly fond of.

But for the most part, I was a self-taught birder, wandering my yard and local woods with a pair of K-Mart special binoculars and a tattered field guide. While my parents facilitated my interest—especially my father, who would take me to parks and nature centers almost every weekend—it was in no small part the adults who volunteered to lead birdwalks for New Jersey Audubon that greatly helped to encourage this particular fledgling birder. Later mentors in high school, college, and beyond were instrumental in taking my skills, experience, and passion to higher levels. Now, it's time to pay it forward. For the majority of birders who haven't picked up birding until later in life, it's never too soon to support our birding community by facilitating the next generation.

Let us not also forget that the ultimate goal in birding with a purpose may be working to protect the very birds themselves. I'll readily admit to a not-so-hidden agenda: the more people I can get excited about birds, the more people who may become bird conservationists. Interest begets appreciation, and appreciation begets compassion—and compassion begets action.

Many, many birds are in trouble. For every species that is increasing and being added to new county, state, and even country lists, multitudes more are declining even more rapidly. This entire chapter, "Birding with a Purpose," can indeed be devoted to bird conservation. Indeed, this entire book, like many other books before and after, can and should be devoted to bird conservation. But I'll leave it to others to tackle those problems at this time.

Bird Conservation Resources

For a few good resources for current information on bird conservation issues, take a look at

- The American Bird Conservancy: www.abcbirds.org
- Birdlife International: www.birdlife.org
- The Bird Conservation Alliance: www.birdconservationalliance.org
- North American Bird Conservation Initiative: http.nabci-us.org
- (National) Audubon: www.audubon.org/bird
- Boreal Songbird Initiative: www.borealbirds.org
- Partners in Flight: www.partnersinflight.org
- Conservation Birding: www.conservationbirding.org

And for non-web must-reads on the topic, I highly recommend

- *Silence of the Songbirds*, by Bridget Stutchbury
- *The Song of the Dodo: Island Biogeography in an Age of Extinctions*, by David Quammen
- *Return to Wild America: A Yearlong Search for the Continent's Natural Soul*, by Scott Weidensaul
- *Bird Conservation Handbook: 100 North American Birds at Risk*, by Jeffrey V. Wells

But for now, I will just implore you to learn more to help protect birds. It's in the best interest of birds, birders, and indeed, all of humanity. At the very, very least, make sure that there is shade-grown, organic, bird-friendly coffee in your cup as you head out the door to enjoy the wonders of the avian world and set out to find some vagrants!

Vagrants

If birds were always where we expected them to be and when we wanted them to be there, birding would not be half the fun, would it? Many birding guides would need to find other jobs, and you certainly would not have needed this book! However, one of the great things about birds is that they can fly (well, most of them), and sometimes they fly to places where they are not expected to be. These wayward wanderers, or vagrants, are the spice of the birding life. While rare birds are indeed rare, with a little effort and focus, you too can discover vagrants.

For most birders, birding is about a lot more than rarities—and well it should be! And, I do want to temper your enthusiasm a bit about this chapter with words of warning—birding isn't all about rarities! We should appreciate the common birds. Some of the most beautiful birds in the world are right on our doorstep, yet are all too often overlooked as we pursue the next big twitch. Have you *really* looked at a Blue or Steller's Jay or even a European Starling in fresh winter plumage? What about a drake Mallard in bright sunlight? A Gray Flycatcher in the East or a Least Flycatcher out West is not going to be as beautiful as these common, ubiquitous, and all-too-underappreciated aesthetic gems.

However, rarities bring much joy—and much consternation from identification quandries to missing chased birds—to birders of all skill levels. For folks who really want to become better birders, simply chasing every rare bird found by others isn't good enough. We want to find those rarities *ourselves* and bask in the thrill of discovery. Even though the excitement of the chase is real, I have never met any birder who wasn't more fulfilled by finding a mega on their own. Finding rare birds is a lot of fun, but it takes a lot of effort and a lot of skill. While almost anyone can stumble onto a rarity now and again, it takes a considerable skill set—and yes, a lot of luck!—to focus one's efforts in order to maximize the greatest chance of needing to reach for your cell phone to call your birding buddies.

Before we talk about locating rarities, we should spend a moment on identifying them. First, keep in mind that migratory species are much, much more likely to occur out of range than nonmigratory ones that rarely travel. If you think you have spotted a bird that is outside its normal or mapped range (and remember that range maps only tell part of the story), then you should double- and triple check the suite of field characteristics (both classic field marks, as well as the characteristics from the "whole bird and more" approach in chapter 1) to be extra certain of your identification. Many a birder makes *mis*identifications by not appreciating when something is out of range or out of season, even if they have studied the identification characteristics and think they know those. A vagrant Scarlet Tanager in Nevada is probably not going to be flycatching from a fencepost (the bright red body and black wings would be those of the Vermillion Flycatcher instead). Likewise, if you think you see "just a sparrow" foraging in the treetops, you might want to look closer!

With digital cameras, "digi-scoping" (taking photos through a spotting scope), "phone-scoping" (taking photos with a cell phone through a spotting scope), "digi-binning" (taking photos through your binoculars), and other modes of snapping images of birds with various apparatuses, it is becoming easier and easier to document unusual occurrences. For example, in the winter of 2008–2009, at least five or six Varied Thrushes appeared for unknown reasons in Maine, and one was photographed via digi-scoping (fig. 7-1). Although the images are not magazine-cover quality, they are sufficient for confirmation and documentation. But even the best photographs in the world are made better and more useful when combined with detailed, copious field notes. Did the camera truly capture the colors that you observed? What was the bird doing? Where was it doing it? Scribble notes on every single feature you can see, no matter how irrelevant you think it is. Leg color, orbital ring color, primary projection, overall plumage, feeding behavior, frequented species of tree—any particular detail may be the one pertinent field mark that our series of photographs happened not to capture.

After getting at least some documentation and confirming to the best of your ability the identification, then you want to get the word out to your fellow birders. By now you probably know another birder or twelve, and their number is probably on speed-dial on your cell phone. If not, or especially when traveling, I implore you to get the observation and the documentation as soon as possible into the right hands so that it can become part of our birding posterity. Search online for a state's Rare Birds Record Committee (or something to that effect). Some now even have online submission forms. Or flip through your now trusty copy of North American Birds and send a note to the regional editor. Or, "eBird" it, and the sighting will pop up instantly. Even if the word gets out months later (e.g., through *North American Birds*), it will still become part of the permanent record.

But before we worry too much about documenting rarities, you need to get out and find some! Whether you have realized it or not, all of the preceding chapters of this book have been teaching you how to find rarities whether you wanted to or not. Finding vagrants isn't just about building a list—although it certainly helps—but it's also about earning the respect of one's birding peers. More importantly, however, the various mechanisms, known and unknown—from mirror migration to storm systems to global climate change—that result in the occurrence and eventual discovery of vagrants, is simply fascinating!

In certain seasons, my blog entries are dominated by the topic of "rarity fever." That is my term for a condition that I suffer from at certain times of the year. Symptoms of rarity fever include insomnia (late nights studying weather maps and birding listserves, early mornings studying radar images and listserves, and early starts in the field), poor diet (days fueled by lots of caffeine—as long as it is via shade-grown coffee of course—and sugar, supplemented usually only by salty junk food), stress ("I have this important meeting today, but there's a first state record at the lake! Ahh, what am I going to do?), and other cold- and flulike symptoms. (I have heard of such excuses as "Uh, boss, I have a fever, I can't come to work today, there's southwest winds, err, I mean, the kids brought something home from school....")

FIGURE 7-1.

For unknown reasons, several Varied Thrushes were present in Maine in the winter of 2008–2009, such as this bird, which was one of two frequenting a Saco, Maine, backyard. The author used the technique of "digi-scoping" to capture this image. While digi-scoped images are not of the highest quality, they suffice for the purposes of confirmation and documentation of rarities. *Digi-scoped image of Varied Thrush, Saco, Maine, 1/09* ©Derek Lovitch.

Personally, I love looking for and finding rarities. And while I never mind adding a new species to any of my various lists, I am more interested in the challenge of predicting, finding, and then interpreting rarities.

Yes, a lot of luck is involved. I know of some very good birds found by not-so-very-good birders. Luck is important, but even more essential is getting out into the field! If you're not out birding, or at least watching your feeders, you're not going to be finding rarities. Although rare birds are indeed rare, just getting out and looking at birds gets you one step closer to discovering the next first state record.

Also important is getting into the field at the right time of year. Rare birds can show up almost anywhere at any time, but there are certain times that are more likely to produce rarities than others. Obviously, during migration, more birds are on the move, and therefore there are more birds of more species to end up in the wrong places. However, it does seem that many, perhaps even most, vagrants are found after the peak season for regular migrants in many areas. Is it simply because there are so many other birds around during migration's peak that we simply fail to find the most exceptional needles in the clichéd haystack? Or do the various mechanisms that produce rarities (such as "miswired" brains) cause the birds to spend more time getting somewhere. I can list all sorts of possibilities, but I have yet to read anything that specifically suggests why rarities seem to be a little less rare past the peak of overall migration.

~~~~~~

Regional Rarity Seasons

Most places in the country have distinctive rarity seasons, and here I will describe a few of the well-known rarity hotspots of the United States. I thank Paul Lehman for his input to these synopses.

1. The Southwest (Arizona and New Mexico) for Mexican strays
   a. May and August: breeding species that may be prospecting or pioneering north of their current range, especially in response to climate change, with fewer (but still some) into the autumn. One wonders how many of these later season "discoveries" have been nearby all along but were only now detected.
   b. Late fall and early winter: annual (or nearly annual) wanderers such as Rufous-backed Robin, Streak-backed Oriole, and Ruddy Ground-Dove.
2. Texas, also for Mexican strays
   Mostly in winter and after Christmas, especially following a freeze that extends into Mexico that can reduce food sources such as insects and nectar causing birds to wander to look for food resources. Smaller numbers of vagrants occur in the time periods mentioned above for Arizona and New Mexico.

3. Florida, for strays from the Caribbean

   April and May during periods of easterly winds in particular.

   Some also occur in fall and winter, perhaps as reverse migrants.

4. Eastern vagrants in the West.

   a. California: mid-May until mid-June, with a few as early as late April, reflecting nicely the timing of most Eastern long-distance migrants in their usual range.

   b. Northern California and Pacific Northwest: mostly mid-June.

   c. Interior West: mid-May through early June, again reflecting the "usual" timing of migration. Farther east and south, such as eastern New Mexico, the occurrences start a little earlier in spring (e.g., early May).

   d. Fall for all regions: early September though early November, again reflecting the typical timing of these species in their "normal" range.

5. Western Alaska, such as St. Paul Island in the Pribilofs, Adak, and Gambell on St. Lawrence Island, for Asian passerine vagrants.

   a. Spring: The last week of May through early to mid-June.

   b. The first half of September through early October.

In much of the country it is in late fall that rarity season really begins. The Northeast is a perfect example, and once again, we'll look at this region in depth primarily because of the author's experiences there, but as noted earlier, many of the concepts that we apply here can be applied everywhere else. Monitoring listserves and skimming a couple of year's worth of your region's seasonal reports in the journal *North American Birds* will yield your area's peak times. In order to be in the right place at the right time so that you can spot those rarities, you'll need to use everything you learned in all of the previous chapters, but especially your knowledge of weather, geography, and habitat.

Weather does indeed play a significant role. For example, in Maine, the peak of rarity season is usually the first couple of weeks of November. When the backside of a high pressure system parks itself just right or the winds pick up ahead of an approaching cold front, extended periods of southwesterly winds get the rarity-fever juices flowing. There's little doubt that many of our rarities during this time period (for example, Cave Swallows from the southwest, western warblers, and southeastern breeders such as Hooded Warblers and Summer Tanagers) arrive during or immediately after periods of southwesterly winds. But southwesterly winds do not make an Allen's Hummingbird fly from the Pacific Coast to eastern Massachusetts. However, it is quite possible that these particular winds help to deposit this wayward waif in a place where birders might find it, such as at a well-watched hummingbird feeder on Cape Cod.

The debate, however, is over exactly how much of a role that winds actually play and whether that role is proximate or ultimate. In chapter 4, I talked about some specific example of birds being displaced by specific weather patterns or systems. More often than not, however, the occurrence of vagrants cannot be tied directly to a weather event.

And, why, exactly, *is* early November so good for finding rarities? Once again, we really don't know, but it is probably a combination of factors. Because most migrants have moved through by this time, it's simply easier to find one in a batch of a hundred birds than in the thousands that are present on a good day in mid-September. So, are vagrants moving through at the peak of migration as well but being missed because they are among the masses?

Since many of our expected migrants have reached their wintering grounds by the time rarities are discovered in New England, then perhaps we're finding these migrants simply because they have stopped migrating (remember the Baltimore Oriole and other overwintering migrants in Nova Scotia discussed in chapter 3?). Or, as the nights get longer and the days colder, food, especially insects and fruit, becomes scarcer, so birds are forced to the warmer microclimates along the heavily developed and more heavily birded coast (see fig. 2-5), where they are more readily found. Additionally, as birders learn about these patterns of occurrence, more birders head out to the right places at the right times, for example, at our annual Rarity Roundup here in Maine (see the introduction), and as a consequence will turn up more rarities.

Once again, however, we come back to the question of how these birds got here, or near here, in the first place. In the past, many of us have thought of vagrants as birds that have been "blown off course." While this no doubt occurs, the explanation is much more complex. A Fork-tailed Flycatcher does not get blown from South America to Florida (e.g., Key West, Apr. 26, 2009), Alabama (e.g., Mobile, May 21, 2009), Ontario (Point Pelee, Oct. 22, 2008) or any of the other one to five-plus locations each year that get graced by this spiffy vagrant. A Purple Martin does not get blown from the southeastern United States to Western Alaska (*four* records from St. Paul in the Pribilofs!). A Prothonotary Warbler that is found in California (up to a dozen a year) in the spring did not get blown there. Beside, if strong winds were the main mechanism of producing vagrants, then why are there so relatively few western birds seen in the East in the spring? Strong cold fronts sweeping across the continent certainly provide winds strong enough to carry a Black-throated Gray Warbler that weighs all of about a third of an ounce (!) well east of its usual range, yet Black-throated Gray Warblers are incredibly rare in the East in the spring (not even one a year).

So, what is happening? Well, we're not really sure! Once again, I am going to avoid a discussion of the complex mechanisms of bird physiology, migration, weather dynamics, etc. Instead, I will just take the easy way out and point you to some references. Also, be sure to refer to the suggested reading list on migration in chapter 4, "Birding and Weather" for more background information on how birds get to where they usually, and not so usually, go.

Suggested Reading on Vagrancy

For those who are interested in learning more about vagrancy and the mechanisms thereof, here are some suggestions for further reading. I would, as always, recommend using the bibliographies of these papers to expand your research.

- A very nice article that summarizes some of the causes and implications of vagrancy appeared in the United Kingdom's *Birdwatch* magazine online edition "The Pioneers" (Alfrey 2011).

- Ned Brinkley's Changing Seasons Article "Oscillations" (2009) discusses, speculates, and pontificates about various mechanisms that may or may not have resulted in some of the rarities of that season across the continent.
- "The Incidence of Vagrant Landbirds on Nova Scotia Islands" (McLaren 1981).
- "Implication of Vagrant Southeastern Vireos and Warblers in California" (Patten and Marantz 1996).

A lot of things happen that combine to bring odd birds to odd places. Some birds are simply "miswired"—to greatly oversimplify things—and flat out fly the wrong way. This is usually done by immature birds making their first fall migration, and they end up on the wrong coast, an offshore island, or even a full 180-degrees in the wrong direction. While most of these miswired vagrants are evolutionary dead ends, vagrancy is not the genetic sink that it might appear to be. Keep in mind that without vagrancy, remote islands such as Hawai'i would be devoid of landbirds (well, at least native ones). If a finch, a thrush, and a flycatcher didn't end up in the middle of the Pacific somehow, we would be devoid of I'iwis, Omaos, and Elepaios and every other native landbird. The Galapagos Islands would be finch-less (and mockingbird-less) and perhaps Darwin would never have "discovered" evolution. (OK, Alfred Wallace would have published it himself eventually, but you get the idea.)

Although relatively new in the birding lexicon, the concept of mirror migration is clearly a significant source of some of the major rarities. Essentially, instead of flying south, a bird flies north. An immature Fork-tailed Flycatcher in Columbia that "should" fly south to Argentina instead flies north and ends up in North Carolina.

Take the case of the ultraexciting and charismatic Brown Hawk-Owl that appeared on St. Paul Island in the fall of 2007. The article documenting this occurrence postulated the route that may have delivered this thrilling first North American record to this remote island in the middle of the Bering Sea (figs. 7-2, 7-3, 7-4; Yerger and Mohlmann 2008).

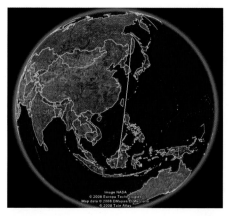

FIGURE 7-2.

A line depicting a hypothetical flight path for a migratory Brown Hawk-Owl from northern Ussuriland to Borneo. Such a flight would involve open-water crossings of about 3,800 kilometers. Image courtesy of National Aeronautics and Space Administration (NASA), TerraMetrics, Europa Technologies, DMapas/ElMercurio, Tele Atlas, and John Yerger/Adventure Birding.

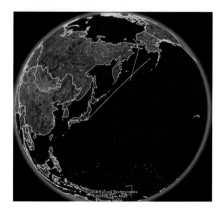

FIGURE 7-3.

The hypothetical flight path (white line) for the Brown Hawk-Owl from eastern Japan to Saint Paul Island. Such a path likely represents the maximal over-water crossing of a misoriented migrant, a distance of some 4,300 kilometers over water. Image courtesy of National Aeronautics and Space Administration (NASA), TerraMetrics, Europa Technologies, DMapas/ElMercurio, Tele Atlas, and John Yerger/Adventure Birding.

FIGURE 7-4.
A line drawn between eastern Japan and southern Borneo. If extended for the same distance 180 degrees away from Japan toward Alaska, the bird would reach Saint Paul Island. Although all models of reverse migration are speculative at this point, they offer a plausible explanation for how some species of long-distance Asian migrants might turn up in the Bering Sea. Image courtesy of National Aeronautics and Space Administration (NASA), TerraMetrics, Europa Technologies, DMapas/ElMercurio, Tele Atlas, and John Yerger/Adventure Birding.

While it only makes sense that more rarities are *found* in coastal migrant traps, we often wonder whether or not more rarities actually *arrive* at the coast than inland. Or is the explanation for the numbers found the result of observer bias, that is, because more birders live along the coast (where most of our population lives), there are simply more people looking and, especially in urbanized areas, fewer places to check. However, mechanisms that concentrate birds inland, such as a small woodlot in an expanse of soybean fields or a few trees around a ranch, should also produce rarities—and they do, but there are fewer people checking them. In other words, you don't have to live in Cape May or at Point Reyes to find a great bird that causes birders from all corners of the country to head straight to the nearest airport. Does a birdfeeder in the middle of Kansas have any less chance of yielding a mega-rarity than one in La Jolla, California, or are more people looking in La Jolla? I could argue both sides, but instead, I am more interested in simply getting you to check those feeders and gardens and that riparian vegetation in La Jolla, Kansas, Cape May, and everywhere in between! After all, I'll rhetorically ask again, if a vagrant lands in the woods and nobody is around to list it, was it there?

In other words, the more birders there are checking more places throughout the continent, then, theoretically at least, the more rarities will be found. While this will benefit our own lists and our collective state, county, region, etc. lists, it will also add to our collective knowledge of bird and vagrant distribution and perhaps even help us understand the changing nature of bird populations, their distribution, and the mechanisms of vagrancy.

Many of us spend unreasonable amounts of time perusing other states' and regions' listserves in order to see what "good" birds are being found. This is a very useful exercise, because it is a great way to learn about distribution and patterns of vagrancy. It can also suggest what we should be looking for. However, just don't be envious of what others are seeing—go out and find something for yourself.

Early in January 2010, I was skimming the listserves of surrounding states and provinces, as I do on a regular basis. I find the easiest way to get this info is to visit www.birdingonthe.net. Jack Siler's excellent site is a wonderful resource, because it hosts links to listserves, chat groups, and message boards from all over the world. Less is more here, and I can quickly skim or study lists on all sorts of birding and bird topics from around the world. Most often I find myself immersed in the various state listserves (especially under the "Regional Specialty" page).

One particular day, after looking at my local weather maps (which I also do on a daily basis, as discussed in chapter 4), I contemplated a very unusual storm system that had just passed through the Northeast and dumped quite a bit of snow on northern New England. The storm then stalled over the Canadian Maritimes for more than a week, yielding a strong and sustained north to northwesterly flow that was originating over the waters around Newfoundland (fig. 7-5).

If such a system were to occur in the fall, I would bet Northern Wheatears would begin to show up across the Eastern Seaboard. However, in the

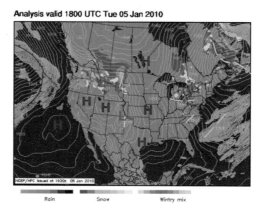

Analysis valid 1800 UTC Tue 05 Jan 2010

Rain   Snow   Wintry mix

FIGURE 7-5.
A deep low pressure system spinning over the Canadian Maritimes in winter has the potential to produce unusual birds in the northeastern United States. *Surface weather map, National Weather Service.*

middle of winter, with fewer birds on the move, I began to think about a few species that could ride these winds toward Maine. Gyrfalcon and Ivory Gull (figs. 7-6 and 7-7) came to mind, but then I started to think bigger. Maine is definitely overdue to add Fieldfare and Redwing, two European thrushes that occur very rarely in North America, with most records coming from Newfoundland. In fact, in a recent rambling blog entry written on a snowy and blustery day, I attempted to prognosticate the next 25 species that I will add to my personal state list, and the next 25 species that will be added to Maine's state list.

This wasn't just an exercise in randomly choosing birds I wanted to see, but instead I was considering distribution. Eastern Screech-Owls are being seen a lot more often in coastal New Hampshire, and therefore if I wander around the woods of southern York County on some calm spring night, I have little doubt that I would add this to my state list (and therefore was number one on my list). Also important to consider are past records of occurrence from surrounding states and provinces. For example, Maine still does not have a Fieldfare on its list, but Nova Scotia has as many as six records of seven birds (but only one was documented sufficiently; see above

FIGURE 7-6.
For unknown reasons, appearances of extra-limital Ivory Gulls have become more regular in the lower forty-eight states and southern Canada. In the winter of 2010, a bird made it as far south as Georgia! However, a year earlier, two birds in Eastern Massachusetts—such as this one in the winter laridphile hotspot of Gloucester—delighted scores. *Digi-scoped image of Ivory Gull, Gloucester, Massachusetts, 1/09* ©Derek Lovitch.

on the importance of documentation!), New Brunswick has a few more records, and even Massachusetts, to our south, has one record. And without a doubt, population changes (especially, but not limited to, increasing populations and range expansions) are playing a major role in what birds show up where. Furthermore, it's just a matter of time for Eurasian Collared Dove to finally be documented in Maine, and Black-bellied Whistling Ducks are showing up with increasing frequency beyond their rapidly expanding breeding range.

Number two on my list of the next birds to be added to Maine's list was the Fieldfare (fig. 7-8), number four was the Redwing, and the Song Thrush,

FIGURE 7-7.
A sample of those scores of birders who delighted in the arrival of this wayward Arctic visitor. Photo of birders looking at *Ivory Gull, Gloucester, Massachusetts, 1/09* ©Derek Lovitch.

which has only one North American record to date, received an honorable mention. Therefore, I began to daydream about an already wayward European thrush that had flown the wrong way (the ultimate cause of its vagrancy) to Newfoundland and then was funneled by the winds of this current storm system (the proximate cause) to Maine.

So, I began to keep a close eye on the Newfoundland/Labrador message board. In early January, I noticed that Northern Lapwings—big, charismatic shorebirds from Europe—were being reported in relatively good numbers (at least three different birds). That could be a sign of things to come for those of us to the south. But then, I noticed a most intriguing post—a link to the Ireland listserve that mentioned that unusually large numbers of Redwings and smaller numbers of Fieldfares and Song Thrushes

were being seen in Western Ireland, and one observer reported seeing large numbers flying off the west coast.

While many, if not most, of these birds would be expected to make a southerly turn and head for the Iberian Peninsula, others could conceivably get caught up in a strong North Atlantic winter storm and follow the winds on the backside of this, or another, low pressure system over to the New World. Then those northerly winds currently over Newfoundland could conceivably usher some—I'd take *one*—of those birds in our direction.

Over the next few weeks, I diligently monitored the listserves to our north. A Redwing did indeed turn up on Newfoundland just a few weeks after the message boards there commented about the Ireland exodus, and that got me even more motivated.

I therefore made a special effort to sift through flocks of American Robins here in Maine. Although I do this on a regular basis anyway, I doubled my effort in checking habitats such as abandoned orchards, city parks with ornamental plantings, and other choice habitats that I know are frequented by winter frugivores. I was especially attentive when we began to see New-foundland ("Newfie") Robins—the blacker-backed and brighter-chested birds that breed in the Canadian Maritimes. Whether or not they are a true subspecies or simply the extreme of clinal variation is subject for debate, but when large flocks of robins appear in midwinter in Maine, and the majority of birds have blacker backs and brighter, brick-red chests, then we can safely assume that these are birds that are arriving from our northeast.

If a Redwing, Fieldfare, or even a Song Thrush is to be found in Maine, chances are that it will be within a flock of these Newfie Robins arriving in late winter after food resources, especially mountain ash, become depleted (and huge irruptions can occur when there are poor American Mountain-Ash crops to our north). After all, records of Fieldfare from Massachusetts (1986), Minnesota (1991), and New Brunswick (1997) all occurred within flocks of American Robins. In fact, the Massachusetts bird was assumed to be part of the same movement that brought a Redwing and at least four Fieldfares to St. John's, Newfoundland, in late December of 1985.

When I began to see more Newfoundland Robins by early February, I increased my effort and anticipation. Now here is where I really, really would like to tell you that my prognostications and concerted efforts paid off. I would like to tell you how great a call I made when I predicted Maine's first Fieldfare was right around the corner. It would be the perfect anecdote, the perfect lesson, to justify all of this soapboxing.

But, alas, even poetic license will not allow me to string such a tale. Despite my best efforts at prognostication and with as much time in the field as I could muster, I did not find any first state record Field-fares, or any other European thrush for that matter. However, I did see lots of robins (and spent a good amount of quality time really studying just how variable this species is, which is a good lesson on its own), plenty of Cedar Waxwings (one of my favorite birds), a hand-ful of Bohemian Waxwings (it was a slow year for them), plus lots of other great birds, like a pioneering Hermit Thrush that was surviving our most bitter cold spell of the season on a small point of land jut-ting into a bay covered by Staghorn Sumac and Asiatic Bittersweet.

Those observations—and many other sightings—were worthwhile, and so my effort was hardly wasted. In fact, no time in the field is ever wasted!

The question is, then, that if I didn't know about a potential influx of European thrushes into Newfoundland two months earlier, would I have bothered checking these areas as diligently? While the thrill of the hunt for vagrants fueled my effort, my greatest consolation prize was some fantastic birding. Much better than sitting around the house watching yet more TV reruns!

Knowing what to expect, when to expect it, and where to expect it goes a long way in preparing you for the next big find. Monitor the listserves of surrounding states and look for patterns. Perhaps a rash of reports of, perhaps, wandering Townsend's Solitaires and Varied Thrushes wandering east will foretell the next big news in your neighborhood. Maybe a series of reports of Old World waterfowl to your north will alert you to checking the local duck hotspot that could yield something along the lines of a Tufted Duck (fig. 7-9).

As I mentioned earlier, I regularly, especially in peak rarity season, keep an eye on all of the listserves of surrounding states at the very least. Once a week or so, I skim all of the eastern states to look for emerging patterns. Cave Swallow reports in the Upper Midwest and Great Lakes usually lead to Cave Swallow sightings on the East Coast (see chapter 4) a few days to a couple of weeks later.

Furthermore, let us keep in mind that with a changing landscape (development, shifts in land use, and the ever-growing human population) and a changing climate, bird populations are changing as well. More and more hummingbirds are wintering in the southeast, drought is causing waterbirds to disperse and is limiting fall seed supplies for grassland sparrows, and an outbreak of pine beetles is denuding hundreds of acres of forest and may push birds to different areas. Countless factors are changing, and birds are reacting in different ways.

Some of those reactions give us hope. Birds are resilient, and although the status and distribution of birds will certainly look much different in a hundred years, I have little doubt that there will still be plenty of birds.

FIGURE 7-9.
The Sacarrappa Falls in Westbrook, Maine, keeps a small stretch of the Presump-scot River open in all but the harshest winters. In addition to a multitude of Mallards and American Black Ducks, this ice-free freshwater habitat often hosts lingering waterfowl, such as Ring-necked Ducks, and in the winter of 2008-2009, this drake Tufted Duck. *Tufted Duck, Westbrook, Maine, 12/08* ©Luke Seitz.

Unfortunately, I also have little doubt that hundreds, perhaps thousands, of species will no longer be with us.

But many others will simply be located in different areas. For example, over the last decade or so, there has been a significant trend of birds moving north. In fact, in recent years, some of the most significant rarities have come from south of our border. The White-crested Elaenia (South Padre Island, Texas, February 2008), Sungrebe (Bosque del Apache National Wildlife Refuge, New Mexico, November 2008), and Sinaloa Wren (Patagonia, Arizona, sighted August 2008, nest building in May 2009, and still present as of the spring of 2010) have been added to the ABA area. This pattern is likely to continue, and so in preparation for your next big discovery, perhaps you should study Howell and Webb's *Guide to the Birds of Mexico and Northern Central America*. As for birds that already occur north of the border, is a Wilson's Plover (fig. 7-10), for example, that shows up

FIGURE 7-10.
A regular spring overshoot north of its usual range, this Wilson's Plover was even further north than usual in the spring of 2010, when it was discovered by biologists monitoring Piping Plovers. *Wilson's Plover, Reid State Park, Georgetown, Maine, 5/10* ©Luke Seitz.

north of its usual range in spring "just an overshoot," or is it a pioneer that foreshadows the future ranges of the species as it responds to climate change and rising sea levels?

A great example of observer attention and awareness has been occurring on the reservoirs of Colorado and elsewhere throughout the arid west. More and more observers are heading to large bodies of water, even organizing "inland pelagics" on the largest lakes, in the fall. The results? Yellow-billed Loons, Sabine's Gulls, phalaropes, jaegers, Black-legged Kittiwakes, regionally rare large gulls, terns, and ducks, and in October of 2007, two Ross's Gulls (on John Martin Reservoir and Lagerman Reservoir in southeastern Colorado). If birders were not out focusing on these man-made oases, many more birders would not be growing their state and county lists significantly. More important, perhaps, is that we would not be closer to understanding the timing and pattern of the continental migration of birds we usually think of being pelagics, such as Sabine's Gulls and jaegers.

All of us from coast to coast can peruse the Regional Reports in *North American Birds*, eBird maps, and state rare-bird alerts and listserves in order to decipher clear and present trends in where birders in the know are heading and what they are finding. Instead of letting others do the work, use what you have learned in this book and from digesting these other resources, and go find some rarities! If birders in Colorado are making so many new sightings on reservoirs in the fall, then why are you sitting at home in Wyoming watching TV? Understanding trends is half of the battle. Then, we can apply our newfound knowledge of how to apply habitat (chapter 2), geography (chapter 3), and weather (chapter 4) to hone our birding effort to put ourselves in the right place at the right time to find rarity gold.

The short version of this chapter on finding vagrants—the "take-home lesson," if you will—is simple and straightforward: go birding! There's little doubt that the continued increase in observer effort and awareness will not only lead to the discovery of more rarities, but perhaps it will help shed some light on why vagrants occur, when, and how.

A New Jersey Case Study

In the preceding chapters, I discussed how using knowledge of subjects such as habitat, geography, meteorology, and more can make you a better birder. So, exactly what does being a better birder mean? Well, it means something different for each of us, but I think we can all agree that becoming a better birder would entail seeing more birds, seeing more "good" birds, and maximizing our time in the field.

Few of us have time and means to go birding every day anywhere we want. Especially when we have the good fortune to take a trip away from home dedicated to birding, we all want to see as many birds as we can, and use our time as efficiently as possible. So, how can we apply our newfound knowledge and expertise when on the road?

Yesteryears

I was born and raised in New Jersey. Disparaging jokes aside, New Jersey is really a wonderful state, with an amazing array of open spaces and great birding destinations. In fact, with the most habitats per square mile of any state, the annual World Series of Birding takes place in New Jersey and is organized by New Jersey Audubon. For 24 hours, from dawn to dusk, from one corner of the state to the other, winning teams often record 225 or more species of birds! In 24 hours! Clearly, there's much more to the state than the turnpike and Newark Airport, where most people's opinions of the state are first formed.

I birded throughout my high school years, dealing with the various peer pressures that come with being known as a birder in your average suburban high school (even teachers called me Bird Man!). OK, it didn't help that I didn't grow until my junior year of high school, we didn't have enough money to have the trendiest overpriced clothes, and well—I was a dork. But happily, I stuck with it, and as I entered my freshman year at Rutgers University, I began to take my birding to the next level.

Between the parties, the football games—and yes, the studying and classwork sometimes—I found time to grow as a birder. Little did I know it at the time, but Helyar Woods and the adjacent Rutgers Display Gardens were fast becoming my first patch list, and the beginning of my appreciation for regularly visiting the same local patch on a regular basis (see chapter 9). Conveniently located about a half-mile from the Cook College (now called the Rutgers School of Biological and Environmental Sciences) campus, my lack of car, lack of money, and lack of time still did not inhibit my development as a birder. By my senior year, there were a few instances where I would go straight from an all-night party to the woods when I expected a good day of migration. (Boy, I wish I still had energy like that!)

I volunteered at the Chimney Rock Hawkwatch and New Jersey Audubon's Owl Haven nature center (now the Sandy Hook Bird Observatory), and in post-college years, I returned to work at the Sandy Hook Hawkwatch and then the Cape May Hawkwatch. In subsequent years and visits, I always squeezed in at least a little birding every time I visited family and friends. One of my goals was to attempt to add a state bird on each of these trips, to help pad my personal New Jersey list as my lists for other states I was living in at the time were rapidly catching up. Other outings were simply to bird with friends or revisit locations that I used to frequent to share with my wife.

But overall, my birding was much more random. Many of my outings were based on when I had a day off, or later, when I had a free morning while visiting for the holidays. I didn't use radar to pick where and when to go birding. I didn't look at the weather patterns—well, perhaps to know if I needed a rain jacket, but not much more than that. What bird was missing from my list? When and where might I find it? If I had the choice, what would be the best date and location to visit for x, y, or z?

Nowadays

My time was always limited, so I needed to focus my attention and effort in a more effective and efficient way. When I began working on this book, I realized how much I had learned (and of course, how much I have yet to learn!), and I decided to take a trip to the motherland (fall of 2009) to spend some time studying with a few of the leaders in the various fields that I was writing about at the time and to demonstrate just how useful these tools can be. Originally, the plan was to spend a night or two with David LaPuma at Rutgers discussing radar, and then some time in Cape May with Cameron Cox observing the famous morning flight at the Higbee Dike, while at the same time picking the brain of Michael O'Brien, especially when it came to nocturnal flight calls and the observation of night-time migration in action.

Once again my time would be limited and there was no chance I could fit in everything I wanted to do. So I had to choose where and when to be at a certain place with a certain person in order to maximize the productivity of my birding and my research. How could I do this? Well, I just had to apply the additional disciplines that I have been discussing in order to make my time in the field more rewarding. Habitat, weather, geography, and more would be applied to my daily decision making. So, with a stack of maps, a list of phone numbers, and a "favorites" list on the laptop jam-packed with weather links, I packed my car and headed south.

"October 18, 2009. 7:00 a.m. Garrett Mountain, New Jersey. Light, intermittent rain. Cold, raw. 39 degrees F." reads my notes.

"Why would I be on Garret Mountain in the fall in cold rain?"you might be asking if you were familiar with Garret Mountain and New Jersey birding. Garret Mountain is a spring migrant trap; few, many fewer birders visit here in the fall. I was spending some time studying all things radar with David LaPuma, the radar guru behind Woodcreeper.com, the website dedicated to monitoring bird migration via radar in New Jersey. On a morning when sleeping in was definitely a consideration, especially following a long drive down from Maine after work, the forecast was calling for cold, rainy, strong northeasterly wind–perfect conditions to catch up on sleep, right? Well, we definitely considered that option, but you don't sleep in during migration! Remember the rule of thumb from "Birding and Weather": if it begins to rain in the middle of night during migration, go birding in the morning!

Therefore, David and I woke up early and pulled up the radar on the computer. The rain had arrived over the course of the night, but it was making very slow progress over and through Central New Jersey. Looking at the radar images to the north, we saw there were a lot of birds "upstream" and despite scattered showers on the radar, there clearly were some other things there as well.

The winds were out of the northeast all night. Looking carefully at both the base reflectivity image and the velocity image, we found that although the rain was moving from south-southwest to north-northeast, the "other" stuff was moving *with* the wind (northeast to southwest) at 10–15 knots faster than the wind was blowing. Birds were on the move! And they were flying right into the rain. Fallout conditions?

The activity seemed to be centered around the inland ridges of New Jersey in the morning, so we chose Garret. Situated at the north end of the first Watchung Ridge and surrounded by densely urban Passaic County, Garret is geographically positioned to receive some of the birds overhead as they descended in the dawn (see chapter 3), and there's enough habitat here to support some of those migrants (see chapter 2).

So we grabbed the Gore-tex, brewed a fresh pot of "liquid brain" (as the New Jersey birding legend and institution Rick Kane calls coffee) and headed out the door. A quick stop for a pork roll, egg and cheese on a bagel (can't get that in Maine!) and we were heading north on the parkway.

We arrived at Garret shortly after dawn, and in a short two-hour loop, tallied a good number of the expected short-distance migrants of the season. Yellow-rumped Warblers were scattered about, with at least 100 encountered that morning. A handful of Palm Warblers and a couple of tardy Northern Parulas joined the mix. Sparrows were more numerous, led by 125-plus White-throated Sparrows, with handfuls of Swamp Sparrows in wet thickets, Song Sparrows at the edge of brush, and Chipping Sparrows on lawns under trees. In addition there was a smattering of Ruby-crowned and Golden-crowned Kinglets fidgeting in the branches, a half-dozen Eastern Phoebes foraging around the ponds (always pumping their tails as they go), and a goodly total of at least 20 Hermit Thrushes poking around on the ground in the woods. Based on the conditions, all in all, this was a very good morning of birding.

The behavior of some of the birds—White-throated Sparrows in tree-tops and Yellow-rumped Warblers flying across large clearings—suggested that these birds had recently arrived and had not yet settled into favorable patches. Essentially, we were in the midst of a mini-fallout, because a relatively light migration had encountered rainfall overspreading the area, and the birds put down to rest, feed, and wait for conditions to improve.

While nothing we saw that day was something to remember for a lifetime, it was a great morning that could easily have been "wasted" doing something like . . . well, anything other than birding! Thanks to the radar, we got out of bed, out the door, and into the field. If you're not in the field, you can't see birds, find rarities, work on your patch list, learn about birds—or any of the myriad of reasons to go birding. And if there had been even more birds in the air the previous night, perhaps we would have had one of those birding experiences of a lifetime.

For more about that morning and the radar images that described this event, see that day's post from David at http.woodcreeper. com/2009/10/18/birds-and-rain/

Over the course of the day, the upper-level low pressure system was slowly pulling away, and high pressure was building. The skies were clearing, and overnight, the winds had become northwesterly. Looking at the radar first thing the next morning, David and I saw that the most activity was over west-central New Jersey, with less activity at the coast (in no small part due to northeasterly winds over Long Island and southern New England). With very light, nearly calm, winds come dawn, we saw that there was little concentration, because the birds had dispersed widely inland. Therefore, instead of heading to the coast, I stayed right there in the New Brunswick area.

Dawn at Hutchenson Memorial Forest with David yielded decent numbers (relatively speaking) of Yellow-rumped Warblers and American

Robins overhead, with an increase in sparrows in the brush. Later I met up with my friend Evan Obercian in his local patches in Oldwick (west-northwest of New Brunswick), where we encountered very good numbers of sparrows.

Cold Brook Preserve, a local hotspot, was quite windy (as it often is, due to open agricultural fields on an exposed small hill/ridge), and so birds were harder to detect. Applying our knowledge of the microclimates offered by another local patch, we found a large number of sparrows, Swamp and Song in particular, in this more sheltered patch (coincidentally, a very similar mix to when Evan and I were birding my local Portland area patches a couple of weeks ago when he was visiting me on my home turf).

After checking a few Canada Goose aggregations for rarities, without success, I headed down to Cape May. After my obligatory stop at the West-side Market for corn fritters, I headed up to the hawkwatch platform, where I was treated to an afternoon full of Merlins, kestrels, and Cooper's and Sharp-shinned Hawks (fig. 8-1). The hawkcount this day, as tallied by Cape May Hawkwatching legend himself, Pete Dunne, was a respectable 1,607 raptors (and the pseudo-raptor New World Vultures) of 13 species. Most of the day's 158 American Kestrels and 120 Merlins passed through in the late afternoon hours—a classic late-day falcon flight that provided spectators with a great show. I enjoyed—and retained for later use, with due credit attributed—yet another great hawkwatching Pete Dunne-ism: "Kestrels are in the present tense, Merlins are in the past tense."

Meanwhile, waves of Double-crested Cormorants were offshore, and Tree Swallows were buzzing all around. An increasing diversity of ducks in Bunker Pond included a single female scaup that was actually called a different species by different people on different days; it was later agreed that it was indeed a Greater, but yes, even the experts in Cape May occasionally make a mistake. There were lots of birds of all sorts in all sorts of places, many of them on the move—it was a glorious end to a very productive day of birding.

However, despite the falling darkness, my birding continued. The winds were dead calm. so, as I so often did when I was an intern in Cape May some years ago, I joined the sunset vigil atop the platform at the South Cape May Meadows, viewing the silhouettes of American Bitterns, Black-crowned

FIGURE 8-1.
The Cape May Hawkwatch, conducted each year by the Cape May Bird Observatory is one of the longest running counts in the East. *View from the Hawkwatch platform, Cape May, New Jersey, 10/09* ©Derek Lovitch.

Night Herons, and Wilson's Snipe as the birds took to the air. And with the absolute last glow of light in the western sky, owls were taking flight. It was early in the owl migration season, but we still were treated to a hunting Barn Owl and two migrant Long-eared Owls. We all agreed, however, that the absolute highlight was a Pied-billed Grebe launching out of the pond and making three wide circles around us, wings buzzing faster than imaginable (although the light, or lack thereof, plays a role in our perception of their actual speed). How often have you seen a "Water Witch" fly? Exactly! And *if* you have seen one fly, you may think it looks like it was shot, fluttering its wings and banking its body desperately, very unlike the fluid and efficient flight that we were treated to that evening as the bird gained altitude before heading south.

Interestingly enough, just before sunset, we also noted a lot of Yellow-rumped Warblers actively moving around, making short flights and sorties and exhibiting other restless behaviors highly suggestive of *zugunruhe*, or migration restlessness. These birds really seemed to be ready to go. And this was just the start of the evening's activities! Later on, I was outside again, standing aside Michael O'Brien and listening to migrants passing overhead. While I was attempting to absorb as much knowledge as possible on the flight calls of migrants, we also spent time discussing some of the concepts and mechanisms at work here.

Michael is one of the leading authorities on the nocturnal flight calls of migrant birds and has been writing the virtual book on listening to nocturnal flight calls. In chapter 5, I discussed many of the attributes of a good listening spot. Well, most of the information came from Michael, and much of it was demonstrated to me that night.

With a very light west wind higher up and clear skies, we drove about Cape May Point, visiting Michael's favorite listening posts. Michael has spent years experimenting with various listening locations around the island of Cape May Point, identifying the best places to hear migrants. I wondered what that group of loitering youths were thinking when we stood there, virtually silently (well, at least when I was not interviewing Michael and peppering him with questions). I'm sure the Striped Skunk that was sauntering up the boardwalk, looking for spilled fries, funnel cake, and the like, was equally surprised to see us; we thought it was best to alert him to our presence at a safe distance.

When we were not listening to the local street punks or plotting our escape from a marauding skunk, we listened to the skies. Yellow-rumped Warblers, Savannah Sparrows, and Palm Warblers made up a large percentage of the audible flight, with a smattering of other species, including a single Dickcissel, whose nocturnal flight call is identical to the "buzzy fart" sound of its diurnal call.

The next morning, I greeted the sunrise atop the dredge spoil dike at Higbee Beach Wildlife Management Area. My good friend Cameron Cox was this year's counter for the Morning Flight Count (fig. 8-2). Also at Higbee is a platform staffed by a seasonal naturalist to help folks enjoy the morning flight phenomena and start them on the track to be identifying

FIGURE 8-2.
Another migration monitoring project is the Morning Flight at the dike at the Higbee Beach Wildlife Management Area. Each dawn during fall migration, observers attempt to identify and tally all individuals that are part of the morning reorientation flight, or redetermined migration. *Higbee Dike at dawn, Cape May, New Jersey, 10/09* ©Derek Lovitch.

these flying blurs as they hurtle by (or, preferably for the birder, pause in the treetops). (fig. 8-3).

Michael reported that nearly 40–50 calls a minute were being heard in the predawn hour, and we had just checked the radar, confirming that birds were on the move. In fact, *a lot* of birds were on the move. With much excitement and anticipation, I climbed the muddy slope of the dike and joined Michael and Cameron as they documented the morning's reorientation flight.

When Cameron finally departed the watch at about 11:30 a.m., almost 6,000 individuals of 101 species were tallied. Almost 4,000 Yellow-rumped

Warblers, more than 600 American Robins, 400 Tree Swallows, and 500 Red-winged Blackbirds led the list, with highlights including a late Connecticut Warbler and an Orange-crowned Warbler, which was identified only later when Michael was sorting through his photos from the morning. (For a complete list of the morning's sightings, visit cmboviewfromthefield. blogspot.com/2009_10_01_archive.html.)

It was simply awesome, scientifically speaking of course. So many birds of so many species in just a few hours of standing in *one* place. I had a great time and was thoroughly excited and enthusiastic. Cameron, however, was just as thoroughly disappointed. It was not the flight that he had hoped for and not the flight that we had expected. Sometimes, it's just plain and simply the fact that the birds don't always do exactly what we think they are "supposed" to do!

Following a little birding in the woods, brush, and grass off the dike at Higbee Beach and enjoying some of the species that were on the move overhead on a more intimate level, I focused on the thicker brush to look for the species that I call "scrubby migrants," such as Ruby-crowned Kinglets, and delighted in the plethora of Carolina Wrens that call this place home. I was also hoping to find a fun vagrant, perhaps a Bell's Vireo. In the weedy, "sparrow-rific" fields, Swamp, Song, and Savannah Sparrows were abundant, punctuated by the occasional White-crowned or Vesper.

As the day rapidly warmed, rising columns of warm air (thermals) became peppered with soaring raptors, including a nice flight of Red-shouldered Hawks, and I continued to skywatch throughout the day. More corn fritters and a cheese steak from Westside Market fueled my skywatching, as I continued to effectively procrastinate from getting work—like the writing of this chapter—completed.

Dark and early the next morning, I was once again atop the Higbee dike with Cameron. An extremely light northwesterly wind was encouraging what (relatively few) migrants were present this morning to reorient into the wind—as is usual here, apparently—and be counted. There were "only" about 1,500 migrants—mostly Yellow-rumps, which are common at this season, but including 1 Dickcissel, 1 Orange-crowned Warbler, and a decent sum for here of 40-plus Blackpoll Warblers.

FIGURE 8-3.
A Yellow-rumped Warbler wings it past the Morning Flight Count atop the dike at the Higbee Beach Wildlife Management Area—one of the most abundant migrants during my visit to Cape May. *Cape May Point, 10/20/09* ©Michael O'Brien.

Next on my itinerary was "The Beanery," or officially, the Rea Farm. This is a unique ecotourism partnership between New Jersey Audubon and the landowner that provides access to some wonderful habitat. Sparrows filled fields planted with seed crops, lingering warblers foraged in the Red Maple swamp, and scrubby migrants poked around the brushy margins. A respectable-for-the-late-date six species of warblers, including truant individual Black-throated Blue and Prairie Warblers were present, and an immature Blue Grosbeak popped out of the weeds to fill out the morning's list.

Cameron, fresh off of his shift at the Morning Flight, and I then checked out the less-frequented Cape Island Creek area, another critical migratory stopover location preserved by the Nature Conservancy. It was downright "birdy" there that day, with a large number of the expected abundant migrants of the season, but also goodly totals of 13 Field Sparrows, 14 White-crowned, and 2 Vesper. The scrubby, food-filled (seeds and fruit of both native and nonnative bushes and trees) edges there provided good foraging habitat for a variety of species.

On our way back to the car (anxiously anticipating a grilled veggie sandwich from The Depot!), a medium-sized yellowish passerine zipped by me. "Whatthehellwasthat?" I blurted as Cameron and I began our search to relocate the bird. With symptoms of rarity fever in full swing, we slowly pieced together a picture of what could have been New Jersey's first ever Hooded Oriole. Unfortunately, our bubble burst when Cameron finally had a good look and confirmed that this was "just" an extraordinarily late Orchard Oriole. Based on the date and location, we concluded that this was probably a reverse migrant that had arrived on the extensive southerly winds that also yielded a late-season day of birding in a t-shirt, and not just a lingering bird. A Hooded Oriole it was not, but the occurrence of this bird certainly fit the pattern that produces oddities, such as reverse migrants from both near (Orchard Oriole) and sometime far (Hooded Oriole).

I spent the afternoon writing—at least to prove to my hosts Michael O'Brien and acclaimed bird artist Louise Zemaitis that I was really in town to work, and not just to play and eat corn fritters—and Michael and I studied the wind and weather maps. A light southerly wind overnight was predicted, and some cloud cover, encouraged us to skip the evening vigil at the South Cape May Meadows platform. Now, I would like to say we found productive birding elsewhere on these conditions, but I'll be honest—we ate pizza and played poker instead!

The next morning, Michael and I greeted the sunrise at Two Mile Landing, with partly cloudy skies and a very light southwesterly wind. We were here to study salt sparrows and perhaps apply a hypothesis of mine that was based on observations of a microhabitat preference I had made in Maine's Scarborough Marsh during the October flood tides, about the perching differences between the interior (*alterus* and/or *nelsoni*) and coastal (*subvirgatus*) subspecies of Nelson's Sparrows. I have observed the interior subspecies seem to prefer—when possible and when all else is equal—to perch on a thicker stem or woody vegetation and usually at a slightly higher level than the coastal subspecies , which usually perches lower and/or seeks out grass-ier patches to relocate to.

We weren't finding many salt sparrows that morning (it was a little early in the season), but what we were noticing was that wave after wave of Yellow-rumped Warblers were on the move overhead, flying west or south-west into the light wind as the sun crested the horizon. "Is this normal on a slow migration morning?" I asked. "No, it most definitely is not," Michael replied. "Maybe we should head over to the dike." Moments later, Cameron called, "Uh, guys, I could use a hand."

Three hours and 23,717 Yellow-rumped Warblers later, we stumbled down, haggard and bedraggled, from the dike, having recorded 2,595 American Robins, 500 Tree Swallows, 125 Red-winged Blackbirds, 92 Chipping Sparrows, 70 Palm Warblers, 70 Sharp-shinned Hawks, and 1,196 other individuals of 75 species. A Parasitic Jaeger chased Laughing Gulls offshore, a truant Bobolink called as it passed overhead, and a possi-ble Cape Island record of 42 White-rumped Sandpipers foraged in the dredge spoils contained in the dike. (Once again, for a complete list of the morning's sightings, you can see the rundown on the Cape May Bird Ob-servatory's website at cmboviewfromthefield.blogspot.com/2009_10_01_archive.html.)

I was one of three counters (along with Cameron and Michael) who were keeping track of migrants this morning. In one hour, I alone clicked off 4,840 Yellow-rumped Warblers—more birds than I have recorded in all on my best morning at Sandy Point, my local morning flight spot in Maine! It was remarkable, it was epic, and it was overwhelming. I had hit the "big one" that I had hoped for— the biggest flight of the season—and I was in the right place at the right time for it. "You have your anecdote for the book!" said Cameron. The only problem was that we *hadn't* predicted this. The winds were southwesterly, the skies were mostly cloudy. This, by con-ventional wisdom, should *not* have happened. So, why were there so many birds?

First, our predictions were based on weather forecasts, and we all know that weather forecasts aren't always perfect. Then, to add another complica-tion, we then were predicting from them how the birds would respond to the weather. Those are two big variables that can change a lot overnight.

So, what had happened? As soon as I got back to Michael and Louise's house, I pulled up the radar and David's Woodcreeper website to look at the overnight radar images (http.woodcreeper.com/2009/10/22/against-the-wind-3/). I also looked at the hourly weather summaries (see chapter 3 and chapter 5). From the second radar loop, from Delaware, you can see that the dark green areas signified a great density of migrants over the water as sunrise approached. Apparently the winds were light enough to get birds moving, but with a light southwesterly wind developing, the migrants were displaced to the east—out over the Delaware Bay and Atlantic Ocean. Come dawn, these birds needed first to get back to land, and then to reorient themselves and find food by moving farther inland.

Essentially, if Michael and I had checked the radar *before* heading out to Two-Mile Landing, we would have realized that we should have been heading straight to the dike instead! I make no claims that predicting where to bird and when is an exact science, and here's an example where we almost made a major mistake. Luckily, Michael recognized that the quantity of Yellow-rumps over Two Mile Landing was unusual, and once again the value of cell phones to the advancement of birding was realized when Cameron started calling.

The great birding and great people of Cape May always make it difficult for a birder to leave, and this time was no different for me. However, we had been spending a lot of time studying the upper-level winds, and they were looking awfully good for producing rarities in New Jersey, and Cape May would of course be a prime spot to see something unusual.

But my time in New Jersey came to a rapid close, and I had to make it back to Maine in time to lead a pelagic trip that weekend, so therefore, after saying goodbye—and having one last cheesesteak—I headed north. The next stop was the Brig, or more formally, the Brigantine Division of the Edwin B. Forsythe National Wildlife Refuge, to enjoy migrant shorebirds

FIGURE 8-4. *(opposite page)*
Increasingly being found north of its usual range, Roseate Spoonbills, such as this one, New Jersey's third, are making headlines in many states. *Digi-scoped image of Roseate Spoonbill, Brigantine Division, Forsythe National Wildlife Refuge, New Jersey, 10/09* ©Derek Lovitch.

but also to hopefully twitch the juvenile Roseate Spoonbill that has taken up residence here for the previous few months. Timing my visit for high tide, where I hoped the bird would be visible as it roosted and not hidden, for example, as it fed at the edge of a deep tidal creek, I located the bird, which was roosting on a dry sod bank with some Snowy Egrets and a Great Egret (fig. 8-4), and enjoyed simply crippling views and digi-scoping opportunities of my first Roseate Spoonbill for New Jersey (and only the third record for the state overall!) and a nice addition to my state list, which at the time was barely holding a lead over that of my new home state of Maine.

Before I began my trip, my mom asked if I would see her on this whirlwind visit. "Hope for cold fronts," was my reply! Well, the cold front didn't happen, but I got the flight at Cape May I needed and wanted, so I made some time for family. But the next morning, I was back in the field visiting my old stomping grounds—and still one of my absolute favorite birding destinations—of Sandy Hook with friend and "Mr. Sandy Hook" himself, Scott Barnes, the Senior Naturalist of the Sandy Hook Bird Observatory.

There are few sure bets in life, but one of those is that if I visit Sandy Hook, there *will* be northeasterly winds! Sure enough, cold, raw northeasterly winds were blowing off the water on this day, and expectedly, landbirding was brutally slow. There was virtually no morning flight (just a few Yellow-rumps) at dawn. Many, if not most, of the landbirds that arrived on the always-productive-here southwesterly winds of the past few days had departed. We did our best to focus our time on sheltered thickets and deeper woodlands, but birding was slow. Only seawatching was going to be fruitful this day—flocks of scoters and Double-crested Cormorants were on the move offshore, and hundreds of Northern Gannets were feeding nearshore. And then, it began to rain.

Here's a perfect example of how, unlike all of my other birding that week, I made a visit based on my time and a friend's availability instead of using weather and radar to focus my attention. The result? Slow birding. On the southwest winds earlier in the week? A Sage Thrasher. The next day, as I drove back to Maine, as southwest winds returned? A Cave Swallow. Well, you can't be everywhere at once!

Luckily, I enjoyed a Rutgers football victory with good friends on my last night in town, so my trip did end on a high note after all. And despite a lackluster day on Sandy Hook, which in its own right was a very useful example, I enjoyed a very productive, very educational, and very exemplifying visit to the great birding state of New Jersey, where I used other disciplines, from meteorology to geography, to maximize my birding experience. So how can you apply these skills on a daily basis without traveling far from home? Enter your local patch, and engage in (my personal obsession) patch listing.

Patch Listing

"Hey, did you hear that?"

"Yeah, there it is again."

"Greater Yellowlegs . . . Yes! . . . Patch bird!"

At my local patch, Hedgehog Mountain Park ("The Hog") in Freeport, Maine, shorebird habitat is limited to a playing field that occasionally hosts a puddle after heavy rains and a small pond at the bottom of an old sand pit. Not exactly prime for species beyond Killdeer, Spotted Sandpiper, and Solitary Sandpiper. Other than a small breeding population of American Woodcock, my patch list (my personal list for all species seen or heard in a specific place, or "patch") for The Hog was limited to those three shorebirds, plus a Lesser Yellowlegs that put down in a large puddle in the playing field during a major storm (see chapter 4).

Therefore, I was quite excited when that Greater Yellowlegs flew overhead and called a couple of times to announce its presence, while a friend and I looked for warblers in the woods on May morning. I must admit that it has been a while since I have been that excited about a vocalizing Greater Yellowlegs! That is just one of the benefits of patch listing—some of the most common birds become major ticks when they show up in your patch. An out-of-habitat vagrant to your patch can become almost as exciting as an out-of-range vagrant to your state.

I've heard a suggestion that all birders are obsessive-compulsive; it's just the degree that differs. For many birders, their obsession-compulsion comes to light with their lists. Life lists, state lists, town lists, county lists, year lists, birds-photographed lists, birds-seen-copulating lists, birds-seen-pooping lists: the list of lists goes on. And none of this is inherently a bad thing, our lists motivate us, our lists record our sightings for posterity, and our lists can bring back great (and yes, not-so-great) memories. And a little friendly competition never hurts either.

Of course, I also suggest that we make sure to remember that the numbers on a list are only there for order—the bird, and not the number, is what is important. Lists, and the "listers" that keep them, are occasionally disparaged when the list becomes too important or a sort of superficial badge of honor. To each their own, but I personally find my lists to be wonderful travelogues, a diary of sorts, and yes, a little extra motivation when a little extra motivation is called for. None of these is a reason for disparagement.

One type of less-common list that I believe can be constructive for birders to keep is the patch list. It can be little more than an excuse to get in the field or an easy solution to birding while getting the dog walked, or it can be taken to a whole new level. It can reduce carbon emissions by keeping you close to home, and it can yield valuable data. And it can be done absolutely anywhere you live, anywhere in the world, at any and all times.

For me, my patch lists provide a little extra motivation when I need that little incentive to get out of bed. I set a goal of seeing 150 species in a given patch, and then I work toward that goal. Sometimes I reach that goal in a few years, sometimes I never do. But I really like the challenge of adding to a patch list, and I believe patch listing can yield quite a bit of knowledge about local bird population, distribution, microhabitat use, timing of migration, and much more.

The concept is simple: see as many birds (or a target number) as you can within the confines of a specific area. This area could be large; it could be small. It could be a well-known hotspot, or it could be your own private woodlot. It doesn't matter what patch you choose, the only "rule," if there is one, is that you need to visit this patch regularly.

I choose the patches that I keep a list for based on a few parameters. You can choose your own parameters if you so desire, or you could even just throw a dart on a map. But for me, a potential patch needs the following characteristics:

1. It must be within a few miles of home or work. It doesn't take much time or effort to get there, so I can squeeze it in before going to work, I don't spend much gas getting there, and it allows me to become intimately familiar with the avifauna and the habitat of my local area.

2. It needs to allow dogs, so I can multitask and get our dog's exercise in while I'm birding. Our Australian Cattle Dog, Sasha, has been raised as a birding dog, so she is not nearly as disruptive in the field as a gallivanting retriever might be. Instead of saying "heel," we simply "pish," and Sasha comes to wait at my feet until we are done birding! It goes without saying that a beach full of migrant shorebirds would not qualify as a potential patch for me. She has, however, accumulated a life list of almost 110 species at this time, and no birds were harmed or intentionally harassed in the process.

3. It needs to be small enough that I can thoroughly comb it in an hour or two, again, so I can get to work on time.

4. It needs at least a little habitat diversity to provide some variety of birdlife.

5. It should have some sort of geographic or habitat feature that could help to produce a vagrant, to spice things up and help build the list of course.

I had a few very successful patches that I combed when I first moved to Portland, Maine. One that I continue to add to now and again is a local city park, actually an abandoned landfill, known to birders as Dragon Field (because it is next to Dragon Cement; not, to my knowledge anyway, to the presence of any dragons). This capped landfill is one of the only tall-grass and weedy areas around, and because it is surrounded by development, it is an absolute magnet for sparrows. What I did not know, however, until I began to work on my patch list, was how productive the back edge was for warblers. A small marsh at the bottom of the sandpit of the cement company is the only open water in the park, and breeding birds are very limited, so my patch list was slow to grow.

Meanwhile, I am fascinated by the subtle distinctions in habitat preferences among the migrant sparrows here. Lincoln's Sparrows tend to prefer the slightly brushier and moist north edge, Savannah Sparrows prefer the shortest, driest grass at the top of the hill, and Swamp Sparrows prefer the wetter spots, especially the margins of the cattail marsh at the western edge (see chapter 2).

A slow walk around Dragon Field in October can yield not only a diversity of sparrows but also a prime opportunity to study subtle habitat variations. Of course, this knowledge can be directly applied to other birding locations, both new and old, as we become more familiar with a species' preferences.

Here's an example. I had a couple of clients out for the day around Portland one October. Their primary interest was studying sparrows, in addition to ticking a few target birds, so I spent a lot of time in various weedy areas around the city. As the morning progressed, the idea of a mini-sparrow-big-day surfaced, and we set out to see as many species of sparrows during the day as we could.

One hole in our list was Lincoln's Sparrow, an uncommon migrant in these parts. After birding Dragon Field without finding a Lincoln's, I decided to make one more concerted effort by focusing our attention on that damp, shrubbier north edge. And sure enough, a few moments later, a spiffy Lincoln's Sparrow with his sharp, fine streaks (as if they were a pen-and-ink drawing), buffy chest, and subtle gray-toned face popped into view. Another satisfied customer!

Meanwhile, my list for Dragon Field was stuck at 149 for a while, and so I made a concerted effort to get one more bird. I looked at the checklist, identified some holes in my list, and formulated my plan. Hmm, no Cape May Warbler? Better pay extra attention to the tallest pines on the rocky hillside behind the dump late in spring migration. Really, no Mourning Warbler yet? I had better check that wet thicket a little more often in late May and early June. And still no Clay-colored Sparrow? Time to double the effort at the margins of the woods during the peak of Chipping Sparrow migration.

By using my knowledge of birds' habitats and preferences and my familiarity with the patch, I was not only able to reach 150, but soon eclipse it. A Cape May Warbler singing from within a tall White Pine on the hillside one May? Check. A Mourning Warbler calling in the wet thicket during the first week of June? Check. And a Clay-colored Sparrow? Well, I saw two together within a small flock of Chipping Sparrows one early October morning.

When we moved to Pownal, a half-hour up the road, I needed some new patches close to home, so I opened up a map, made a few notes, and began to explore. Once my parameters were met, I began my investigation of a few new places to truly get to know them.

While I have only seen one Greater Yellowlegs at Hedgehog Mountain, I see 12 species of warblers breeding here every year. This knowledge became quite useful one day when I had clients out for a day of birding seeking an array of life birds, including a number of breeding warblers.

Although this seemed a fairly typical assignment, one of the clients showed up with a broken leg! While she said she was happy to wait at the car, I did my best to get all of their target birds within a short hobble of the car so that they both could build their lists. Using my knowledge of the breeding territories of various species in my patches (knowledge gained only by visiting them very often), I found the vast majority of their lifers within 100 feet of the car! For example, I found the Canada Warbler along the main entrance trail at Florida Lake Park and the Black-throated Blue Warbler on the first hillside along the main trail at the Hog. And with regard to Black-throated Blue Warblers, I had never noticed this species' affinity for dense stands of young Striped Maple until I started wondering why "B.T.-Blues" were so patchily distributed in my local patches.

"So, that's all well and fine," you might say, "but I have enough lists. What can patch listing do for me?" Well, first of all, it is a chance to apply your newfound knowledge of using geography and habitat to improve your birding to help choose a potentially productive patch. Next, whatever patch I am currently working on at a given time, I make sure to visit at least once a week, all year long, even in the "slow" seasons. You can't add to a patch list if you're not in your patch, and some of my more unusual patch birds have occurred in seasons that are not usually productive at that given patch. If I had not been patch listing, I might not have been at Hedgehog Mountain Park that early June morning when I found a singing Clay-colored Sparrow.

By visiting a place frequently and regularly, we not only build our patch list, but by becoming so familiar with a specific place, there is much that can be learned about seasonal distribution, temporal changes in bird migration, and even population fluctuations.

Here are a few examples:

- Red-eyed Vireos seem to be declining in my patch at Hedgehog Mountain Park. I decided that I better keep an eye on this trend, and so I devised an annual "census" route to be performed in early June to see if I could quantify my observations.
- Portland's Eastern Promenade used to host a greater density of overwintering Song Sparrows than anywhere else that I have found in Maine. (When was the last time you paid attention to Song Sparrows?) Then the city changed its management practices, reduced the amount of woody cover, and mowed the fields more frequently. Now, only a few Song Sparrows overwinter.
- My Winslow Park Patch List (Freeport) has made me rather familiar with the comings and goings of Barrow's Goldeneyes, which are listed as Threatened by the State of Maine. The southernmost wintering flock of this bird in the eastern United States occurs here in South Freeport most winters. There have been noticeably fewer of this charismatic bird here in the past few years, perhaps part of a long-term decline or perhaps as a result of reduced ice in winter around Casco Bay, or even in the Gulf of St. Lawrence. Regardless, my regular observations and hypothesis have been tapped by the state's biologists for data on the species.
- If not for my patch listing, I might not have been out in the woods of Hedgehog Mountain Park one late spring morning (even though little migration had been detected by radar overnight), and I would have missed only my second-ever observation of a Fisher—one of the coolest, yet most incredibly secretive—mammals around!

How about the weather? How do specific conditions change the birdlife at your patch? Which winds are most productive in yielding a good wave of migrants? In the longer-term, have you noticed any effects on bird populations due to climate change? Here in Southern Maine, there are now Carolina Wrens and Red-bellied Woodpeckers on occasion in my patches—birds that were quite rare less than a decade ago when I first began my Portland patch lists. You can then take what you have learned about links with climate and apply it to your birding at all other locations, in your area, and beyond.

When I worked at Whitefish Point in Michigan's Upper Peninsula, I worked hard on my Point LaBarbe List. Point LaBarbe is a small, south facing point that juts out into the north end of Lake Michigan immediately west of the massive Mackinac Bridge. For most Michigan birders, Point LaBarbe was nothing more than another place to speed by as they raced up to Whitefish to twitch the latest awesome "Point bird." Although I too enjoyed keeping a Whitefish Point List, I joked with friends about my "Anti–Whitefish Point List" that I worked almost as hard at.

Therefore, on days off when weather conditions suggested that Point LaBarbe might be fruitful (boy, I wish I had known about birding by radar back then!), I headed south, probably passing birders racing north. When I departed Michigan a couple of years later, my Point LaBarbe list included such treats as Yellow Rail (in migration!), Marbled Godwit, Golden-winged Warbler (four in one morning!), and a total of 151 species in less than two years.

In a way, this chapter is the antithesis to chapter 7, "Vagrants." With patches, the focus is less on the rare and more on the common, such as a flyover Greater Yellowlegs. But is it really? I mean, after all, if we choose a patch correctly, exploit it to its fullest potential, and bird it regularly, chances are we'll turn up a vagrant or two over time.

And this could be valuable for more than just building our lists. By checking more places more of the time, we could add to our collective knowledge of rarity distribution and perhaps answer the question of whether or not vagrants are actually more common along the coast or whether they are just found there because there are more people looking.

Graphing and charting tools in eBird (which were introduced to in chapter 6) can yield a wealth of information about birds in our patches, and our data can add to our collective knowledge by providing consistent, steady data from a variety of locations around the continent.

For birders, I believe that "patch working" (birding your patch regularly) can yield a number of educational rewards, as I have touched upon in the various anecdotes and examples earlier. First, we combine many of the disciplines explored in previous chapters to find and identify a patch, and then we work to exploit it to its fullest potential. By developing a set of patch lists and birding them frequently, we can enhance our knowledge of local birds, their habitats, their occurrences, and so on. Second, we can challenge ourselves and our friends to build our lists without a large expenditure of carbon or money! Frankly, it doesn't get much cheaper than patch listing, especially if your patch is within walking or biking distance! In fact, I believe that as our culture slowly begins to shift away from a dependency on fossil fuels, staying near home is going to be more of an interest and more of a need.

Who knows, you might just put your local park "on the map!" So take what you've learned in this book and take you new skills for a test drive in your local patch. You might find a vagrant, you might spot a rare mammal, or perhaps, you might even learn something new.

References and Additional Reading

Able, K. 1999. *Gatherings of Angels: Migrating Birds and Their Ecology*. Cornell University Press: Ithaca, NY.

Alderfer, J., and J. L. Dunn. 2007. *Birding Essentials*. National Geographic Society: Washington, D.C.

Alfrey, P. 2011. "The Pioneers." Parts 1 and 2. Birdwatch: The Home of Birding. www.birdwatch.co.uk/categories/articleitem.asp?item=727

Barth, R., and N. Ratzlaff. 2004. *Field Guide to Wildflowers: Fontenelle Forest and Neal Woods Nature Centers*. Fontenelle Nature Association: Bellevue, NE.

Bennett, D. 2010. Easy = True: How 'Cognitive Fluency' Shapes What We Believe, How We Invest, and Who Will Become a Supermodel. Ideas. *Boston Sunday Globe*, January 31, C1–C2.

Blomdahl, A., B. Breife, and N. Holmstrom. 2003. *Flight Identification of European Seabirds*. Christopher Helm: London.

Brinkley, E. S. 2006a. The Changing Seasons: Far Fetched. *North American Birds* 60: 332–339.

———. 2006b. The Changing Seasons: The Winter That Wasn't. *North American Birds* 60: 184–193.

———. 2009. The Changing Seasons: Oscillations. *North American Birds* 63: 370–382.

Buler, J. J., and R. H Diehl. 2009. Quantifying Bird Density during Migratory Stopover Using Weather Surveillance Radar. *IEEE Transactions on Geoscience and Remote Sensing* 47: 2741–2751.

Clemants, S., and C. Gracie. 2006. *Wildflowers in the Field and Forest: A Field Guide to the Northeastern United States*. Oxford University Press: New York.

Cooper, A. W. 2008. Life Zones. *Access Science*. http://accessscience.com/content/Life-zones/381100.

Crossley, R. 2011. *The Crossley ID Guide*. Princeton University Press: Princeton, NJ.

Davis, R., T. Day, V. W. Fazio, N. L. Martin, R. O. Paxton, B. Pranty, R. R. Veit, and R. Wiltraut. 2007. Special Interregional Report: Tropical Storm Ernesto. *North American Birds* 61: 10–17.

Dinsmore, S. J., and A. Farnsworth. 2006. The Changing Seasons: Weatherbirds. *North American Birds* 60: 14–26.

Dunn, J., and J. Alderfer, eds. 2006. *Field Guide to the Birds of North America.* 5th ed. National Geographic Society: Washington, D.C.

Dunne, P., D Sibley, and C. Sutton. 1988. *Hawks in Flight.* Houghton Mifflin: Boston.

———. 2006. *Pete Dunne's Essential Field Guide Companion: A Comprehensive Resource for Identifying North American Birds.* Houghton Mifflin Harcourt: Boston.

Epple, A. O. 1995. *A Field Guide to the Plants of Arizona.* Globe Pequot Press: Guilford: CT.

Evans, W. R., and M. O'Brien. 2002. *Flight Calls of Migratory Birds.* Old Bird Inc.: New York. CD-ROM.

Evans, W. R., and K. V. Rosenberg. 2000. Acoustic Monitoring of Night-migrating Birds: A Progress Report. In *Strategies for Bird Conservation: The Partners in Flight Planning Process,* ed. R. Bonney, D. N. Pashley, R. J. Cooper, and L. Niles. USDA, Forest Service, Rocky Mountain Research Station: Ogden, UT. Available at http://birds.cornell.edu/pifcapemay.

Farnsworth, A. 2009. Flight Calls and Their Value for Future Ornithological and Conservation Research. *Auk* 122(3): 733–746.

Farnsworth, A., and S. A. Gauthreaux, Jr., and D. van Blaricom. 2004. A Comparison of Nocturnal Call Counts of Migrating Birds and Reflectivity Measurements on Doppler Radar. *Journal of Avian Biology* 35: 365–369.

Farnsworth, A., and R.W. Russell. 2007. Monitoring Flight Calls of Migrating Birds from an Oil Platform in the Northern Gulf of Mexico. *Journal of Field Ornithology* 78(3): 279–289.

Gagnon, F., M. Belisle, J. Ibarzabal, P. Vaillancourt, and J. L. Savard. 2010. A Comparison between Nocturnal and Aural Counts of Passerines and Radar Reflectivity from a Canadian Weather Surveillance Radar. *Auk* 127: 119–128.

Gagnon, F., J. Ibarzabal, J. P. Savard, P. Vaillancourt, M. Belisle, and C. M. Francis. 2011. Weather Effects on Autumnal Migration of Passerines on Opposite Shores of the St. Lawrence Estuary. *Auk* 128(1): 99–112.

Gauthreaux, S. A., Jr., and C. G. Belser. 2003. Radar Ornithology and Biological Conservation. *Auk* 120(2): 266–277.

Gauthreaux, S. A., Jr., C. G. Belser, and D. van Blaricom. 2003. Using a Network of WSR-88D Weather Surveillance Radars to Define Patterns of Bird Migration at Large Spatial Scales. In *Avian Migration*, ed. P. Berthold, E. Gwinner, and E. Sonnenschein, 335–346. Springer-Verlag: Berlin.

Gauthreaux, S.A., Jr., and J. W. Livingston. 2006. Monitoring Bird Migration with Fixed-beam Radar and a Thermal-imaging Camera. *Journal of Field Ornithology* 77: 319–328.

Gauthreaux, S. A., Jr., J. W. Livingston, and C. G. Belser. 2008. Detection and Discrimination of Fauna in the Aerosphere Using Doppler Weather Surveillance Radar. *Journal of Integrated Comparative Biology* 48(1): 12–23.

Green, P. 1998. Possible Anywhere: Fieldfare. *Birding* 30(3): 213-219.

Haines, A., and T. F. Vining. 1998. *Flora of Maine*. V. F. Thomas: Bar Harbor, ME.

Harrington, H. D. 1964. *Manual of the Plants of Colorado*. Sage Books: Denver, CO.

Hickman, J. C., ed. 1993. *The Jepson Manual: Higher Plants of California*. University of California Press: Berkeley.

Horn, D., D. Dahl, T. E. Hemmerly, T. Cathcart, and Tennessee Native Plant Society. 2005. *Wildflowers of the Tennessee, Ohio Valley, and the Southern Appalachians*. Lone Pine Publishers: Auburn, WA.

Howell, S.N.G. 2003. *Hummingbirds of North America*. Princeton University Press: Princeton.

———. 2010. *Molt in North American Birds*. Houghton Mifflin Harcourt: Boston.

Howell, S.N.G., and J. Dunn. 2007. A *Reference Guide to Gulls of the Americas*. Houghton Mifflin: Boston.

Howell, S.N.G., and S. Webb. 1995. *A Guide to the Birds of Mexico and Northern Central America*. Oxford University Press: Oxford.

Iliff, M. J., and D. Lovitch. 2007. The Changing Seasons: Food for Thought. *North American Birds* 61: 208-224.

Irons, D. S., and D. Fix. 2008. The Changing Seasons: The Times They Are A'Changin'. *North American Birds* 62: 14–30.

Kaufman, K. 1990. *Advanced Birding*. Houghton Mifflin: Boston.

———. 2011. *Field Guide to Advanced Birding*. Houghton Mifflin: Boston.

Kroodsma, D.. 2005. *The Singing Life of Birds*. Houghton Mifflin: Boston.

Lehman, P. E., and E. S. Brinkley. 2009. The Changing Seasons: Cornucopia. *North American Birds* 63: 16–32.

Liechti, F., B. Bruderer, and H. Paproth. 1995. Quantification of Nocturnal Bird Migration by Moonwatching: Comparisons with Radar and Infrared Observations. *Journal of Field Ornithology* 66(4): 457–468.

Ligouri, J. 2005. *Hawks from Every Angle*. Princeton University Press: Princeton, NJ.

———. 2011. *Hawks at a Distance*. Princeton University Press: Princeton, NJ.

Lowery, G. H., and R. J. Newman, 1966. A Continentwide View of Bird Migration on Four Nights in October. *Auk* 86(4): 547–586.

MacKinnon, A., J. Pojar, and P. B. Alabeck. 2004. *Plants of the Pacific Northwest Coast*. Lone Pine Publishing: Auburn, WA.

McLaren, I. A. 1981. The Incidence of Vagrant Landbirds in Nova Scotia Islands. *Auk* 98: 243–257.

McLaren, I. A., and J. D. McLaren. 2009. An Analysis of Unusual Flights of Neotropical Migrants to Northeastern North America in April 2009. *North American Birds* 63: 364–368.

Merriam, C. H. 1894. Laws of Temperature Control of the Geographic Distribution of Terrestrial Animals and Plants. *National Geographic Magazine* 6: 229–238.

Nelson, G. 2005. *East Gulf Coast Plain Wildflowers*. Globe Pequot Press: Guilford, CT.

———. 2006. *Atlantic Coastal Plain Wildflowers*. Morris Book Publishing: Guilford, CT.

Newton, I. 2008a. *Bird Migration*. Vol. 13 of *Handbook of the Birds of the World*, ed. J. Hoyo, A. Elliot, and D. Christie. Lynx Edicions: Barcelona.

———. 2008b. *The Migration Ecology of Birds*. Academic Press: Maryland Heights, MO.

O'Brien, M., R. Crossley, and K. Karlson. 2006. *The Shorebird Guide*. Houghton Mifflin: Boston.

Parish, R., R. Coupe, D. Lloyd, and J. Antos. 1996. *Plants of Southern Interior British Columbia*. Lone Pine Publishing: Auburn, WA.

Patten, M. A., and C. Marantz. 1996. Implications of Vagrant Southeastern Vireos and Warblers in California. *Auk* 113(4): 911–923.

Paulson, D. 1993. *Shorebirds of the Pacific Northwest*. University of Washington Press: Seattle.

Pyle, P. 1997. *Identification Guide to North American Birds: Part 1*. Slate Creek Press: Bolinas, CA.

———. 2008. *Identification Guide to North American Birds: Part 2*. Slate Creek Press: Bolinas, CA

Quammen, D. 1996. *The Song of the Dodo*. Scribner: New York.

Ratzlaff, N. S., and R. E. Barth. 2007. *Field Guide to Trees, Shrubs, Woody Vines, Grasses, Sedges, and Rushes: Fontenelle Forest and Neal Woods Nature Centers.* Fontenelle Nature Association: Bellevue, NE.

Rideout, C., and B. Holiman. 2010. Smith's Longspur—Have You Seen One Lately? *Bird Conservation, Fall 2010.*

Schmoker, B., and T. Leukering. 2007. The Changing Seasons: Wheatears, Flycatchers, and Plovers. *North American Birds* 61: 18–27.

Sibley, D. A. 2000. *The Sibley Guide to Birds.* Alfred A. Knopf: New York.

———. 2002. *Sibley's Birding Basics.* Alfred A. Knopf: New York.

———. 2009. *The Sibley Guide to Trees.* Alfred A, Knopf: New York.

Strausbaugh, P. D., and E. L. Cove. 1978. *Flora of West Virginia.* Seneca Books: Grantsville, WV.

Stutchbury, B. 2007. *Silence of the Songbirds.* Walker and Company: New York.

Symonds, G.W.D. 1958. *The Tree Identification Book.* Harper Collins: New York.

———. 1963. *The Shrub Identification Book.* Harper Collins: New York.

Thobish, T. 2008. Alaska. *North American Birds* 62: 129–135.

Turner, M., and P. Gustafson. 2006. *Wildflowers of the Pacific Northwest.* Timber Press: Portland, OR.

Weidensaul, S. 1999. *Living on the Wind: Across the Hemisphere with Migratory Birds.* North Point Press: New York.

———. 2005. *Return to Wild America.* North Point Press: New York.

Wells, J. V. 2007. *Birder's Conservation Handbook.* Princeton University Press: Princeton, NJ.

Yerger, J., and J. Mohlmann. 2008. First Record of Brown Hawk-Owl on St. Paul Island, Alaska. *North American Birds* 62: 4–8.

Index

part four:
Engage the World

part five:
Be at Peace

introduction
Using Your Mind to Change Your Brain

This is a book of practices—simple things you can do routinely, mainly inside your mind, that will support and increase your sense of security and worth, resilience, effectiveness, well-being, insight, and inner peace. For example, they include *taking in the good, protecting your brain, feeling safer, relaxing anxiety about imperfection, not knowing, enjoying your hands, taking refuge,* and *filling the hole in your heart.*

At first glance, you may be tempted to underestimate the power of these seemingly simple practices. But they will gradually change your brain through what's called *experience-dependent neuroplasticity.*

Moment to moment, whatever you're aware of—sounds, sensations, thoughts, or your most heartfelt longings—is based on underlying neural activities; the same goes for unconscious mental processes such as the consolidation of memory or the control of breathing. Exactly *how* the physical brain produces nonphysical consciousness remains a great mystery. But apart from the possible influence of transcendental factors—call them God, Spirit, the Ground, or by no name at all—there is a one-to-one mapping between mental and neural activities.

It's a two-way street: as your brain changes, your mind changes; and as your mind changes, your brain changes. This means—remarkably—that what you pay attention to, what you think and feel and want, and how you work with your reactions to things all sculpt your brain in multiple ways:

- Busy regions get more blood flow, since they need more oxygen and glucose.

- The genes inside neurons get more or less active; for example, people who routinely relax have improved expression of genes that calm down stress reactions, making them more resilient (Dusek et al. 2008).

- Neural connections that are relatively inactive wither away; it's a kind of neural Darwinism, the survival of the busiest: use it or lose it.

- "Neurons that fire together, wire together." This saying from the work of the psychologist Donald Hebb means that active synapses—the connections between neurons—get more sensitive, plus new synapses grow, producing thicker neural layers. For example, cab drivers who have to memorize the spaghetti snarl of streets in London have a thicker *hippocampus*—a part of the brain that helps make visual-spatial memories—at the end of their training (Maguire et al. 2000). Similarly, people who routinely practice mindfulness meditation develop thicker layers of neurons in the *insula*—a region that activates when you tune in to your body and your feelings—and in parts of the *prefrontal cortex* (in the front of your brain) that control attention (Lazar et al. 2005).

The details are complex, but the key point is simple: *how you use your mind changes your brain*—for better or worse.

There's a traditional saying that the mind takes the shape it rests upon; the modern update is that the *brain* takes the shape the mind rests upon. For instance, you regularly rest your mind upon worries, self-criticism, and anger, then your brain will gradually take the shape—will develop neural structures and dynamics—of anxiety, low sense of worth, and prickly reactivity to others. On the other hand, if you regularly rest your mind upon, for example, *noticing you're all right right now, seeing the good in yourself,* and *letting go*—three of the practices in this book—then your brain will gradually take the shape of calm strength, self-confidence, and inner peace.

You can't stop your brain from changing. The only question is: Are you getting the changes you want?

All It Takes Is Practice

That's where practice comes in, which simply means taking regular action—in thought, word, or deed—to increase positive qualities in yourself and decrease negative ones. For example, studies have shown that *being mindful* (chapter 22) increases activation of the left prefrontal cortex and thus lifts mood (since that part of the brain puts the brakes on negative emotions) (Davidson 2004), and it decreases activation of the *amygdala*, the alarm bell of the brain (Stein, Ives-Deliperi, and Thomas 2008). Similarly, *having compassion for yourself* (chapter 3) builds up resilience and lowers negative rumination (Leary et al. 2007; Neff 2009).

Basically, practice pulls weeds and plants flowers in the garden of your mind—and thus in your brain. That improves your garden, plus it makes you a better gardener: you get more skillful at directing your attention, thinking clearly, managing your feelings, motivating yourself, getting more resilient, and riding life's roller-coaster.

Practice also has built-in benefits that go beyond the value of the particular practice you're doing. For example, doing *any* practice is an act of kindness toward yourself; you're treating yourself like you matter—which is especially important and healing if you have felt as a child or an adult that others haven't respected or cared about you. Further, you're being active rather than passive—which increases optimism, resilience, and happiness, and reduces the risk of depression. At a time when people often feel pushed by external forces—such as financial pressures, the actions of others, or world events—and by their reactions to these, it's great to have at least some part of your life where you feel like a hammer instead of a nail.

Ultimately, practice is a process of personal transformation, gradually pulling the roots of greed, hatred, heartache, and delusion—broadly defined—and replacing them with contentment, peace, love, and clarity. Sometimes this feels like you're making changes inside yourself, and at other times it feels like you're simply uncovering wonderful, beautiful things that were always already there, like your natural wakefulness, goodness, and loving heart.

Either way, you're in the process of developing what one could call a "buddha brain," a brain that understands, profoundly, the causes of suffering and its end—for the root meaning of the word "buddha," is "to know, to awake." (I'm not capitalizing that word here in order to distinguish my general focus from the specific individual, the great teacher called the Buddha.) In this broad sense, anyone engaged in psychological growth or spiritual practice—whether Christian, Jewish, Muslim, Hindu, agnostic, atheist, or none of these—is developing a buddha brain and its related qualities of compassion, virtue, mindfulness, and wisdom.

The Law of Little Things

Now, if a practice is a hassle, most people (including me) are not going to do it. So the practices in this book involve either brief actions a few times a day—like *finding beauty* (chapter 17)—or simply a general attitude or perspective, such as *relaxing anxiety about imperfection* (chapter 46) or *not taking life so personally* (chapter 48).

Each moment of practice is usually small in itself, but those moments really add up. It's the law of little things: because of slowly accumulating changes in neural structure due to mental activity, lots of little things can wear down your well-being—and lots of little things can get you to a better place. It's like exercise: any single time you run, do Pilates, or lift weights won't make much difference—but over time, you'll build up your muscles. In the same way, small efforts made routinely will gradually build up the "muscle" of your brain. You really can have confidence, grounded in the latest brain science, that practice will pay off.

How to Use This Book

But you have to stick with it—so it really helps to focus on one main practice at a time. Life these days is so busy and complicated that it's great to have *just one thing* to keep in mind.

Of course, it's got to be the right "one thing." For forty years, I've been doing practices—first as a young person looking for happiness, then as a husband and father dealing with work and family life, and now as a neuropsychologist and meditation teacher—and teaching them to others. For this book, I've picked the best practices I know to build up the neural substrates—the foundations—of resilience, resourcefulness, well-being, and inner peace. I didn't invent a single one: they're the fundamentals that people make New Year's resolutions about but rarely do—and it's the *doing* that makes all the difference in the world.

6

You can do these practices in several ways. First, you could find one particular practice that by itself makes a big difference for you. Second, you can focus on the practices within a section of the book that addresses specific needs, such as part 1 on being good to yourself if you're self-critical, or part 5 on being at peace if you're anxious or irritable. Third, you could move around from practice to practice depending on what strikes your fancy or feels like it would help you the most right now. Fourth, you could take a week for each one of the fifty-two practices here, giving yourself a transformational "year of practice."

Whatever your approach is, I suggest you keep it simple and focus on one practice at a time—whether that time is an event or situation (e.g., a ticklish conversation with your mate, a crunch project at work, a meditation), a day, or longer. And in the back of your mind, other practices and their benefits can certainly be operating; for example, *not taking things personally* (chapter 48) could be in the foreground of awareness while *taking refuge* (chapter 28) is in the background.

Know what your practice is each day; the more you keep it in awareness, the more it will benefit you. Besides simply thinking about this practice from time to time, you could rest your mind even more upon it by putting up little reminders about it—such as a key word on a sticky note—or journaling about it or telling a friend what you're doing. You could also weave your practice into psychological or spiritual activities, such as psychotherapy, yoga, meditation, or prayer.

Working with just fifty-two practices, I've had to make some choices:

- The practices are super-succinct; more could be said about each one of them. The title of each chapter is the practice. Chapters begin by answering *why* to do that practice, and then tell you *how* to do it. Chapter lengths vary depending on their subject.

- With the exception of the very last practice, I've emphasized things done within yourself—such as *being grateful* (chapter 18)—rather than between yourself and others. (If you're interested in interpersonally focused practices in the *Just One Thing* (*JOT*) style, you might like my free e-newsletter by that name at www.RickHanson.net.) Meanwhile, you could apply the practices in this book to one or more relationships, or engage in them with a buddy—such as a friend or a mate—or as a group (e.g., family, team at work, reading group).

- Most practices here involve taking action inside your mind—and of course it's also important to take action in your body and in the world around you.

- There are three fundamental phases to psychological and spiritual growth: *being with* difficult material (e.g., old wounds, anger); *releasing* it; and *replacing* it with something more beneficial. In a nutshell, you let be, let go, and let in. You'll find practices for each of these phases, though I've concentrated on the third one because it's often the most direct and rapid way to reduce stress and unhappiness and develop positive qualities in yourself.

◀ While I experience and believe that something transcendental is involved with both mind and matter, I've stayed here within the frame of Western science.

As you engage these practices, have some fun with them. Don't take them (or yourself) too seriously. Feel free to be creative and adapt them to your own needs. For example, the *How* sections usually contain multiple suggestions, and you don't have to do all of them; just find the ones that do the most for you.

Throughout, take good care of yourself. Sometimes a practice will be too hard to sustain, or it will stir up painful issues. Then just drop it—for a while, or indefinitely. Draw on resources for practices; for example, deepening your sense of being cared about by others will help you *forgive yourself* (chapter 7). Remember that practice does not replace appropriate professional mental or physical health care.

Keep Going

People recognize that they've got to make an effort over time to become more skillful at driving a truck, running a department, or playing tennis. Yet it's common to think that becoming more skillful with one's own mind should somehow come naturally, without effort or learning.

But because the mind is grounded in biology, in the physical realm, the same laws apply: the more you put in, the more you get back. To reap the rewards of practice, you need to *do* it, and keep doing it.

Again, it's like exercise: if you do it only occasionally, you'll get only a little improvement; on the other hand, if you do it routinely, you'll get a large improvement. I've heard people talk like making efforts inside the mind is some kind of lightweight activity, but in fact it's always a matter of resolve and diligence—and sometimes it's very challenging and uncomfortable. Practice is not for wusses. You will *earn* its benefits.

So honor yourself for your practice. While it's down-to-earth and ordinary, it's also aspirational and profound. When you practice, you are nourishing, joining with, and uncovering the very best things about you. You are taking the high road, not the low one. You're drawing on sincerity, determination, and grit. You're taming and purifying the unruly mind—and the jungle that is the brain, with its reptilian, mammalian, and primate layers. You're offering beautiful gifts to your future self—the one being in the world you have the most power over and therefore the greatest duty to. And the fruits of your practice will ripple outward in widening circles, benefiting others, both known and unknown. Never doubt the power of practice, or how far your own chosen path of practice can take you.

I wish you the best on your path!

part one:

Be Good
to Yourself

1

Be for Yourself

To take any steps toward your own well-being—such as the practices in this book—you have got to be on your own side. Not against others, but *for* yourself.

For many people, that's harder than it sounds. Maybe you were raised to think you didn't count as much as other people. Maybe when you've tried to stick up for yourself, you've been blocked or knocked down. Maybe deep down you feel you don't deserve to be happy.

Think about what it's like to be a good friend to someone. Then ask: Am I that kind of friend to *myself*?

If not, you could be too hard on yourself, too quick to feel you're falling short, too dismissive of what you get done each day. Or too half-hearted about protecting yourself from mistreatment or telling others what you really need. Or too resigned to you own pain, or too slow about doing those things—both inside your head and outside it, in the wider world—to make your life better.

Plus, how can you truly help others if you don't start by helping yourself?

The foundation of all practice is to wish yourself well, to let your own sorrows and needs and dreams *matter* to you. Then, whatever you do for yourself will have real oomph behind it!

How

Several times a day, ask yourself: Am I on my own side here? Am I looking out for my own best interests? (Which will often include the best interests of others.)

Good times to do this:

- If you feel bad (e.g., sad, hurt, worried, disappointed, mistreated, frustrated, stressed, or irritated)

- If someone is pushing you to do something

- If you know you should do something for your own benefit but you're not doing it (like asserting yourself with someone, looking for a new job, or quitting smoking)

At these times, or in general:

- Bring to mind the feeling of being with someone who cares about you. This will help you feel like you matter and have worth, which is the basis of being for yourself.

◄ Recall what it feels like to be for someone. Perhaps a child, pet, or dear friend. Notice different aspects of this experience, such as loyalty, concern, warmth, determination, or advocacy. Let the sense of being on someone's side be big in your awareness. Let your body shift into a posture of support and advocacy: perhaps sitting or standing a little more erect, chest coming up a bit, eyes more intent; you're strengthening the experience of being for someone by drawing on embodied cognition, on the sensorimotor systems in your brain that underlie and shape your thoughts and feelings.

◄ Recall a time when you had to be strong, energetic, fierce, or intense on your own behalf. It could be as simple as the experience of the last part of an exercise routine, when you had to use every last ounce of willpower to finish it. Or it could be a time you had to escape from a serious danger, or stand up for yourself against an intimidating person, or doggedly grind out a big project in school or work. As in the bullet point just above, open to this experience and shift into embodying it so it is as real as possible for you, and so that you are stimulating and thus strengthening its underlying neural networks.

◄ See yourself as a young child—sweet, vulnerable, precious—and extend this same attitude of loyalty, strength, and caring toward that little boy

14

or girl. (You could get a picture of yourself as a kid and carry it in your wallet or purse, and look at it from time to time.)

⋈ Imagine having this same sense and stance of loyalty, strength, and caring for yourself today.

⋈ Be mindful of what it feels like in your body to be on your own side. Open to and encourage that feeling as much as possible. Notice any resistance to it and try to let it go.

⋈ Ask yourself: *Being on my own side, what's the best thing to do here?*

⋈ Then, as best you can, do it.

Remember:

⋈ Being for yourself simply means that you care about yourself. You wish to feel happy instead of worried, sad, guilty, or angry. You want people to treat you well instead of badly. You want to help your future self—the person you'll be next week, next year, next decade—to have as good a life as possible.

⋈ Your experience *matters*, both for the moment-to-moment experience of living and for the lasting traces that your thoughts and feelings leave behind in the structure of your brain.

⋈ It is moral to treat people with decency, respect, compassion, and kindness. Well, "people" includes you! You have as many rights, and your opinions and needs and dreams have as much standing, as those of anyone else in the world.

❧ When you take good care of yourself, then you have more to offer others, from the people close to you to the whole wide world.

2

Take in the Good

Scientists believe that your brain has a built-in *negativity bias* (Baumeister et al. 2001; Rozin and Royzman 2001). This is because, as our ancestors dodged sticks and chased carrots over millions of years of evolution, the sticks had the greater urgency and impact on survival.

This negativity bias shows up in lots of ways. For example, studies have found that:

- The brain generally reacts more to a negative stimulus than to an equally intense positive one (Baumeister et al. 2000).

- Animals—including us—typically learn faster from pain than from pleasure (Rozin and Royzman 2001); once burned, twice shy.

- Painful experiences are usually more memorable than pleasurable ones (Baumeister et al. 2001).

- Most people will work harder to avoid losing something they have than they'll work to gain the same thing (Rozin and Royzman 2001).

- Lasting, good relationships typically need at least a 5:1 ratio of positive to negative interactions (Gottman 1995).

In your own mind, what do you usually think about at the end of the day? The fifty things that went right, or the one that went wrong? Such as the driver who cut you off in traffic, or the one thing on your To Do list that didn't get done . . .

In effect, the brain is like Velcro for negative experiences, but Teflon for positive ones. That shades *implicit memory*—your underlying feelings, expectations, beliefs, inclinations, and mood—in an increasingly negative direction.

Which is not fair, since most of the facts in your life are probably positive or at least neutral. Besides the injustice of it, the growing pile of negative experiences in implicit memory naturally makes a person more anxious, irritable, and blue—plus it gets harder to be patient and giving toward others.

But you don't have to accept this bias! By tilting *toward* the good—toward that which brings more happiness and benefit to oneself and others—you merely level the playing field. Then, instead of positive experiences washing through you like water through a sieve, they'll collect in implicit memory deep down in your brain.

You'll still see the tough parts of life. In fact, you'll become more able to change them or bear them if you take in the good, since that will help put challenges in perspective, lift your energy and spirits, highlight useful resources, and fill up your own cup so you have more to offer to others.

And by the way, in addition to being good for adults, taking in the good is great for children, too, helping them to become more resilient, confident, and happy.

How

1. Look for good facts, and turn them into good experiences.

Good facts include positive events—like finishing a batch of e-mails or getting a compliment—and positive aspects of the world and yourself. Most good facts are ordinary and relatively minor—but they are still real. You are not looking at the world through rose-colored glasses, but simply recognizing something that is actual and true.

Then, when you're aware of a good fact—either something that currently exists or has happened in the past—let yourself *feel* good about it. So often in life a good thing happens—flowers are blooming, someone is nice, a goal's been attained—and you know it, but you don't feel it. This time, let the good fact affect you.

Try to do this step and the two that follow at least a half dozen times a day. When you do this, it usually takes only half a minute or so—there is always time to take in the good! You can do it on the fly in daily life, or at special times of reflection, like just before falling asleep (when the brain is especially receptive to new learning).

Be aware of any reluctance toward having positive experiences. Such as thinking that you don't deserve to, or that it's selfish, vain, or shameful to feel pleasure. Or that if you feel good, you will lower your guard and let bad things happen.

Then turn your attention back to the good facts. Keep opening up to them, breathing and relaxing, letting them move your needle. It's like sitting down to a meal: don't just look at it—taste it!

2. Really enjoy the experience.

Most of the time, a good experience is pretty mild, and that's fine. Simply stay with it for ten, twenty, even thirty seconds in a row—instead of getting distracted by something else.

Soften and open around the experience; let it fill your mind; give over to it in your body. (From a meditative perspective, this is a kind of concentration practice—for a dozen seconds or more—in which you become absorbed in a positive experience.) The longer that something is held in awareness and the more emotionally stimulating it is, the more neurons that fire and thus wire together, and the stronger the trace in implicit memory.

In this practice, you are not clinging to positive experiences, since that would lead to tension and disappointment. Actually, you are doing the opposite: by taking them in, you will feel better fed inside, and less fragile or needy. Your happiness will become more unconditional, increasingly based on an inner fullness rather than on external conditions.

3. Intend and sense that the good experience is sinking in to you.

People do this in different ways. Some feel it in the body as a warm glow spreading through the chest like the warmth of a cup of hot cocoa on a cold wintry day. Others visualize things like a golden syrup sinking down inside; a child might imagine a jewel going into a treasure chest in his or her heart. And some might simply know that while this good experience is held in awareness, its related neural networks are busily firing and wiring together.

Any single time of taking in the good will usually make just a little difference. But over time those little differences will add up, gradually weaving positive experiences into the fabric of your brain and your whole being.

In particular, as you do the practices in this book—or engage any process of psychological healing and growth, or spiritual development—really take in the fruits of your efforts. Help them stick to your mental/neural ribs!

3

Have Compassion
for Yourself

Life is full of wonderful experiences. But it has its hard parts as well, such as physical and mental discomfort, ranging from subtle to agonizing. This is the realm of suffering, broadly defined.

When someone you care about suffers, you naturally have *compassion*: the wish that a being not suffer, usually with a feeling of sympathetic concern. For example, if your child falls and hurts himself, you want him to be out of pain; if you hear that a friend is in the hospital, or out of work, or going through a divorce, you feel for her and hope that everything will be all right. Compassion is in your nature: it's an important part of the neural and psychological systems we evolved to nurture children, bond with mates, and hold together "the village it takes to raise a child" (Goetz, Keltner, and Simon-Thomas 2010).

You can also have compassion for yourself—which is *not* self-pity. You're simply recognizing that "this is tough, this hurts," and bringing the same warmhearted wish for suffering to lessen or end that you would bring to any dear friend grappling with the same pain, upset, or challenge as you.

Studies have shown that self-compassion has many benefits (Leary et al. 2007; Neff 2009), including:

- Reducing self-criticism

- Lowering stress hormones like cortisol

- Increasing self-soothing, self-encouragement, and other aspects of resilience

- Helping to heal any shortages of caring from others in your childhood

That's a pretty good list!

Self-compassion usually takes only a handful of seconds. And then—more centered and heartened—you can get on with doing what you can to make your life better.

How

Maybe your back hurts, or you've had a miserable day at work, or someone has barked at you unfairly. Or, honestly, maybe you just feel bad, even depressed. Whatever it is, some self-compassion could help. Now what?

Self-compassion comes naturally for some people (particularly those with a well-nurtured childhood). But it's not that easy for a lot of us, especially those who are self-critical, driven, stoic, or think it's self-indulgent to be caring toward themselves.

So here are some steps for calling up self-compassion, which you could blend together as self-compassion becomes easier for you:

- Take a moment to acknowledge your difficulties: your challenges and suffering.

- Bring to mind the feeling of being with someone you *know* cares about you. Perhaps a dear friend, a family member, a spirit, God . . . even a pet. Let yourself feel that you matter to this being, who wants you to feel good and do well in life.

- Bring to mind your difficulties, and imagine that this being who cares about you is feeling and expressing compassion for you. Imagine his or her facial expression, gestures, stance, and attitude toward you. Let yourself receive this compassion, taking in its warmth, concern, and goodwill. Open to feeling more understood and nurtured, more peaceful and settled. The experience of *receiving* caring primes circuits in your brain to *give* it.

- Imagine someone you naturally feel compassion for: perhaps a child, or a family member. Imagine how you would feel toward that person if he or she were dealing with whatever is hard for you. Let feelings of compassion fill your mind and body. Extend them toward that person, perhaps visualized as a kind of light radiating from you (maybe from your heart). Notice what it's like to be compassionate.

❧ Now, extend the same sense of compassion toward yourself. Perhaps accompany it with words like these, heard softly in the back of your mind: *May this pain pass . . . may things improve for me . . . may I feel less upset over time.* Have some warmth for yourself, some acknowledgment of your own difficulties and pain, some wish for things to get better. Feel that this compassion is sinking in to you, becoming a part of you, soothing and strengthening you.

4

Relax

It's easy to feel stressed these days. Or worried, frustrated, or irritated about one thing or another, such as finances, work, the health of a family member, or a relationship.

When you get stressed or upset, your body *tenses up* to fight, flee, or freeze. That's Mother Nature's way, and its short-term benefits kept our ancestors alive to pass on their genes.

But today—when people can live seventy or eighty years or more, and when quality of life (not mere survival) is a priority—we pay a high, long-term price for daily tension. It leads to health problems like heart disease, poor digestion, backaches and headaches, and hormonal ups and downs. And to psychological problems, including anxiety, irritability, and depression.

The number one way to reduce tension is through relaxation. Besides its benefits for physical and mental health, relaxation feels great. Just recall how nice it feels to soak in a tub, curl up in bed, or plop on the couch after the dishes are done.

Whether you're stuck in traffic, wading through an overflowing in-box, or having a tough conversation, being able to relax your body at will is a critically important inner skill.

How

Here are some good ways to activate the "rest-and-digest" *parasympathetic nervous system* (PNS) that calms down the fight-or-flight *sympathetic nervous system*:

- PNS fibers, involved with digestion, fill the mouth. So relax your tongue and jaw; perhaps touch your lips. (If I'm having a hard time sleeping, sometimes I'll rest a knuckle against my lips, which has a soothing and calming effect.)

- Open your lips slightly. This can help ease stressful thinking by reducing subvocalizations, the subtle, unconscious movements of the jaw and tongue often associated with mental speech.

- Do several long exhalations, since the PNS handles exhaling. For example inhale for a count of three, and exhale for a count of six.

- For a minute or more, breathe in such a way that your inhalation and exhalation are equally long; count mentally up to five for each inhalation and each exhalation. This creates small but smooth changes in the interval between heartbeats—since the heart speeds up slightly with inhalation and slows down slightly with exhalation—which is associated with relaxation and well-being (Kristal-Boneh et al. 1995).

❧ Relax your diaphragm—the muscle underneath your lungs that helps suck air into them—by putting your hand on your stomach, just below your rib cage, and then trying to breathe in a way that pushes your hand half an inch or so away from your backbone. (This is especially helpful if you're feeling anxious.)

❧ Try these methods in stressful situations, or any time you're feeling worried or frustrated; they really work! Also use them "offline," when things are more settled, such as by setting aside a few minutes each day—perhaps just before bed—to practice relaxation. The resting state of your body-mind will become more peaceful, and you'll become more resilient when things hit the fan. For example, researchers have found that practicing relaxation actually increases the expression of genes that calm down the stress response (Dusek et al. 2008).

5

See the Good in Yourself

There is good in every person—but it's often easier to see in others than in yourself. For example, think about a friend: What do you like about him or her? Including qualities such as sense of humor, fairness, honesty, intelligence, soul, patience, passion, helpfulness, curiosity, determination, talent, spunk, or a good heart.

Seeing these positive characteristics in your friend feels reassuring, comfortable, and hopeful. It's good to recognize what's good in someone.

Including you!

Each of us is like a mosaic, with lots of lovely tiles, some that are basically neutral, and a few that could use a little—ah—work. It's important to see the whole mosaic. But because of the brain's negativity bias, we tend to fixate on what's wrong with ourselves instead of what's right. If you do twenty things in a day and nineteen go fine, what's the one you think about? Probably the one that didn't go so well.

Your brain builds new structures primarily based on what you pay attention to; neurons that fire together, wire together. Focusing on the "bad" tiles in the mosaic you are reinforces an underlying sense of being mediocre, flawed, or less than others. And it blocks the development of the confidence and self-worth that come from recognizing the good tiles. These results of the negativity bias are not fair. But they're sure powerful, and a big reason most of us have feelings of inadequacy or self-doubt; I've had to work with these issues myself.

Knowing your own strengths and virtues is just a matter of seeing yourself *accurately*. Then, recognizing the good in yourself, you'll feel better inside, reach out to others with less fear of rejection, and pursue your dreams with more confidence that you'll have success.

How

Pick one simple good thing about yourself. Maybe you are particularly friendly, open, conscientious, imaginative, warm, perceptive, or steadfast. Be aware of the experience of that positive characteristic. Explore its body sensations, emotional tones, and any attitudes or viewpoints that go with it.

Take a little time to register that you do indeed have this good quality. Let yourself become convinced of it.

Look for signs of it for a day or a week—and feel it when you find it.

Notice any difficulty in accepting that you have this good quality, such as thoughts like *But I'm not that way all the time.* Or *But I have bad parts, too.* Try to get on your own side here and see yourself realistically, including your good qualities. It's okay that you don't live from those qualities every minute: that's what it means to be a mosaic; that's what it means to be human.

Repeat this process for other strengths or virtues that you have.

Also open to the good things that *others* recognize in you. Start with a friend, and look at yourself through his or her eyes. What does that person like about you? Or appreciate, enjoy, respect, or admire? If your friend were telling someone else about your good qualities, what might he or she say? Do this again with several other people from different parts—and perhaps times—of your life, such as other friends or a family member, partner, teacher, coach, or coworker. Then allow other people's knowing of your good characteristics to become your own. Soften your face and body and mind to take in this knowing of the truth, the whole truth, of your personal mosaic.

Whether it starts with your own recognition of yourself or from other people, let the knowing of good things about you become feelings of worth, confidence, happiness, and peace.

Sense a quiet voice inside you, coming from your own core, firmly and honestly listing some of your good qualities. Listen to it. Let what it's saying sink in. If you like, write down the list and go over it from time to time; you don't have to show it to anyone.

As you go through life, look for examples of your decency, endurance, caring, and other good qualities. When you see these facts, open to feeling good about yourself.

Let these times of feeling good about yourself gradually fill your heart and your days.

6
Slow Down

Most of us are running around way too much. Say you bump into a friend you haven't seen for a while and ask, "How are you?" Twenty years ago, a typical answer would be "fine." But today the reply is more likely to be "busy!"

We're caught up in e-mails, phone calls, long hours working, schlepping kids from here to there, and trying to match velocities with everyone else who has speeded up.

Whatever the particular causes may be in your own life, it's easy to feel like a short-order cook at the lunch rush.

There's a place for revving up occasionally, whether it's dealing with an emergency or cheering like a maniac because your fourth-grade daughter has finally taken a shot while playing basketball (that was me).

But chronic speediness has many bad effects:

- It activates the same general stress-response system that evolved in the brain to protect us from charging lions, which releases nerve-jangling hormones like adrenaline and cortisol, weakens your immune system, and wears down your mood.

- It puts the alarm system of the brain on red alert, scanning for threats and often overreacting. Have you ever noticed that when you speed up, you're quicker to find things to worry or get irritated about?

- It gives you less time to think clearly and make good decisions.

Even though "the need for speed" may have become a way of life, it's always possible to make a change. Start with little things. And then let them grow. Honestly, slowing down is one of those seemingly small actions that could really change your life.

How

Here are some ways to slow down. I suggest doing just a few of them: don't rush to slow down!

- Do a few things more slowly than usual. Leisurely lift the cup to your lips, don't rush through a meal, let others finish talking before jumping in, or stroll to a meeting instead of racing. Finish one task before moving on to another. A few times a day, take a long, *slow* breath.

- Back off the gas pedal. One time, as I zoomed down the freeway, my wife murmured, "What's the rush?" She made me realize that slowing down a few miles per hour meant arriving just a few minutes later, but with lots more ease along the way.

- When the phone rings, imagine that it is a church or temple bell reminding you to breathe and slow down. (This suggestion is from the Vietnamese monk Thich Nhat Hanh.)

- Resist the pressure of others to get things done sooner than you really need to. As the saying has it, their lack of planning does not make it your emergency.

- Find what's good about this moment as it is, so you'll have less need to zip along to the next thing. For example, if you're stuck on hold on a phone call, look around for something that's beautiful or interesting, or enjoy the peacefulness of simply breathing.

Over time, wrap up existing commitments and be careful about taking on new ones. Notice and challenge any internal pressure to always be doing and getting more and more. What's the net bottom-line effect on your quality of life: Does racing about make you happier? Or more stressed and worn out?

All the while, soak in the ease and well-being that come from slowing down—and don't be surprised if people say you look more confident, rested, dignified, and happy.

It's *your* life, no one else's. Slow down and enjoy it!

7

Forgive Yourself

Everyone messes up. Me, you, the neighbors, everybody. It's important to acknowledge mistakes, learn from them so they don't happen again, and feel appropriate remorse. But most people keep beating themselves up way past the point of usefulness: they're unfairly self-critical.

Inside the mind are many subpersonalities. For example, one part of me sets the alarm clock for 6 a.m. to get up and exercise . . . and then when it goes off, another part of me grumbles: *Who set the darn clock?!* More broadly, there are an inner critic and an inner protector inside each of us. For most people, that inner critic is continually yammering away, looking for something, anything, to find fault with. It magnifies small failings into big ones, punishes you over and over for things long past, ignores the larger context, and doesn't credit you for your efforts to make amends.

That's why you need your inner protector to stick up for you: to put your weaknesses and misdeeds in perspective, to highlight your many good qualities surrounding your lapses, to encourage you to return to the high road even if you've gone down the low one, and—frankly—to tell that inner critic to Hush Up Now.

How

Start by picking something relatively small that you're still being hard on yourself about, and try the methods below. Then work up to more significant issues.

Here we go:

- Start by getting in touch with the feeling of being cared about by someone in your life today or from your past. Get a sense that this person's caring for you, and perhaps other aspects of him or her, have been taken into your own mind as parts of your inner protector. Do this with other beings who care about you, and open to a growing sense of your inner protector.

- Staying with feeling cared about, bring to mind some of your many good qualities. You could ask the protector what it knows about you. These are facts, not flattery, and you don't need a halo to have good qualities like patience, determination, fairness, or kindness.

❧ This step and the one above it will help you face whatever needs forgiving, and actually forgive yourself.

❧ If you yelled at a child, lied at work, partied too hard, let a friend down, cheated on a partner, or were secretly glad about someone's downfall—*whatever* it was—acknowledge the facts: what happened, what was in your mind at the time, the relevant context and history, and the results for yourself and others.

❧ Notice any facts that are hard to face—like the look in a child's eyes when you yelled at her—and be especially open to them; they're the ones that are keeping you stuck. It is always the truth that sets us free.

❧ Sort what happened into three piles: moral faults, unskillfulness, and everything else. Moral faults deserve *proportionate* guilt, remorse, or shame, but unskillfulness calls for correction, no more. (This point is *very* important.)

You could ask others—including people you may have wronged—what they think about this sorting (and about other points below), but you alone get to decide what's right. For example, if you gossiped about someone and embellished a mistake he made, you might decide that the lie in your exaggeration is a moral fault deserving a wince of remorse, but that casual gossip (which most of us do at one time or another) is simply unskillful and should be corrected (i.e., not done again) without self-flagellation.

❧ In an honest way, take responsibility for your moral fault(s) and unskillfulness. Say in your mind or out loud (or write): *I am responsible for* _____ , _____ , *and* _____ . Let yourself *feel* it.

Then add to yourself: *But I am NOT responsible for* _____ , _____ , *and* _____ . For example, you are not responsible for the misinterpretations or overreactions of others. Let the relief of what you are NOT responsible for sink in.

❧ Acknowledge what you have already done to learn from this experience, and to repair things and make amends. Let this sink in. Appreciate yourself.

Next decide what, if anything, remains to be done—inside your own heart or out there in the world—and then do it. Let it sink in that you're doing it, and appreciate yourself for this, too.

Now check in with your inner protector: is there anything else you should face or do? Listen to the still, quiet voice of conscience, so different from the pounding scorn of the critic. If you truly know that something remains, then take care of it. But otherwise, know in your heart that what needed learning has been learned, and that what needed doing has been done.

❧ And now actively forgive yourself. Say in your mind, out loud, in writing, or perhaps to others statements like *I forgive myself for* _____ , _____ , *and* _____ . *I have taken responsibility and done what I could to make things better.* You could also ask the inner protector to forgive you, or others out in the world, such as the person you wronged.

❧ You may need to go through one or more of the steps above again and again to truly forgive yourself, and that's alright. Allow the experience of being forgiven—in this case, by yourself—to take some time to sink in. Help it sink in by opening up to it in your body and heart, and by reflecting on how it will help others if you stop beating yourself up.

May you be at peace.

8
Get More Sleep

You need more sleep.

That is, unless you really are that rare person these days who's truly getting enough sleep. (Disclosure: that person is definitely not me.)

Without sufficient sleep, risks go up for car accidents, diabetes, heart disease, depression, and unwanted weight. And performance goes down in paying attention, learning, and staying motivated. Plus, it just feels bad to be foggy, groggy, tired, and irritable.

People don't get enough sleep for a variety of reasons. It's common to stay up too late and get up too early, and drink too much coffee to get going in the morning and too much alcohol to relax at night. Sleep problems are also a symptom of some health conditions—such as depression and sleep apnea—so talk with your doctor if you have insomnia or if you still feel tired after seemingly getting enough sleep.

The right amount of sleep varies from person to person—and from time to time: if you're stressed, ill, or working hard, you need more sleep. Whatever it is that you need, the key is consistency: getting good rest every night, not trying to catch up on weekends or holidays.

After I left home, I often went back to visit my parents. They frequently told me I looked tired and needed more sleep. It bugged me every time they said it. But you know what?

They were right. Almost everyone needs more sleep.

How

Two things get in the way of sufficient sleep: not setting enough time aside for it, and not having deep and continuous sleep during the time allotted.

In terms of the first problem:

- Decide how much time you want to sleep each night. Then, look at your schedule, see when you need to wake up, and work backwards to give yourself a bedtime. Figure out what you need to do during the hour before your bedtime to get to sleep on time; it probably includes not getting into an argument with anyone!

- Observe the "reasons" that emerge to stay up past your bedtime. Most if not all of them will boil down to a basic choice: what's more important, your health and well-being—or watching another hour of TV, doing housework, or (fill in the blank)?

-◄ Really enjoy feeling rested and alert when you get enough sleep. Take in those good feelings, so your brain will want more of them in the future.

In terms of the second problem, issues with sleep itself, here are some suggestions; pick the ones that work for you:

-◄ Consider the advice of organizations like the National Sleep Foundation: have a bedtime routine; relax in the last hour or two before bed; stop eating (particularly chocolate), drinking coffee or alcohol, exercising, or smoking cigarettes two or three hours before bedtime; make sure the environment of your bedroom supports sleep (e.g., cool and quiet, good mattress, earplugs if your partner snuffles or snores).

-◄ Do what you can to lower stress. Chronic stress raises hormones like cortisol, which will make it hard to fall asleep in the first place, or wake up early in the morning.

-◄ Make a deal with yourself to worry or plan during the next day, after you get up. Shift your attention to things that make you feel happy and relaxed, or simply to the sensations of breathing itself. Bring to mind the warm feeling of being with people who care about you. Have compassion for yourself.

-◄ Really relax. For example, take five to ten *long* exhalations; imagine your hands are warm (and tuck them under the pillow); rest a finger or knuckle against your lip; relax your tongue and jaw; imagine you are in a very peaceful setting; progressively relax each part of your body, starting with your feet and moving up to your head.

⋇ Certain nutrients are important for sleep. Unless you're sure you're getting these in your daily diet, consider supplementing magnesium (500 milligrams/day) and calcium (1200 milligrams/day). If you can, take half in the morning and half before bed.

⋇ The neurotransmitter serotonin aids sleep; it is made from an amino acid, tryptophan, so consider taking 500–1000 milligrams of tryptophan just before bed. If you wake up in the middle of the night and can't easily fall back to sleep, consider 1 milligram of melatonin taken sublingually (under the tongue). You could also eat a banana or something else that's quick and easy; rising blood sugar will lift insulin levels, which will help transport more tryptophan into your brain. You can usually get tryptophan and melatonin at a health food store; do not supplement either of these if you are breastfeeding or taking psychiatric medication (unless your doctor tells you it's fine).

Good night!

9

Befriend Your Body

Imagine that your body is separate from you, and consider these questions:

- How has your body taken care of you over the years? Such as keeping you alive, giving you pleasure, and taking you from place to place.

- In return, how well do you take care of your body? Such as soothing, feeding, and exercising it, or taking it to the doctor. On the other hand, in what ways might you run it down, feed it junk food, or intoxicate it?

- In what ways are you critical of your body? For example, are you disappointed in it or embarrassed by it? Do you feel let down by it, or wish it were different?

- If your body could talk to you, what might it say?

⊰ If your body were a good friend, how would you treat it? Would that be different from how you treat it now?

Personally, I can't help squirming a little when I face these questions myself. It's common to push the body hard, ignore its needs until they get intense, and tune out from its signals. And then drop the body into bed at the end of another long day like—as my father would say, having grown up on a ranch—"a horse rid hard and put up wet."

People can also get mad at the body, and even mean to it. Like it's the body's fault if it weighs too much or is getting old.

But if you do any of these things, you'll end up paying a big price, since you are not separated from your body after all. Its needs and pleasures and pains are your own. Its fate will be your own someday.

On the other hand, if you treat your body well, like a good friend, you'll feel better, have more energy, be more resilient, and probably live longer.

How

Remember a time when you treated a good friend well. What was your attitude toward your friend, and what kinds of things did you do with him or her? How did it feel inside to be nice toward your friend?

Next, imagine a day of treating your body like another good friend. Imagine loving this friend—your body—as you wake up and help it out of bed: being gentle with it, staying connected to it, not rushing about . . . what would this feel like?

Imagine cherishing your body as you move through the morning—such as helping it kindly to some water, giving it a nice shower, and serving it healthy and delicious food. Imagine treating your body with love as you do other activities, such as driving, caring for children, exercising, working with others, doing dishes, having sex, or brushing your teeth.

How would this approach feel?

You'd probably experience less stress, more relaxation and calm, more pleasure, more ease, and more of a sense of being in control of your life. Plus an implicit sense of being kind to yourself, since in a deep sense you don't just have a body, you are your body; treating it well is treating *you* well.

If your body could speak, what might it say to you after being treated with love for a day?

Then, for real, treat your body well for a day (or even for just a few minutes). What's this like? In what ways does it feel good? Notice any reluctance to be nice to your body. Maybe a feeling that doing so would be self-indulgent or sinful. Explore that reluctance, and see what it's about. Then decide if it makes any sense. If it doesn't, return to treating your body well.

If you could talk to your body, what might you say? Perhaps write a letter to your body, telling it how you've felt about it in the past, and how you want to be nicer to it in the future.

Make a short list of how to care better for your body, such as quitting smoking, or leaving work sooner, or taking more time for simple bodily pleasures. Then commit to treating your body better.

Kindness begins at home.

Your home is your body.

10

Nourish Your Brain

Your brain contains about a hundred billion neurons plus another trillion support cells. Most neurons fire five to fifty times a second—even when you're asleep. Consequently, even though your brain weighs only three pounds, about 2 to 3 percent of bodyweight, it needs about 25 percent of the glucose in your blood. No wonder it's hungry!

And it needs other nutrients besides glucose. For example, about 60 percent of the dry weight of the brain consists of healthy fats. Or consider the neurotransmitters that carry information from one neuron to another. Your body builds these complex molecules from smaller parts, assisted by other biochemicals. For instance, serotonin—which supports your mood, digestion, and sleep—is made from tryptophan with the aid of iron and vitamin B_6.

Significant shortages in any one of the dozens of nutrients your brain needs will harm your body and mind. For example:

Shortage	Effect
Vitamins B_{12}, B_6, folate	Depressed mood (Skarupski, et al, 2010)
Vitamin D	Weaker immune system; dementia; depressed mood (Nimitphong and Holick 2011)
DHA	Depressed mood (Rondanelli et al. 2010)

On the other hand, filling up your neural cupboard with good supplies will bring you more energy, resilience, and well-being.

How

At every meal, especially breakfast, have three to four ounces of protein—about the size of a deck of cards—from one source or another. This will give you vital amino acids plus help regulate blood sugar and insulin.

Speaking of blood sugar, eating lots of sweets and white-flour carbohydrates raises insulin levels . . . which then crash, leading to the weary/cranky/foggy state of hypoglycemia. Routinely high insulin also puts you on the slippery slope to type 2 diabetes. So keep these foods to a minimum, aiming for no more than twenty-five grams a day of refined sugar, and avoiding refined flours as much as possible.

Eat lots of dark-colored fruits and vegetables, such as blueberries, kale, beets, carrots, and broccoli. These foods contain important nutrients that support memory (Krikorian, et al. 2010), protect your brain against oxidation (Guerrero-Beltran, et al. 2010), and may reduce the risk of dementia (Gu, et al. 2010).

Take a broad-spectrum, high-potency, multivitamin/ mineral supplement. It would be great if you could get all the nutrients for optimal health from three meals a day, but most people don't have the time to get and prepare all the fresh vegetables and other complex foods this would take. Plus we need more of these nutrients to help metabolize the hundreds of man-made molecules we're exposed to each day. In addition to eating as healthily as you can, it's simple to toss a few supplement capsules a day down the hatch, which takes less time than brushing your teeth. To identify a high-quality supplement—whose daily dose probably involves two to three capsules—look for one that has about five to ten times the "daily values" (DVs) of B vitamins and 100 percent of the DVs of minerals.

Also take two to three capsules a day of high-quality fish oil, enough to get at least 500 milligrams of both DHA (decosahexaenoic acid) and EPA (eicosapentaenoic acid); check the label. If you don't want fish oil, an alternative is a combination of flax oil and DHA from algae, but fish oil is the most effective way to get omega-3 oils into your body and brain.

Meanwhile, as you take these actions, enjoy knowing that as you "feed your head," you're in fact feeding your life.

11
Protect Your Brain

Your brain controls your other bodily systems, and it's the basis for your thoughts and feelings, joys and sorrows. No question, it is the most important organ in your body. Small changes in its neurochemistry can lead to big changes in your mood, resilience, memory, concentration, thoughts, feelings, and desires.

So it's vital to protect it from negative factors like toxins, inflammation, and stress.

If you take good care of your brain, it will take good care of you.

How

Avoid toxins. Besides the obvious actions—like don't sniff glue, and stand upwind when pumping gas—be careful about alcohol, which works by depriving brain cells of oxygen: that buzz is the feeling of neurons drowning.

Minimize inflammation. When your immune system activates to deal with an infection or allergen, it sends chemical messengers called *cytokines* throughout your body. Unfortunately, cytokines can linger in your brain, leading to a slump in mood and even depression (Maier and Watkins 1998; Schiepers, Wichers, and Maes 2005).

So take practical steps to reduce colds and flu, such as washing your hands often, and avoid any foods that set off your immune system. For example, many people have inflammatory reactions to gluten grains (e.g., wheat, oats, rye) and/or dairy products; it's not surprising, since these foods were introduced just 10,000 years ago, a tiny moment in the 200 million-year evolution of the mammalian, primate, and human diet. You don't need overt symptoms of allergies for a medical lab blood test to show that gluten or dairy foods aren't good for you. On your own, try going to zero with both these food groups for two weeks and see if you notice a difference in your mental or physical health; if you do, keep staying away from them: I do myself, and there are plenty of delicious alternatives.

Get regular exercise, which promotes the growth of new neural structures, including via the birth of new brain cells.

Relax. The stress hormone cortisol both sensitizes the fight-or-flight alarm bell of the brain—the amygdala—and weakens (even shrinks) a region called the hippocampus, which helps put the brakes on stress reactions. Consequently, in a vicious cycle, stress today makes you more sensitive to stress tomorrow. Additionally, since the hippocampus is also critical for making memories, a daily diet of stress (even from just feeling frustrated, irritated, or anxious) makes it harder to learn new things or put your feelings in context. One major antidote to stress is relaxation, which activates the soothing and calming parasympathetic wing of the nervous system; see chapter 4 for good ways to relax.

part two:

Enjoy Life

12
Take Pleasure

When you find pleasure in life, you are not pushing away things that are hard or painful. You are simply opening up to the sweet stuff that's already around you—and basking, luxuriating, and delighting in it.

This activates the calming and soothing parasympathetic wing of your autonomic nervous system, and quiets the fight-or-flight sympathetic wing and its stress-response hormones. Besides lifting your mood, settling your fears, and brightening your outlook, the stress relief of taking pleasure offers physical health benefits, too: strengthening your immune system, improving digestion, and balancing hormones.

How

Relish the pleasures of daily life, starting with your senses:

- *What smells good?* The skin of an orange, wood smoke on the air, dinner on the stove, a young child's hair . . .

- *Tastes delicious?* Strong coffee, delicate tea, French toast—chocolate!—tossed salad, goat cheese . . .

- *Looks beautiful?* Sunrise, sunset, full moon, a baby sleeping, red leaves in autumn, images of galaxies, fresh fallen snow . . .

- *Sounds wonderful?* Waves on the seashore, wind through pine trees, a dear friend laughing, Beethoven's Ode to Joy, silence itself . . .

- *Feels good on your skin?* Newly washed sheets, a good back scratch, warm water, a fresh breeze on a muggy day . . .

Next, include the mind: What do you like to think about or remember. For example, bring to mind a favorite setting—a mountain meadow, a tropical beach, a cozy living room chair—and imagine yourself there.

Last, *savor* these pleasures. Sink into them, take your time with them, and let them fill your body and mind. Marinate in pleasure! Notice any resistance to feeling really good, any thought that it is foolish or wrong . . . and then see if you can let that go. And fall back into pleasure.

Enjoy yourself!

13
Say Yes

When our son was doing theater in high school, I learned about an exercise for improvisational acting ("improv"): no matter what another actor says or does to you, you are always supposed to figuratively (and sometimes literally) say yes to it. In other words, if someone on stage turns to you and says, "Doctor, why does my baby have two heads?" you should respond with something like, "Because two heads are better than one."

Real life is like improv: the script's always changing, and saying yes keeps you in the flow, pulls for creativity, and makes it more fun. Try saying no out loud or in your mind. How's that feel? Then say yes. Which one feels better, opens your heart more, and draws you more into the world?

Saying yes to some part of life—to a condition or situation, to a relationship, to your history or personality, or to something happening inside your own mind—does not necessarily mean that you *like* it. You can say yes to pain, to sorrow, to the things that aren't going well for you or others.

Your yes means that you accept the facts as they are, that you are not resisting them emotionally even if you are trying with all your might to change them. This will usually bring some peace—and will help any actions you take be more effective.

How

Say yes to something you like. Then yes to something neutral. Both of these are probably easy.

Then say yes to something you don't like. Can you do that, too? As you do this, try to feel a sense that you are okay, fundamentally, even though what you dislike exists. Also try to feel some acceptance in your yes, some surrender to the facts as they are, whether you like them or not.

Try saying yes to more things that are not your preference. You're not saying yes that you approve of them, but —for example—yes it's raining at my picnic, yes people are poor and hungry across the planet, yes my career has stalled, yes I miscarried, yes my dear friend has cancer. Yes that's the way it is. Yes to being in traffic. Yes to the job you have. Yes to the body you have.

Yes to the twists and turns in your life so far: large and small; good, bad, and indifferent; past, present, and future. Yes to the younger sibling whose birth toppled you from your throne. Yes to your parents' work and your family circumstances. Yes to your choices after leaving home. Yes to what you had for breakfast. Yes to moving someplace new. Yes to the person you are sleeping with—or yes to not sleeping with anyone. Yes to having children—or to not having them.

Say yes to what arises in the mind. Yes to feelings, sensations, thoughts, images, memories, desires. Yes even to things that need to be restrained—such as an angry impulse to hit something, undeserved self-criticism, or an addiction.

Say yes to *all* the parts of the people in your life. Yes to the love in your parents and also yes to the parts that bothered you. Yes to a friend's flakiness amidst her good humor and patience, yes to another friend's sincerity amidst her irritability and criticalness. Yes to every bit of a child, a relative, a distant acquaintance, an adversary.

And yes to different parts of yourself—whatever they are. Not picking and choosing right now, but saying yes— YES—to whatever is inside you.

Play with different tones of yes (out loud or in your mind) related to different things—including the ones you don't like—and see how this feels. Try a cautious yes, as well as a yes that is confident, soft, rueful, or enthusiastic.

Feel your yes in your body. To adapt a method from Thich Nhat Hanh: Breathing in, feel something positive; breathing out, say yes. Breathe in energy, breathe out yes. Breathe in calm, breathe out yes.

Say yes to your needs. Yes to the need for more time to yourself, more exercise, more love, fewer sweets, and less anger. Try saying no to these needs in your mind or out loud, and see how that feels. And then say yes to them again.

Say yes to actions. To this kiss this lovemaking this reaching for the salt this brushing of teeth this last good-bye to someone you love.

Notice your nos. And then see what happens if you say yes to some of the things you've previously said no to.

Say yes to being alive. Yes to life. Yes to your own life. Yes to each year, each day. Yes to each minute.

Imagine that life is whispering yes. Yes to all beings, and yes to you. Everything you've said yes to is saying yes to you. Even the things you've said no to are saying yes to you!

Each breath, each heartbeat, each surge across a synapse: each one says yes. Yes, all yes, all saying yes.

Yes.

14
Take More Breaks

As we evolved in hunter-gatherer bands over millions of years, life moved at the pace of a walk, in rhythm with the seasons and with the rising and setting of the sun each day. In many of the hunter-gatherer cultures still existing today, it takes only a few hours a day to find food and shelter. It's a good guess that our ancient ancestors lived similarly, and spent the rest of their time relaxing, hanging out with friends, and looking at the stars.

Sure, life was tough in other ways, like dodging saber-tooth tigers, yet the point remains that the human body and mind evolved to be in a state of rest or leisure—in other words, *on a break*—much of the time.

But now, in the twenty-first century, people routinely work ten, twelve, or more hours a day—when you count commuting, working from home, and business travel—to put bread on the table and a roof over their heads. Much the same is true if a person is a stay-at-home parent, since "the village it takes to raise a child" usually looks more like a ghost town these days. Many of us are on the job and on the go from soon after we wake up in the morning and check e-mails or feed children (or both!) to the last time we pull phone messages at night.

It makes you wonder who is "advanced" and who is "primitive"!

The modern, pedal-to-the-metal lifestyle produces chronic stress and tension, and related physical and mental health issues. It also crowds out creative pursuits, friendships, recreation, spiritual life, and time for children and mates. As a therapist, I often see families where one or both parents are dealing with work sixty-plus hours a week; the job is an elephant in the living room, pushing everything else to the margins.

Imagine for a moment that you are sitting comfortably somewhere in your old age and looking back on your life and reflecting. Do you think you are going to wish you had spent more time on the job or doing housework?

Or wish you had spent more time relaxing, hanging out with friends, and looking at the stars?

How

So promise yourself that you'll take more breaks. Most of them will be brief, even a minute or less. But their accumulating effects will be really good for you.

Here are some methods for getting more breaks; pick the one(s) you like best:

- **Give yourself permission**—Tell yourself that you have worked hard and deserve a little rest; that it's important for your health; that your productivity will actually increase with more breaks; that even cavemen/women got more breaks than you!

- **Renounce everything else**—When it's time for a break, drop everything else for that time. Truly "clock out."

- **Take lots of microbreaks**—Many times a day, step out of the stream of doingness for at least a few seconds: close your eyes for a moment; take a couple of deep breaths; shift your visual focus to the farthest point you can see; repeat a saying or prayer; stand up and move about.

- **Shift gears**—Maybe you have to keep grinding through your To Do list, but at least take a break from task A by doing a different kind of task B.

- **Get out**—Look out the window; go outside and stare up at the sky; find a reason to walk out of a meeting.

- **Unplug**—If only for a few minutes, stop answering your phone(s); shut down e-mails; turn off the TV or radio; take off the earphones.

- **Make your body happy**—Wash your face; eat a cookie; smell something good; stretch; lie down; rub your eyes or ears.

- **Go on a mental holiday**—Remember or imagine a setting (mountain lake? tropical beach? grandma's kitchen?) that makes you feel relaxed and happy. When you can, go there and enjoy yourself. As I've told myself in certain situations, "They may have my body, but they don't get my mind."

- **Keep your stress needle out of the red zone**—If you find yourself getting increasingly frustrated or tense in some situation, disengage and take a break before your head explodes. Staying out of "red zone" stress is a serious priority for your long-term health and well-being.

To get at the underlying causes of your busy life and lack of breaks, consider all the things you think you have to do. Can you drop or delegate some of these? And can you take on fewer commitments and tasks in the future?

Personally, I've been slowly learning how to say no. No to low priority activities, no to great things I just don't have time for, no to my appetite for filling up my calendar.

Saying no will help you say yes to your own well-being, to friends, to activities that really feed you, to an uncluttered mind. To the stars twinkling high above your head.

15
Be Glad

In order to keep our ancestors alive in harsh and often lethal settings, neural networks evolved that continually look for, react to, store, and recall bad news—both "out there," in your environment, and "in here," inside your own head.

As a consequence, we pay a lot of attention to threats, losses, and mistreatment in our environment—and to our emotional reactions, such as worry, sadness, resentment, disappointment, and anger. We also focus on our own mistakes and flaws—and on the feelings of guilt, shame, inadequacy, and even self-hatred that get stirred up.

There's a place for noticing and dealing with things that could harm you or others. And a place for improving your own mind and character.

But because of the negativity bias of the brain, most of us go way overboard.

Which is really *unfair*. It's not fair to zero in on a bit of bad news and ignore or downplay all the good news around it. The results of that unfairness include uncalled-for anxiety, pessimism, blue moods, and self-doubt. Emphasizing the bad news also primes us to be untrusting or cranky with others.

But if you compensate for the brain's bias by actively looking for good news—especially the little things you are *glad* about—then you will feel happier, more at peace with the world, more open to others, and more willing to stretch for your dreams. And as your growing gladness naturally lowers your stress, you'll likely get physical health benefits as well, such as a stronger immune system.

Now, that's good news . . . about good news!

How

Look for things to be glad about, like:

- Bad things that never happened, or were not as bad as you feared

- Relief that hard or stressful times are over

- Good things that have happened to you in the past

- Good things in your life today, such as: friends, loved ones, children, pets, the health you have, stores stocked with food, public libraries, electricity, positive aspects of your work and finances, activities you enjoy, sunsets, sunrises . . . ice cream!

◄ Good things about yourself, such as positive character traits and intentions

Sink into feelings of gladness:

◄ "Glad" means "pleased with" or "happy about." So notice what it feels like—in your emotions, body, and thoughts—to be *pleased* with something or *happy* about it. When you create a clear sense-memory of a positive mental state, you can find your way back to it again.

◄ Be aware of small, subtle, mild, or brief feelings of gladness.

◄ Stay with the good news. Don't change the channel so fast!

◄ Notice if your feelings of gladness get hijacked by doubt or worry. Also be honest with yourself, and consider if you are kind of attached to your resentments, grievances, or "case" about other people. It's okay if it's hard for you to stay with gladness; it's really common. Just try to name to yourself what has happened in your mind—such as "hijacking" . . . "brooding" . . . "grumbling"— and then freely decide if you want to spiral down into the bad news, or if you want to focus on good news instead. Make a conscious decision, acknowledge it to yourself, and then act upon it.

❧ Sometime every day, before going to bed, name to yourself at least three things you are glad about.

Share your feelings of gladness:

❧ Make a point of mentioning to others something that you are pleased or happy about (often the little stuff of everyday life).

❧ Look for opportunities to tell another person what you appreciate about him or her.

16
Have Faith

Try a little experiment: in your mind or out loud, complete this sentence a few times: "I have faith in _____ ." Then complete another sentence a few times: "I have no faith in _____ ." What do faith—and no faith—feel like?

In your experience of faith, there's probably a sense of *trusting* in something—which makes sense since the word comes from the Latin root, "to trust." ("Faith" can also mean a religion, but my meaning here is more general.) Faith feels good. To have confidence is to have faith; "con+fide" means "with+faith."

Faith comes from direct experience, reason, trusted sources, and sometimes from something that just feels deeply right and that's all you can say about it. You could have faith in both biological evolution and heaven. Sometimes faith seems obvious, like expecting water to yield each time you prepare to dive in; other times, faith is more of a conscious choice—an act of faith—such as choosing to believe that your child will be all right as he or she leaves home for college.

What do you have faith in—out there in the world or inside yourself?

For example, I have faith in the sun coming up tomorrow, my partner while rock climbing, science and scholarship, the kindness of strangers, the deliciousness of peaches, the love of my wife, God, and the desire of most people to live in peace. And faith in my determination, coffee-making skills, and generally good intentions.

In your brain, faith (broadly defined to include assumptions and expectations) is an efficient way to conserve neural resources by not figuring things out each time from scratch. The visceral sense of conviction in faith integrates prefrontal logic, limbic emotion, and brainstem arousal.

Without faith in the world and in yourself, life feels shaky and scary. Faith grounds you in what's reliable and supportive; it's the antidote to doubt and fear. It strengthens you and supports you in weathering hard times. It helps you stay on your chosen paths, with confidence they will lead to good places. Faith fuels the hope and optimism that encourage the actions that lead to the results that confirm your faith, in a lovely positive cycle. Faith lifts your eyes to the far horizons, toward what's sacred, even Divine.

How

Sure, some skepticism is good. But going overboard with it leads to an endless loop of mistrusting the world and doubting yourself. You need to have faith that you'll make good choices about where to have faith! Which means avoiding two pitfalls:

- Putting too much trust in the *wrong* places, such as in people who won't come through for you, in a business or job that's unlikely to turn out well, in dogmas and prejudices, or in a habit of mind that harms you—like a guardedness with others that may have worked okay when you were young but is now like walking around in a suit of armor that's three sizes too small.

- Putting too little trust in the *right* places, such as in the willingness of most people to hear what you really have to say, in the results that will come if you keep plugging away, or in the goodness inside your own heart.

So, first make a list of what you *do* have faith in—both in the world and in yourself. You can do this in your mind, on paper, or by talking with someone.

Next, ask yourself where your faith might be misplaced—in dry wells or in dogs that won't hunt. Be sure to consider too much faith in certain aspects of your own mind, such as in beliefs that you are weak or tainted, that others don't care about you, or that somehow you're going to get different results by doing pretty much the same old things.

Then pick one instance of misguided faith, and consciously step away from it: reflect on how you came to develop it and what it has cost you; imagine the benefits of a life without it; and develop a different resource to replace it. Repeat these steps for other cases of misplaced faith.

Second, make another list, this one of what you *could* reasonably have faith in—in the world and in yourself. These are missed opportunities for confidence—such as in people who could be trusted more (including children), in the basic safety of most days for most people, and in your own strengths and virtues.

Then pick one and see if you can have more faith in it. Remember the good reasons for relying upon it. Imagine how more trust in it will help you and others. Consciously choose to believe in it.

Third, consider some of the good qualities and aspirations in your innermost heart. Give yourself over to them for a moment—or longer. What's that like?

Try to have more faith in the best parts of yourself. They've always been faithful to you.

17
Find Beauty

Beauty is that which *delights* the senses—including the "sixth sense" of the mind.

Different people find beauty in different forms and places. You don't have to go to a museum, listen to a symphony, or eat a gourmet meal to be in the presence of beauty.

For example, here are some of the (maybe strange) things I find beautiful: A clump of grass in a sidewalk crack. The horn of a train as it moves away. The smell of cinnamon. The curve of highway cloverleafs. Kitchen knives. The faces of nurses. Courage. Falling water. A glazed donut. The touch of cashmere. Foam. Frisbees. Snakes. Geometrical proofs. Worn pennies. The feeling of catching a football.

What are some things that are beautiful to you?

There's so much beauty all around us. But I think that for many people, there is little sense of this. That was certainly true for me before I started deliberately looking for beauty. And then we wonder why life doesn't seem very delightful!

What do you feel when you encounter beauty, including in its everyday forms? Perhaps your heart opens, something eases in the mind, there's pleasure, and your spirits lift. The experience of beauty relieves stress, nourishes hope, and reminds us that there's much more to life than grinding through tasks. The sense of beauty can also be shared—have you ever admired a sunset with a friend?—bringing you closer to others.

How

Take a few moments each day to open to beauty. Really *look* at the things around you—particularly at the ordinary things we tend to tune out, such as the sky, appliances, grass, cars, weeds, familiar views, bookshelves, or sidewalks. Try the same with everyday sounds, smells, tastes, and touches. Also seek out lovely memories, feelings, or ideas.

Hunt for beauty like a child looking for seashells on a bountiful beach. Be open to things outside the frame of "nice" or "pretty." Let yourself be surprised. Find beauty in unexpected places.

When you find beauty, feel it. Open to a growing sense of boundless beauty above and below and stretching in all directions, like you're floating in a sea of rose petals.

Recognize the beauty in others, in their character, choices, sacrifices, aspirations. Understand the beauty in noble failures, quiet determination, leaps of insight, and joy at the good fortune of others. Hear the beauty of a parent's voice soothing a child, of friends laughing, of the click and clack of a teacher's chalk on the blackboard. See the beauty in the face of someone at the very beginning of this life, and see it in the face of someone at the very end.

Recognize the beauty in your own heart. Don't duck this one: as others are beautiful, so are you.

Make beauty with your hands, your words, and your actions.

Even the breath is beautiful. Breathing in beauty, let beauty breathe you.

18
Be Grateful

We experience gratitude when we are freely given something good.

Therefore, looking for opportunities for gratitude—developing an "attitude of gratitude"—is a great way to notice and enjoy some of the gifts you've received.

Gratitude does not mean ignoring difficulties, losses, or injustice. It just means *also* paying attention to the offerings that have come your way. Especially the little ones of everyday life.

When you do this, you're resting your mind increasingly on good things moving toward you, on being supported, on feelings of fullness—on the sense of having an open heart that moves toward an open hand.

Fuller and fuller, more and more fed by life instead of drained by it, you naturally feel like you have more of value inside yourself and more to offer to others.

And that is a very good thing. For example, studies by Robert Emmons and others have shown that gratitude is associated with greater well-being, better coping, and even better sleep (McCullough et al. 2001).

How

Prime your pump by bringing to mind someone you naturally feel grateful toward. Perhaps a friend, parent or grandparent, teacher, spiritual being, or pet.

Next, *look around and notice*, both here and now, and in the past:

- The gifts of the physical world, including the stars in the sky, the colors of the rainbow, and the remarkable fact that the seemingly arbitrary constants that determine how atoms stick together in our universe are just right for planets to form and life to develop—enabling you to be here today

- The gifts of nature, like the flight of a bird, the creatures that die so we may live, and your amazing brain

- The gifts of life, including the marvelous instructions for building a human being woven into the strands of DNA

- The gifts of nurturance, helpfulness, good counsel, and love from other people

These gifts are freely offered; no one can possibly earn them. All we can do is be grateful for these gifts, and do what we can in our own little corner of the world to use them well each day.

Let yourself *accept* these gifts. It would be rude—ungrateful!—to refuse them.

Remember that gratitude is not guilt or indebtedness —both of which actually make it harder to feel grateful. You may feel moved to be generous in turn—including in new directions, such as giving to some out of appreciation for what you have been given by others—but it will come from large-heartedness, not because you think you owe something. Gratitude moves us away from let's-make-a-deal exchanges in relationships toward a sense of abundance, in which you feel fed beyond measure and in turn give with all your heart without keeping score.

Then *recognize the benefits* to you of what has been given. Reflect on how it helps you and those you care about, makes you feel good, and fuels your own generosity in turn.

And *recognize the benevolence of the giver*, whether it is a person, Mother Nature, or the physical universe—or, if this is meaningful to you, something Divine. Don't minimize the benevolence to avoid feeling unworthy or indebted; open up to it as a telling of the truth, as a giving back to the giver, and as a joyful leaning toward that which is truly gift-giving in your world.

Last, *soak up the gifts coming to you*, whatever they are. Let them become part of you, woven into your body, brain, and being. As you inhale, as you relax, as you open, take in the good that you've been given.

19
Smile

Smiling has many benefits:

- Thinking of things that make you smile—like people you love, silly moments, stupid pet tricks, funny movies—helps you feel better right on the spot. Plus it calms down the stress response and releases wholesome neurochemicals like dopamine and natural opioids (e.g., endorphins).

- Researchers have found that the facial movements of smiling—independent of what a person actually feels inside—prompt the person to evaluate the world more positively (Niedenthal 2007).

- Smiling and the good feelings it encourages promote *approach behaviors*, a fancy term for paying more attention to the opportunities around you, going after your dreams with more confidence, and reaching out to others.

❧ Through what's called *emotional contagion*, when you smile and thus feel and act better, that influences others to feel and act better, too. Then nice positive cycles start rolling through a group—perhaps a family, a team at work, or simply a bunch of friends—in which your smile gets others to smile and be more positive, which snowballs into an even bigger grin for you.

❧ When you smile—authentically, to be sure, not in a false or Dr. Evil sort of way—that tells people you are not a threat, which calms the ancient, evolutionary tendency to be wary of others, and thus inclines them to be more open to you.

How

This is definitely *not* about putting a happy shiny face on depression, grief, fear, or anger. Smiling then would be phony, and would probably feel awful. But when you feel neutral or experience mild well-being, shifting into a small smile while thinking of good facts that make it real can naturally lift your mood and help you act more effectively.

So, in your mind or on paper, make a list of things that make you smile. Several times a day, look for moments to bring that list to mind . . . and a soft smile to your face.

Then notice the results, in how you feel inside, and in how you act toward others and how they respond to you. Savor these good feelings and successes, taking them in.

Smiling a few more times each day may not seem like much, but it will send wonderful ripples through your brain, body, mind, and relationships.

Now, isn't that something to smile about?

20

Get Excited

Excitement is energy plus positive emotion, and it is part of joy, passion, and having fun. It may be mild—but it still moves your needle. For example, on my personal 0-10 "thrillometer," seeing the stars on a clear night is about a 2 while the San Francisco Giants winning the World Series in 2010 was a 10.

When you consider excitement in this expanded way, what moves your own needle, even a little bit? How about the sound of bagpipes, a child's first steps, traveling someplace new, finishing a project that's gone well, dancing, laughing, finding something you've wanted on super-sale, or hearing a neat idea?

Of course it's hard, if not impossible, to feel excitement if you are ill or psychologically burdened. The inability to get excited is a sign that something's not right.

But under normal conditions, without excitement about *something*, life feels flat, bland, and inert. Passion helps ignite and sustain creativity, entrepreneurship, political action, and committed relationships. Getting excited about something *together* is bonding; shared enthusiasm makes a movie, concert, political rally, conversation, or lovemaking a lot more rewarding.

As you grew up, your natural liveliness may have been criticized, dampened, or squelched. In particular, passion is woven into both strong emotions and sex; if either of these has been shamed or numbed, so has excitement. Did any of this happen to you? If it did, then gradually making more room for passion in your life—more room for delight, eagerness, and energy—is a joyful way to express yourself more fully.

How

Find something that excites you, even just a bit. Feel the enjoyment in it. See if you can intensify the experience through a quick inhalation, a sense perhaps of energy rising in your body. Lift your chest and head, and let more aliveness come into your face. Register this feeling of excitement, and make room for it in your body. Then as you go through your day, notice what moves your own thrillometer, particularly in subtle ways. Look for things to get excited about!

Tell yourself that it's okay to get excited, thrilled, or aroused. Take a stand for a life that's got some juiciness in it. Reflect on your passions as a younger person: What's happened to them? Should you dust one of them off and recommit to it?

Pick a part of your life that's become static, perhaps stale—such as cooking, a job, housework, repetitive parts of parenting, even sex—and really pursue ways to pep it up. Try new dishes, turn up the music, get goofy, dance with the baby, vary your routines, and so on.

Be aware of how you might be putting a damper on excitement, such as tightening your body, deadening your feelings, or murmuring thoughts like *Don't stand out . . . Don't be "too much" for people . . . Don't be uncool.* As you become more mindful of the wet blankets in your own mind, they'll dry out.

Consider some of the practices for raising energy from yoga, martial arts, or other forms of physical training. These include taking multiple deep breaths (not to the point of lightheadedness), sensing energy in the core of your body a few inches below the navel, jumping up and down a few times, making deep guttural sounds (don't try this at work!), or visualizing bright light.

Join with the excitement of others. Focus on something that lights up a friend or your partner, and look for things that could be fun, enlivening, or interesting about it for *you*. Don't fake anything, but nudge your own energy upwards; get more engaged with the other person's passion, which may ignite your own.

Don't rain on other people's parade—and don't let them rain on yours. Sure, if you're getting too revved up, read the social signals and either dial down your energy or take it elsewhere. But be aware that excitement makes some people uncomfortable—to keep their own passions bottled up, they put a lid on those of others—and honestly, that's their problem, not yours. With this sort of person, you may need to disengage, find others who share your interests, and walk to the beat of your own drummer.

For me, the essence of excitement is *enthusiasm*—whose root meaning is quite profound: "moved by something extraordinary, even divine."

part three:

Build Strengths

21
Find Strength

To make your way in life—to enjoy the beautiful things it offers, to steer clear of hazards and protect yourself and others, and find friendship and love—you need strength. Not chest-thumping pushiness, but determination and grit.

Strength comes in many forms, including endurance, losing on the little things in order to win on the big ones, and restraint. For example, if you want to move a boat at the edge of a dock, don't run into it with a big smash; you'll just hurt yourself. Instead, stand on the edge of the dock, put your hand on the boat, and lean into it. *Strength keeps leaning.*

Inner strength is not all or nothing. You can build it, just like a muscle.

How

Mental strength draws on physical health, which is fueled by: eating protein at every meal; taking vitamin and mineral supplements daily; exercising several times a week; setting aside seven to nine hours a day for sleep; using intoxicants in moderation or not at all; and addressing and resolving chronic health problems, even seemingly mild ones. If you are not doing these, how about starting today?

Make a list of your strengths, such as intelligence, honesty, bearing pain, natural talents, recognizing good in others, or just surviving. Be accurate—not unfairly self-critical. Recognizing your strengths will help you feel stronger. If it's appropriate, ask someone what he or she thinks some of your strengths are.

Think about some of the good things you use your strengths for, such as earning a living, raising a family, growing as a person, or making our world better. Tell yourself, *It is good for me to be strong. My strength helps good things happen. Good people want me to be strong; anyone who wants me to be weak is not on my side.* Notice any beliefs that it is bad to be strong . . . and then turn your attention back to the good reasons for being strong.

To increase your sense of strength, recall times you felt strong. (For me, many of these have involved standing up for others, or physical activities like hiking in wilderness.) What did your body feel like then? What was your posture, point of view, or intention? Explore embodying strength right now: maybe lifting your chin, widening your stance, or breathing deeply. Take in these physical sensations and attitudes of strength so you can tap into them again.

Notice how good it feels to be strong. Feel the pleasure in your body, perhaps a quiet fierceness and resolve. Enjoy the confidence that strength brings, the sense of possibility. Appreciate how your strength empowers your caring, protectiveness, and love.

Tell yourself that you are strong. That you can endure, persist, cope, and prevail. That you are strong enough to hold your experience in awareness without being overwhelmed. That the winds of life can blow, and blow hard, but you are a deeply rooted tree, and winds just make you even stronger.

And when they are done blowing, there you still stand. Offering shade and shelter, flowers and fruit. Strong and lasting.

22
Be Mindful

As we saw in the introduction to this book, the movements of information through your nervous system—which is what I mean by "mental activity," most of which is unconscious—can create lasting changes in brain structure: "neurons that fire together, wire together." In particular, this rewiring is accelerated for what's in the field of focused attention. In effect, attention is like a combination spotlight and vacuum cleaner: it illuminates what it rests upon and then sucks it into your brain.

Since attention is largely under volitional control—you can direct it with conscious effort—you have an extraordinary tool at your disposal all day long to gradually sculpt your brain in positive ways. Unfortunately, most people do not have very good control of their attention: it's hard for them to rest it where they want and keep it there—such as an important but boring meeting, or the sensations of one breath after another—and hard to pull it away from things that aren't helpful, like senseless worry, self-critical rumination, or too much TV. The reasons include temperament (for example, anxious, spirited), personal history (for example, losses or traumas that keep them on edge), and our hyper-stimulating, ADD-ish culture.

Happily, attention is very trainable. You really can develop better control of your spotlight/vacuum cleaner. This is where mindfulness comes in—which simply means being steadily aware of something. As you practice being mindful, you will gain more control over your attention.

You could be mindful of what's around you—perhaps key details at work, the deeper wants of your partner, flowers blooming and children smiling, or where you left the car keys. You could also be mindful of your inner world, such as soft feelings of hurt underneath brittle anger, your good intentions and basic decency, or unrealistic expectations that set you up for disappointment.

Mindfulness has lots of benefits. It brings important information about what's happening around you and inside you. It helps you witness your experience without being swept away by it, and to hold it in a larger context; as your mindful awareness increases, negative experiences have less impact on you. And the duration and intensity of what you are paying attention to tends to increase its traces in your brain. Consequently, mindfulness really helps you take in positive experiences.

To some extent, mindfulness has become associated with Buddhism, but all the world's religions and moral traditions value being mindful—rather than mindless!

Additionally, mindfulness is increasingly taught in secular settings such as hospitals, corporations, classrooms, professional sports, and military training.

Studies have shown that regular practices of mindfulness:

- Thicken cortical layers in regions of the brain that control attention (so you get better at attention itself) (Lazar et al. 2005)

- Add neural connection in the insula, a part of the brain that supports both self-awareness and empathy for the emotions of others (Lazar et al. 2005)

- Increase the relative activation of the left prefrontal cortex (behind the left side of your forehead), which helps control and reduce negative emotions (Davidson 2004)

- Strengthen your immune system (Davidson et al. 2003)

- Reduce the impact of pain and accelerate post-surgical recovery (Kabat-Zinn 2003; Kabat-Zinn, Lipworth, and Burney 1985)

Pretty great for a simple method—mindfulness—that you can use, privately and effectively, anywhere you go.

How

Mindfulness is natural. You are already mindful of many things each day. The problem is that most of us remain mindful for only a few seconds at a time. The trick is to have more "episodes" of mindfulness, and to lengthen and deepen them.

So, set aside a minute or more every day to be deliberately mindful—focusing on a specific object of attention (e.g., the sensations of breathing) or opening wide to whatever moves through awareness. You could extend these moments of mindfulness into a longer period of meditation, letting your mind become increasingly clear and peaceful.

Then, throughout the day, add some additional times of mindfulness when you remain stably present with whatever is happening around you and inside you. If you like, use recurring events such as meals, a telephone ringing, or walking through a doorway as reminders to be mindful.

It will support and deepen your mindfulness to bring an attitude of curiosity, openness, non-judgmental acceptance, and even a kind of friendliness to the things you're aware of. Also try to develop a background awareness of how mindful you are being; in effect, you are paying attention . . . to attention, in order to get better at it.

These practices will gradually train your brain to be more mindful, which will bring you many rewards. For as William James—the first major American psychologist—wrote over a century ago (1890, p. 424): "The faculty of voluntarily bringing back a wandering attention, over and over again, is the very root of judgment, character, and will . . . An education which should improve this faculty would be *the* education *par excellence*."

23
Be Patient

It's fine to want things to happen in a proper and timely way. But what if you need to hang in there for several years in your current job before you can move on to a better one, or you're stuck on hold listening to elevator music, going to the mailbox each day for a long-awaited letter, or trying to get a squirming toddler into a car seat? Now what?

Patience means handling delay, difficulty, or discomfort without getting aggravated. Circumstances are what they are, but patience protects you from their impact like a shock absorber.

In contrast, impatience interprets circumstances as you being hindered or mistreated, so you feel frustrated, let down, or annoyed. Then insistence comes in: "This must change!" But by definition you can't fulfill that commandment (otherwise, there'd be nothing to get impatient about). Impatience combines all three ingredients of toxic stress: unpleasant experiences, pressure or urgency, and lack of control.

Impatience with others contains implicit criticism and irritation—and people want to get away from both of these. Just recall how you feel when someone is impatient with you. Or consider how others react when you are impatient with them.

Impatience is dissatisfaction; it is resistance to the way it is. Patience senses a fundamental alrightness, the doorway to contentment. Impatience is angry; patience is peaceful. Impatience narrows down onto what's "wrong," while patience keeps you wide open to the big picture. Impatience can't stand unpleasant feelings; patience helps you tolerate physical and emotional discomfort. Impatience wants rewards *now*; patience helps you tolerate delayed gratification, which fosters increased success and sense of worth.

Patience may seem like a superficial virtue, but actually it embodies a deep insight into the nature of things: they're intertwining, messy, imperfectible, and usually not about you. Patience also contains a wonderful teaching about desire: wish for something, sure, but be at peace when you can't have it. Patience knows you can't make the river flow any faster.

How

For an overview, reflect on these questions:

- What does patience feel like? Impatience?

- How do you feel about someone who's really patient? And about someone who's really impatient?

- What makes you impatient?

- What helps you stay patient?

In challenging situations:

- Try to step back from thoughts that make you impatient, such as righteousness, superiority, or insistence. Remember that standards differ among persons and cultures. Remind yourself that there is (usually) nothing truly urgent.

- Be aware of any body sensations or emotions triggered by delay or frustration—and see if you can tolerate them without reacting with impatience. Relax your body, come into the present moment, and open to feeling that you are basically all right right now.

- Rather than feeling that you are "wasting" time, find things that are rewarding in situations that try your patience; for example, look around and find something beautiful. Pay attention to your breath while relaxing your body, and wish others well. Similarly, rather than viewing yourself as "waiting in" situations, explore the sense of "being in" them. Enjoy the time being.

- Try to have compassion for others who seem to be in the way or taking too long. For example, a pet peeve of mine is people who stand in the middle of public doorways, but lately I've been realizing they have no idea they're blocking others.

- Pick a conversation—or even a relationship altogether—and deliberately bring more patience to it. You could react more slowly and thoughtfully (and never interrupt), let the other person have more time to talk, and allow minor issues to slide by.

- Play with routine situations—such as a meal—and take a few extra seconds or minutes before starting, in order to strengthen your patience muscles.

- Offer patience as a *gift*—to others, dealing with their own issues, and to yourself, wanting true happiness. Life is like a vast landscape with both soft grass and sharp thorns; impatience rails at the thorns; patience puts on a pair of shoes.

24
Enjoy Humility

Some might think that humility means being less than others, a doormat, second-class, or self-effacing.

But actually, it's none of these. *Humility* just means that you're stepping out of the rat race of self-glorification. You're not trying to build up your ego, impress people, or compete with others for status. You're not preoccupied with yourself. What a relief!

The root of the word "humble," comes from the Latin for "ground." With humility, you abide like the earth itself: solid, unpretentious, creating value without fanfare.

Humility is not humiliation. In fact, relaxed humility builds your confidence: you know your intentions are honorable, and you expect that others will probably be supportive.

In relationships, humility creates comfort and ease. It's like an open hand, empty of the weapons of superiority, scorn, or self-importance. You're receptive to others, not presuming your own infinite wisdom; as a result, they're less likely to feel criticized, and less likely to get defensive or competitive with you. Not chasing praise, you become more aware of your natural worth—which becomes easier for others to see as well; the less you focus on being appreciated, the more appreciation you'll get.

Humility embodies wisdom. It recognizes that everyone, including the grandest, is humbled by needing to depend on a vast web—of people, technology, culture, nature, sunlight, and biochemistry—to live a single day. Fame is soon forgotten. At the end of it all, we're each reduced to dust. Humility helps you be at peace with these facts.

How

Healthy humility is grounded in healthy self-worth. Feeling humble does *not* mean feeling inadequate. If you're like me and self-worth has been an issue, take steps over time to deepen your felt recognition of your own good qualities with the practices of *taking in the good* and *seeing the good in yourself* (chapters 2 and 5). Be mindful of any challenges to self-worth that could lead you to compensate with overconfidence, puffing up your reputation, or preemptive strikes of superiority.

Nor does being humble mean tolerating mistreatment. Speak up and do what you can. Knowing that you are prepared to be assertive makes it easier to relax into the unguardedness of humility.

A humble person wishes all beings well—including oneself. You can still dream big dreams (chapter 40) and help them come true. With humility, you pursue excellence, not fame.

Be honest with yourself about any ways you are *not* humble, any times you've been cocky, pretentious, promoting yourself with exaggerations, or entitled. In particular, try to catch any antihumility in your relationships, such as acting one-up or better-than, or being (even subtly) dismissive or devaluing. Instead, flow more with others: be modest, don't always try to win the point, don't interrupt, and don't claim more than your share of air time or credit.

In your brain, the background murmurings of self-centered preoccupations—*I sounded really good there . . . Hope they thought so . . . I wish people praised me more . . . I want to be special*—are supported by networks in the top middle portions of your cortex. When you step out of that stream and are simply present with what is, without turning it into a story about yourself, different networks come to the fore, on the sides (especially right) of your head (Farb et al. 2007). You can stimulate these networks and thus strengthen some of the neural substrates of humility by:

- Taking a panoramic, big-picture view of situations and your part in them
- Sensing your breath as a unified whole, with all the sensations of it appearing in awareness as a

single gestalt (rather than attention skipping from sensation to sensation as it typically does)

Explore humility on a global scale. For example, notice any beliefs that your political viewpoint, nation, or spirituality is superior to that of others. Also consider your consumption of the planet's resources from the perspective of humility; are there any changes you'd like to make?

Throughout, be aware of the rewards of humility. Enjoy how it makes your day simpler, keeps you out of conflicts with others, and brings you peace.

25
Pause

Doing therapy with a child who's learning better self-control, sometimes I'll ask if he or she would like to ride a bike with no brakes. The answer—even from the most spirited ones—is always no. They understand that no brakes mean either a boring ride or a crash; paradoxically, brakes let you go fast and have the most fun.

It's the same in life. Whether you're faced with criticism at work, a partner whose feelings are hurt, an internal urge to lash out verbally, or an opportunity for some gratification that will cost you later, you've got to be able to put on the brakes for a moment—to *pause*. Otherwise, you'll likely crash, one way or another.

Your brain works through a combination of excitation and inhibition: gas pedals and brakes. Only about 10 percent of its neurons are inhibitory, but without their vital influence, it's your brain that would crash. For example, individual neurons that are over-stimulated will die, and seizures involve runaway loops of excitation.

In daily life, pausing provides you with the gift of time. Time to let other people have their say without feeling interrupted. Time for you to find out what's really going on, calm down and get centered, sort out your priorities, and craft a good response. Time both to bring cool reason to hot feelings, and to enable wholeheartedness to soften hard-edged positions. Time for the "better angels of your nature" to take flight in your mind.

How

Let yourself *not* act. Sometimes we get so caught up in nev-erending doing that it becomes a habit. Make it okay with yourself to simply *be* from time to time.

A few times a day, stop for a few seconds and tune in to what's going on for you, especially beneath the surface. Use this pause to make space for your experience, like airing out a long-closed closet into a big room. Catch up with yourself.

Before beginning a routine activity, take a moment to become fully present. Try this with meals, starting the car, brushing your teeth, taking a shower, or answering the phone.

After someone finishes speaking to you, take a little longer than usual before you reply. Let the weight of the other person's words—and more importantly, the person's underlying wants and feelings—really sink in. Notice how this pause affects you—and affects the other person's response to you.

If an interaction is delicate or heated, slow it down. You can do this on your own even if the other person keeps rat-a-tat-tatting away. Without being deliberately annoying, you could allow a few seconds more silence (or even longer) before you respond, or speak in a more measured way.

If need be, pause the interaction altogether by suggesting you talk later, calling time out, or (last resort) telling the other person you're done for now and hanging up the phone. In most relationships, you do not need the permission of the other person to end an interaction! Of course, pausing a conversation (which may have become an argument) midstream is more likely to go well if you also propose another, realistic time to resume.

Before doing something that could be problematic—like getting high, putting a big purchase on a credit card, firing off an irritated e-mail, or talking about person A to person B—stop and forecast the consequences. Try to imagine them in living color: the good, the bad, and the ugly. Then make your choice.

Last, for a minute or more each day, pause globally. Just sit, as a body relaxed and breathing. Letting thoughts and feelings come and go as they will, not chasing after them. Nowhere you need to go, nothing you need to do, no one you need to be. Paused from doing, sinking into being.

26
Have Insight

By *insight*, I mean understanding yourself, particularly how your mind constructs your reactions to things.

Let's say I've just come home from a frazzling day of work, and my wife gives me a hug and then asks in passing, "Did you get any eggs?" (which we had not discussed; I hadn't known we needed any)—and I get irritated, tense in my body, and a little sad. What's happening here?

Her casual, neutral question about the eggs—the *stimulus*—led to a *response* of irritation, tension, and sadness *due to* several factors at work in my mind: stress, a sensitivity to possible criticism (that I had forgotten the eggs) from growing up with a fault-finding (although very loving) mother, and my guilt about not doing enough housework. If those factors disappeared, so would my upset.

Recall a moderately irritating or worrying situation of your own: what were your reactions to it, and *why* were you reacting that way? Consider stress, fatigue, your temperament, how you interpret certain events, your history with the others involved, and the impact of your childhood.

As with everybody else, your reactions come from *causes* inside your mind. Therefore, if you can change the causes, you can change your reactions for the better:

- Seeing, in the moment, how your mind has colored your perceptions and turbocharged your emotions can transform your reactions—sometimes rapidly and dramatically, like waking up from a bad dream.

- Over time, you can gradually alter or get better control over the mental factors that wear on your well-being, relationships, and effectiveness.

How

Begin by shifting attention away from the external causes of your reactions—like what someone said to you—and toward the causes *inside your own mind,* such as how you interpret what was said, attribute intentions to the speaker, or feel especially prickly because of your history with that person.

The mind is like a great mansion, with cozy dens, dusty closets, and dank cellars. Insight explores it, opening closed doors and making sense of what it finds: sometimes a treasure chest, sometimes smelly old shoes—though truly, it's usually treasure, including your natural goodness, sincere efforts, and lovingkindness.

Nonetheless, it can feel scary to look around (especially in those cellars); these suggestions could help you keep going:

- Remember the benefits of insight. For example, I'm very independent, so I remind myself that the main forces controlling me are actually inside my own head (e.g., beliefs left over from childhood); understanding them reduces their power over me.

- Bring to mind the feeling of being with someone who cares about you—like a friend walking with you down a dark street. As they say in AA: "The mind is a dangerous neighborhood; don't go in alone."

- Regard what you find without making it good or bad. It's not *you*. It's only a sensation, feeling, thought, or want arising in a room in your mind. Try to be accepting rather than self-critical, compassionate rather than shaming. Everybody, me included, has wild stuff in the mind; it's a jungle in there!

Drawing on the resources in the bullet points just above, look around inside your mind. Now sense beneath the surface and ask yourself one or more of these questions:

- What is softer—such as hurt, sadness, or fear—below hard and defended stuff like anger or justifications?

- What am I really wanting, deep down? What are the good desires underlying bad behaviors? Such as the normal desire for safety at the root of anxious rumination.

- What material here is from a time when I was younger? (For example, because I was often excluded from groups in school, I still sometimes feel like an outsider in groups when I'm really not.)

- What am I getting stuck on? Like fixating on a position or goal—or even a word. What am I trying to control that's not controllable (e.g., whether someone loves me)?

- How is my gender shaping my reactions? Or my temperament, cultural and ethnic background, or personality?

You can use these methods for insight on the fly, when things come up for you. And you can use them to drill down into a specific issue, such as sensitivity to criticism, longing for approval, tension with your parents, or efforts to get into a good relationship

Whatever you find, try to relax and open to it. Helpful or unhelpful, it's just furniture in the mansion of your mind.

27

Use Your Will

Life has challenges. To meet them, you need to be able to push through difficulties, stretch for other people, restrain problematic desires while pursuing wholesome ones, and do the hard thing when you must.

This means using your will.

We commonly equate will with willpower—the deliberate application of vigorous effort, such as lifting the last, strenuous rep of weight in a gym.

But will is a larger matter: it's a *context of commitment*, as for a mother devoted to the care of her family. Will is giving yourself over to your highest purposes, which lift you and carry you along. This kind of will feels like being pulled by inspiration rather than pushed by stubbornness. Surrendered rather than driven.

How

What does it actually mean, to make your highest purposes the engine of your life? As a framework for the answer, I'd like to draw on four qualities of a strongly dedicated person identified by the Buddha which have meant a lot to me personally: *ardent, resolute, diligent,* and *mindful.* Please consider how each of these could help you be more willful in one or more key areas, such as being braver in intimate relationships, completing your education, doing your fair share of housework, or sticking with a diet.

Ardent (a variation on ardor) means wholehearted, enthusiastic, and eager. Not dry, mechanical, or merely dogged. For example, why do you *care* about what happens in this aspect of your life, why does it *matter*? Let yourself be heartfelt and passionate about your aims and activities here.

Resolute means you are wholly committed and unwavering. Bring to mind an experience of absolute determination, such as a time you protected a loved one. You may feel a firming in the chest, a sense of every bit of you pulling for the same thing. Explore this feeling as it might apply to a particular part of your life. Imagine yourself staying resolute here as you face temptations—saying no, for example, to the donuts offered in a meeting—and take in the ways this would feel good to you. Get in touch with your resolve each morning, surrender to it, and let it guide you through the day.

Diligent means you are conscientious and thorough. Not as a grind, not from guilt or compulsion, but because—from the Latin root for "diligence"—you "love, take delight in" the stepping stones toward your higher purposes. This is where ardency and resolution often break down, so to help yourself:

- Keep in mind the reasons for your efforts; open to and try to feel their rewards, such as knowing that you are doing the best you can in the service of a good cause and deserve what's called "the bliss of blamelessness."

- Translate big purposes into small, doable daily actions. Don't let yourself get overwhelmed.

- Find the structures, routines, and allies that help you keep going.

- Tell the truth to yourself about what's actually happening. Are you doing what you had intended to do? If you're not, admit it to yourself. Then start over: re-find your wholehearted commitment, see what there is to do, and do it.

Mindful means that you know if you're being willful or lackadaisical. You're aware of your inner world, of the mental factors that block the will (e.g., self-doubt, lethargy, distractibility) and those that fuel it (e.g., enthusiasm, strength, grit, tenacity). You recognize if you've grown willful to a fault, caught up in purposes that are outdated or not worth their cost. You're able to make skillful course corrections that keep you aligned with your highest purposes.

Last, *enjoy* your will. Exercising it can get kind of grim if you're not careful. But actually, a person can be both lighthearted and strong-willed. Take pleasure in the strength in your will, and the fruits it brings you.

28
Take Refuge

In Hawaii one time, my wife Jan and I visited a "place of refuge." People fleeing for their lives could come there and be sheltered. Related customs exist around the world; for example, in medieval Europe, a person could take refuge in a church and be protected there.

Less formally, we all need everyday refuges from challenges, sorrows, and the occasional sheer craziness of the world. Otherwise, you get too exposed to the cold winds of life, and too drained by the daily round. Without refuge, after awhile you can feel like you're running on empty.

Refuges include people, places, memories, and ideas—anyone or anything that provides reliable sanctuary and protection, that's reassuring, comforting, and supportive, so you can let down your guard and gather strength and wisdom.

A refuge could be curling up in bed with a good book, having a meal with friends, or making a To Do list to organize your day. Or remembering your grandmother, feeling strength in your body, trusting the findings of science, talking with a trusted friend or counselor, having faith, or reminding yourself that although you're not rich, you're financially okay.

The world's religions also have refuges that may speak to you, such as sacred settings, texts, individuals, teachings, rituals, objects, and congregations.

Personally, one of my favorite refuges is *practice* itself: the theme of this book. It makes me feel good to trust that if I keep plugging away, then I can gradually become happier and more loving.

What gives you a sense of refuge?

How

Make a written or mental list of at least a few things that are refuges for you. And if you can, take a moment each day to consciously take refuge in those things.

You can "take refuge" in several ways:

- *Go to* a refuge

- *Come from* a refuge

- *Abide as* a refuge

- Sense a refuge *at work in your life*

Personally, it's been a breakthrough to imagine that my refuges already exist inside me, that I can live *from* them, as an expression of them in this life. When you take refuge in this way, you are giving yourself over to wholesome forces, and letting them work through you and carry you along.

You can take refuge explicitly, with words, by saying things in your mind like *I take refuge in* _____ . Or *I abide as* _____ . Or _____ *flows through me.*

Or just sense the refuge without words: feel what it is like for you to be in it, safe and supported, *home.*

Then repeat your way of taking refuge for each of your refuges. Try to do this every day, as soon as you remember to do so. It only takes a few minutes or less. And you can even do it in the middle of traffic or a meeting.

Once you have finished taking refuge, sense the good feelings and thoughts sinking deeply into you, filling you up, and weaving themselves into your being—a resource and inner light that you'll take with you wherever you go.

29

Risk the Dreaded Experience

When things happened to you as a child—or you saw them happening to others—you naturally formed expectations about what you'd likely feel in similar situations in the future. Based on these expectations, you developed responses: do *this* to get pleasure, do *that* to avoid pain. Then experiences in adulthood added additional, related expectations and responses.

Consequently, the following sequence routinely happens inside you, me, and everyone else many times a day—usually within a few seconds and often unconsciously:

1. A feeling or desire emerges in the mind, seeking expression.

2. This activates an associated expectation of emotional pain (from subtle unease to extreme

trauma) if the feeling or desire is expressed; this pain is the "dreaded experience."

3. This expectation triggers an inhibition of the original feeling or desire in order to avoid risking the dreaded experience.

For example, (1) you'd like more caring from someone, but (2) your childhood has led you to be cautious about revealing those vulnerable longings, so (3) you play it safe and don't ask for anything.

Take a moment to find one or more ways that this sequence—(1) an *emerging self-expression* leads to (2) an *associated expectation*, which leads to (3) an *inhibiting response*—unfolds in your mind. Here are some examples:

- (1) You want to get closer (e.g., emotionally, physically) to someone, but (2) moving closer exposes you to the risk of rejection, so (3) you do something that is distancing.

- (1) A feeling comes up (e.g., sadness, anger) but (2) expressing this feeling (or feelings in general) was discouraged in your childhood, so (3) you change the subject, make a joke, or otherwise move away from the emotion.

- (1) A desire arises to make something happen (e.g., aim for a new goal at work, write a song, plant a garden), but (2) you fear being unsuccessful, unsupported, scorned, or thwarted if you stick your neck out, so (3) you set aside your dream one more day.

Sometimes this is reasonable. For instance, (1) the urge to tell your boss to stuff it (2) prompts an expectation of big trouble if you do, (3) so you keep quiet.

But if you're like me and most people, your expectations of pain are often unreasonable. The negativity bias of the brain makes you overestimate both the likelihood of a bad outcome from self-expression and the amount of pain you'll feel if something bad actually happens. Further, the deep-down expectations that most shape self-expression developed when you were a child, so it is normal for them to be:

- Concrete, simplistic, and rigid—even though now you can think in more abstract, complex, and flexible ways

- Based on a time when you (a) were stuck with certain people (e.g., family members, peers), (b) had few resources, and (c) felt pain keenly—even though now you have much more (a) choice in your relationships, (b) assertiveness, money, and other resources, and (c) capacity to cope with pain.

These unreasonable expectations lead to responses that are needlessly pinched and cramped: we numb out internally, muzzle ourselves, stay safe and distant in relationships, and shrink our dreams. The experiences we dread hem us in, like taboo lands surrounding a shrinking little pasture, controlling us, telling us: "Don't chance that, live smaller." And most of the time, we suffer these costs without even realizing it.

What's the alternative?

It's to risk the dreaded experience—and reap the rewards that result. For example:

⚜ (1) Wishing for something from an intimate partner, (2) you feel nervous about saying it, yet you know it's likely to be well-received and that you'll be fundamentally all right if it's not, so (3) you decide to speak up and risk feeling let down—and with some zigs and zags, it works out pretty well.

⚜ (1) You don't feel your boss fully appreciates your abilities, but (2) he reminds you of your critical father and you dread those old feelings of hurt and low worth if you ask for more challenging (and interesting) assignments. So you plan carefully and identify a project he'll probably support, and you bring to mind, again and again, positive experiences of feeling seen and valued by others to help you cope if he is dismissive of you. (3) Having done your homework, you approach your boss with strength and clarity, which increases your odds of success.

⚜ (1) You want to start a business. (2) Even though you worry about looking like a fool if it fails, you remind yourself that most people respect those who stick their necks out and have an entrepreneurial spirit. (3) So you start that business and do your best, at peace with whatever may happen.

How

Start by *observing* how this sequence proceeds in your mind: (1) self-expression → (2) expectation of pain → (3) inhibition. This is the most important step (which is why the explanation above is longer than usual). You'll frequently see it in retrospect, when you replay a response you had in a situation—a (3)—and realize that its *function* was to shut down your self-expression. At bottom, many of our reactions are strategies (often unconscious ones) for avoiding a dreaded experience.

Next, *challenge your expectations.* Are they really true? Help yourself appreciate the *fact* that expressing your emotions and wants—in reasonably skillful ways—will usually lead to good results. Speak to yourself like a wise, firm, and encouraging swim coach talking you through the first time you dove into a pool, with lines like *Other people have done this; it turned out okay for them and it can be the same for you. You have the abilities to make this work. Yes, it won't be perfect and might be uncomfortable, but you will be all right. I believe in you. Believe in yourself.*

Then, move out of your comfort zone by *taking calculated risks.* Start with easy situations in which the odds of self-expression causing a bad result are small—and even if the bad result were to occur, it would be only mildly uncomfortable for you. Then work your way up the ladder of increasingly vulnerable and high-stakes self-expression. A wonderful freedom grows in the heart as you do this; you're less cowed by dreaded experiences and not clipping your wings to avoid them. If a particular self-expression does lead to a painful result for you, notice that you can cope with this pain and that it soon comes to an end, and absorb the reasonable lessons (e.g., it's not wise to confide in a certain friend). Overall, you could well decide that it's worth occasionally feeling some pain in order to gain the much greater pleasures of fuller self-expression.

Last, *take it in* when you risk self-expression and it turns out fine (as it usually does). Really highlight it in your mind when pessimistic expectations don't come true, or when feared events do occur but they're not all that upsetting. Open to the satisfaction of expressing yourself, and let it sink in. Feel the healthy pride and self-respect earned by being brave enough to dive in.

30
Aspire without Attachment

To live is to pursue goals. Out of healthy self-interest and kindness to yourself, it's natural and fine to seek security, success, comfort, enjoyment, creative expression, physical and mental health, connection, respect, love, self-actualization, and spiritual development.

The question is whether you go after your goals with stress and drivenness—in a word, with *attachment*—or with outer effort and inner peacefulness, rewarded by the journey itself no matter the destination: with *aspiration*.

The difference between attachment and aspiration got really clear for me one time in Boulder, Colorado, where I'd gone with my old friend Bob for a week of rock climbing. Our guide, Dave, asked us what our goals were, and I said I wanted to climb 5.11 (a stiff grade) by the end of the week; at that point I could barely climb 5.8. Bob stared at me and then said this was crazy, that I'd only get frustrated and disappointed (Bob's pretty driven, and doesn't like falling short). I said no, that it would be a win for me either way: my goal was so ambitious that if I failed to reach it there'd be no shame, and if I did manage to fulfill it, wow, that would be a ton of fun. So I kept banging away, getting steadily better: 5.8, 5.9, easy 5.10, hard 5.10 . . . and then on the last day, I followed Dave without a fall on solid 5.11. Yay!

At the heart of attachment is *craving*—broadly defined—which contains and leads to many kinds of suffering (from subtle to intense). And while it may be an effective goad for a while—the stick that whips the horse into a lather—in the long run it is counterproductive, when that horse keels over. On the other hand, aspiration—working hard toward your goals without getting hung up on the results—feels good, plus it helps you stretch and grow without worrying about looking bad. Paradoxically, holding your goals lightly increases the chance of attaining them, while being attached—and thus fearing failure—gets in the way of peak performance.

If you sit on the couch your whole life and never take care of or go after anything important, you can avoid the pitfalls of attachment. But if you have a job, intimate relationship, family, service, art, or spiritual calling, the challenge is to stay firm in your course, with dedication and discipline, centered in aspiration.

How

Aspiration is about *liking,* while attachment is about *wanting*—and these involve separate systems in your brain (Berridge and Robinson 1998; Pecina, Smith, and Berridge 2006). Liking what is pleasant and disliking what is unpleasant are normal and not a problem. Trouble comes when we tip into the craving and strain inherent in wanting, wanting, wanting what's pleasant to continue and what's unpleasant to end. So learn to recognize the differences between liking and wanting in your body, emotions, attitudes, and thoughts. I think you'll find that liking feels open, relaxed, and flexible while wanting feels tight, pressed, contracted, and fixated.

Then, see if you can stay with liking without slipping into wanting:

- Help little alarm bells to go off in your mind— Alert! Caution!—when you get that familiar feeling of wanting/craving, especially when it's subtle and floating around in the back of your mind.

- Relax any sense of "gotta have it." Feel into the ways your life is and will be basically all right even if you don't attain a particular goal. Seek results from a place of fullness, not scarcity or lack.

◦ Try to remain relatively peaceful—even in the midst of passionate activity—since intensity, tension, fear, and anger all fuel strong wanting.

◦ Release any fixation on a certain outcome. Recognize that all you can do is tend to the causes, but you can't force the results (chapter 37).

◦ Keep the sense of "me" to a minimum. Success or failure will come from dozens of factors, only a few of which are under your control. Win or lose, don't take it personally.

Along the way, watch out for the widespread belief that if you're not fiercely driven toward your goals, you're kind of a wimp. Remember that you can have strong effort toward your aims without falling into attachment to the results. Consider the description I once heard of Thich Nhat Hanh, a Vietnamese monk who has accomplished many things as a peace advocate and teacher:

A cloud, a butterfly, and a bulldozer

31
Keep Going

I once attended a workshop led by Joseph Goldstein, a Buddhist teacher. I had realized something about the lack of a fixed self, and shared the insight with him. He nodded and said, "Yes, right." I felt seen for taking a step forward. Then he smiled and added something I've never forgotten: "Keep going."

Of all the factors that lead to happiness and success—such as class origins, intelligence, personality, character, looks, luck, race,—the one that typically makes the most difference over time is *persistence*. Knocked down ten times, you get up ten times.

If you keep going, you *might* not reach your goal—but if you stop, you'll *never* reach it.

We respect people who persist. There's a magic in determination that draws others toward it and elicits their support.

And you just don't know when your day will finally come. There are so many stories of "overnight success" that actually arrived after many years of effort, often including some failures. For example, Dwight Eisenhower was an obscure colonel in 1939—and nearly forty-nine years old—when Germany invaded Poland to begin World War II; four years later he was in charge of all Allied forces in Europe; nine years after that he was elected president.

How

Make sure your goals are worthy of your perseverance. You can be determined to a fault. Don't "keep going" down a tunnel with no cheese. Consider the collateral damage: are you winning battles but losing the "war" of overall health, well-being, integrity, and welfare of others?

Know the feeling of tenacious persistence. It could be fierce, strong, stubborn, unyielding, clear, inspired, surrendered, on-mission, purposeful, focused, committed— or all of these. Recall a time you had this feeling, and know it again in your body. Call it up whenever you need to draw on resources inside to keep going.

Take the step that's right in front of you—one after another. I've taught many people to rock climb: Beginners will often have one foot down low and one foot at knee level, on solid placements, plus two good handholds, yet they can't find any new holds, so they feel stuck. But when they simply stand up on the higher foothold—taking the step that's available—that brings higher handholds and footholds within reach.

Find the pace you can sustain; life's a marathon, not a sprint. For example, on my first Boy Scout backpack trip, I was a skinny, nerdy, unathletic kid. But I wanted to be the first to our campsite. We set out and the burly "alpha" boys raced ahead, while I kept up a slow-but-steady pace. After a few miles, I passed them sitting down on the side of the trail. They were startled to see me trucking along and soon got up and raced past me. But after another few miles, once again they were laid out by the side of the trail, this time really fried as I walked past them—and I was very happy to get the first, really cool tent spot.

Keep going in your mind even if you can't make any headway in the world. Maybe you're truly stuck in some situation—a job, an illness, a certain sort of marriage. But at least you can continue to reflect on what's happening, learn to cope with it better, and love the people around you. And over time maybe things will improve. As Winston Churchill said, "If you're going through hell, keep going."

Have faith that your efforts will pay off. You may have heard this teaching story: A bunch of frogs fell into a vat of cream. They couldn't jump out, and one after another drowned. But one frog refused to quit and kept swimming and staying alive, even after all the other frogs had died. Finally its movements churned the cream to solid butter—and it hopped out to safety.

Keep churning!

part four:

Engage the World

32

Be Curious

A couple years ago, my father and I were driving to the ocean, near where I live north of San Francisco. Born on a ranch in North Dakota in 1918, he's a retired zoologist who loves birds, and I wanted to show him some wetlands.

The twisting road was carved from the side of coastal hills plunging to the sea. After a while we paused at a pull-out for a pit stop. Returning from the bushes, I found my dad scrutinizing dried, scraggly grasses sticking out from the mini-cliff next to our car. "Look, Rick," he said excitedly, "see how the layers of dirt are different, so the plants growing in them are different, too!" He sounded like a little kid who'd discovered an elephant in his backyard.

But that's my dad: endlessly curious, never bored. I and ten thousand other drivers had sped around that turn seeing nothing but another meaningless road cut. But he had not taken the commonplace for granted. He wondered about what he saw and looked for connections, explanations. For him, the world wears a question mark.

This attitude of wonder, interest, and investigation brings many rewards. For example, engaging your mind actively as you age helps preserve the functioning of your brain. Use it or lose it!

Plus you gather lots of useful information—about yourself, other people, the world—by looking around. You also see the larger context, and thus become less affected by any single thing itself: not so driven to get more of what you like, and not so stressed and unsettled by what you don't like.

As our daughter once pointed out, curious people are typically not self-centered. Sure, they are interested in the inner workings of their own psyche—curiosity is a great asset for healing, growth, and awakening—but they're also very engaged with the world and others. Maybe that's why we usually like curious people.

How

To begin with, curiosity requires a *willingness* to see whatever is under the rocks you turn over. Usually it's neutral or positive. But occasionally you find something that looks creepy or smells bad. Then you need courage, to face an uncomfortable aspect of yourself, other people, or the world. In this case, it helps to observe it from a distance, and try not to identify with it. Surround it with spaciousness, knowing that whatever you've found is just one part of a larger whole and (usually) a passing phenomenon.

With that willingness, curiosity expresses itself in action, through looking deeper and wider—and then looking again.

Much of what we're curious about is really neat, such as the development of children, the doings of friends, or the workings of a new computer. And sometimes it pays to be curious about some sort of issue. As an illustration, let's say you've been feeling irritable about a situation. (You also can apply the practices below to different aspects of your mind, or to other people or to situations in the world.)

Looking deeper means being interested in what's under the surface. For example, what previous situations does it remind you of—particularly ones when you were young and most affected by things?

Looking wider means broadening your view:

- What are other aspects of the situation, such as the good intentions of others, or your own responsibility for events?

- What factors could be at work in your mind? For example, have you worked too much lately, or felt underappreciated, or not eaten or slept well? Did you appraise the situation as a lot worse, or a lot more threatening, than it actually was? Did you take it personally?

Looking again means being active in your investigating. You keep unraveling the knot of whatever you're curious about, teasing apart the threads, opening them up and seeing what's what. You don't take the first explanation as the final one. There's an underlying attitude of wonder and fearlessness. Like a child, a cat, a scientist, a saint, or a poet, you see the world anew.

Again.

And again.

33
Enjoy Your Hands

Sometimes it's worth remembering the obvious: you engage the world with your *body*—often with your *hands*.

Human hands are unique in the animal kingdom in their dexterity and sensitivity. Their capacity for skilled action helped drive the evolution of the neural networks that handle sophisticated planning, decision-making, and self-control.

Your hands reach, touch, caress, hold, manipulate, and let go. They type, stir pots, brush hair, wash dishes, shift gears, scratch ears, open doors, throw stones, hold loved ones, and help you snuggle into bed. They may not be perfect, and with aging, they may sometimes be in pain, but they're always lovely and vital.

Appreciating your hands makes you appreciate living. Being mindful of them—paying attention to what they're feeling and doing—is a simple and available way to drop down into a more sensual, in-the-body connection with the world, including the people you touch.

How

Right now, take a moment to be aware of your hands. What are they doing? What are they touching? They are always touching something, if only the air. What are they sensing? Warm or cool? Hard or soft?

Move your fingertips. Notice how incredibly sensitive they are, with about 20,000 nerve endings per square inch. Play with the sensations of your fingers stroking your palm, your thumb touching each finger in turn, the fingers of one hand caressing the fingers of the other one.

Soak up the enjoyment your hands give you. Use your hands to draw you into pleasure such as the warmth of holding a cup of coffee, the relief of scratching an itchy head, or the satisfaction of getting a pesky button through its hole.

As appropriate, touch others more. Feel the grip of a handshake, a friend's shoulder, a lover's skin, a child's hair, a dog's or cat's fur.

Feel the skillfulness of your hands: steering a car, writing a note, replacing a lightbulb, sawing wood, planting bulbs, measuring garlic, peeling an onion. Feel their strength in holding a knife, making a fist, lugging a suitcase.

Watch your hands talk: pointing, rising and falling, opening and closing, thumbs-up, okay, waving hello and goodbye.

Many times a day, try to sink awareness into your hands.

Feel them feeling your life.

34
Don't Know

Once upon a time, a scholar and a saint lived on the same street, and they arranged to meet. The scholar asked the saint about the meaning of life. She said a few words about love and joy, then paused to reflect, and the scholar jumped in with a long discourse on Western and Eastern philosophy. When the scholar was finished, the saint proposed some tea, prepared it with care, and began pouring it slowly into the scholar's cup. Inch by inch the tea rose. It approached the lip of the cup, and she kept pouring. It ran over the top of the cup and onto the table, and she still kept pouring. The scholar burst out: "What are you doing?! You can't put more into a cup that's already full!" The saint set down the teapot and said, "Exactly."

A mind that's open and spacious can absorb lots of useful information. On the other hand, a mind that's already full—of assumptions, beliefs about the intentions of others, preconceived ideas—misses important details or contexts, jumps to conclusions, and has a hard time learning anything new.

For example, let's say a friend says something hurtful to you. What benefits would come from an initial attitude that's something like this: *Hmm, what's this about? I'm not sure, don't entirely know.* First, you'd buy yourself time to figure things out before putting your foot in your mouth. Second, you'd naturally investigate and learn more: Did you hear correctly? Did you do something wrong you should apologize for? Is something bothering your friend unrelated to you? Did your friend simply misunderstand you? Third, she'd probably be more open and less defensive with you; a know-it-all is pretty irritating.

The great child psychologist Jean Piaget proposed that there are essentially two kinds of learning:

- *Assimilation*—We incorporate new information into an existing belief system.

- *Accommodation*—We change a belief system based on new information.

Both are important, but accommodation is more fundamental and far-reaching. Nonetheless, it's harder to do, since abandoning or transforming long-held beliefs can feel dizzying, even frightening. That's why it's important to keep finding our way back to that wonderful openness a child has, seeing a cricket or toothbrush or mushroom for the very first time: child mind, beginner's mind . . . don't-know mind.

How

For a few minutes, or for a day, a week—or a lifetime—let yourself not know:

- Be especially skeptical of what you're sure is true. These are the beliefs that often get us in the most trouble.

- In conversation, don't assume you know where other people are headed. Don't worry about what you're going to say; you'll figure it out just fine when it's your turn. Remember how you feel when someone acts like they know what you're "really" thinking, feeling, or wanting.

- Let your eyes travel over familiar objects—like the stuff on a dinner table—and notice what it's like during that brief interval, maybe a second or so, after you've focused on an object but before the verbal label (e.g., "salt," "glass") has come into awareness.

- Or go for a walk. Notice how the mind tries to categorize and label—to know—the things around you, so it can solve problems and keep you alive. Appreciate your mind—"Good boy! Good girl!"—and then explore letting go of needing to know.

- Ask yourself if it's important to you to be a person with the right answers, the one who knows. What would it be like to lay down that burden?

❦ This may seem a little cosmic, but it's down-to-earth: Look at something and ask yourself if you know what it *is*. Suppose it's a cup. Do you really know what a "cup" is, deep down? You say it's made of atoms, of electrons, protons, quarks. But do you know what a quark is? You say it's energy, or space-time, or sparkling fairy dust beyond human ken, or whatever—but really, do you ever, can you ever, actually know what energy or space-time truly is?? We live our lives surrounded by objects that we navigate and manipulate—spoons, cars, skyscrapers—while never truly knowing what any of it actually *is*. And neither does anyone else, even the world's greatest scientists.

❦ Since you don't really know what a spoon is, do you even know what you are? Or what you are truly capable of? Or how high you could actually soar? Consider any limiting assumptions about your own life . . . how you've "known" that your ideas were not very good, that others would laugh (or that it would matter if they did), that no one would back you, that swinging for the fences just means striking out. What happens if you apply "don't know" to these assumptions?

❦ Notice how relaxing and good it feels to lighten up about needing to know. Take in those good feelings so you'll feel more comfortable hanging out in don't-know mind.

May you know less after this practice of not-knowing than when you began.

And therefore, know more than ever!

35
Do What You Can

Researchers have shown that it is remarkably easy to produce "learned helplessness" in dogs, whose neural circuitry for motivation and emotion is quite similar to ours. Then it takes much, much more training to get the dogs to unlearn their helpless passivity (Seligman 1972).

People are much the same. We, too, can be easily trained in learned helplessness, which can be tough to undo. Think about some of the ways you've felt pushed around by external forces, and how that's affected you. Learned helplessness fosters depression, anxiety, pessimism, low self-worth, and less effort toward goals.

As a human being like any other, your biological vulnerability to learned helplessness makes it very important that you *recognize* where you do in fact have some power, and that you take the actions that *are* available to you—even if they must be only inside your own head.

How

Begin by considering a useful idea from Stephen Covey's book *The Seven Habits of Highly Effective People*. Imagine a circle containing the things you have influence over, and another circle containing the things you're concerned about. Where those circles overlap is the sweet spot where you can actually make a difference in the things that matter to you.

To be sure, sometimes there are things we care about but can't change personally, like people going hungry. I'm not saying just ignore those things or be indifferent to them. We should focus on what we *can* do, such as bearing witness to the suffering of others and letting it move our hearts, staying informed, and looking for opportunities to make a material difference, such as helping at a homeless shelter.

But trying to control things that are out of your hands will plant seeds of helplessness, make you suffer, and undermine your capacity to exercise the influence you do have.

Ask yourself: How could I pull my time, money, energy, attention, or worry away from stones that will never give blood or houses built on sand—and instead, shift these resources to where they will *actually* make a difference?

Then take an inventory of the key strengths and other resources you *do* have. Your circle of influence is probably a lot bigger than you think it is!

Consider how you could draw on some of those resources to take beneficial actions in ways you haven't ever done, or have never sustained. Challenge assumptions, like: "Oh, I just couldn't do *that*." Are you sure? Bring to mind someone you know who is very self-confident, and then ask yourself: "If I were that confident, what new things would I do?"

In particular, think about actions you could take inside your own mind. Compared to trying to change the world or your body, usually your mind is where you have the most influence, where the results are most enduring and consequential, and where you have the greatest opportunity for a sense of efficacy and a chance to undo feelings of helplessness. For example, how could you nudge your emotional reactions in a better direction over time, or develop more mindfulness or warm-heartedness? These are all within your reach.

When I don't know what to do about some difficulty, sometimes I think of a saying from a boy named Nkosi Johnson, who lived in South Africa. Like many children there, Nkosi was born with HIV, and he died when he was twelve. Before that happened, he became a nationally known advocate for people with AIDS. His "mantra," as he called it, always touches my heart: "Do all you can, with what you have, in the time you have, in the place where you are."

That's all anyone can ever do.

36
Accept the Limits of Your Influence

The previous practice was to exercise the influence you *do* have: to do what you can.

Of course, it's also true that each one of us is very limited in what we can do or change. You can't change the past, or even this present moment. Looking to the future—the only thing you can actually affect—you have little influence over other people, including their thoughts, actions, or suffering. And even less influence over the economy, government policies, or international affairs. Things happen due to causes—and of the ten thousand causes upstream of this moment, most of them are out of your control.

You don't have the power to make something happen if the prerequisites aren't present. For example, you can't grow roses without good soil and water.

If you've been pounding your head against a wall for a while, it's time to stop, accept the way it is, and move on. As I sometimes tell myself: *Don't try to grow roses in a parking lot.*

How

In general, when faced with some fact you can't change—like you're stuck in traffic, or you feel sad, or your young daughter has just poured milk on the floor (speaking of some of my own experiences)—ask yourself, *Can I accept that this is the way it is, whether I like it or not?*

Understand that acceptance does *not* mean approval, acquiescence, overlooking, or forgiveness. You are simply facing the facts, including the fact of your limited influence.

Notice the good feelings that come with acceptance, even if there are also painful feelings about various facts. Notice that acceptance usually brings you more resources for dealing with life's difficulties.

If you cannot accept a fact—that it exists, that it has happened, whatever your preferences may be—then see if you can accept the fact that you cannot accept the fact!

More specifically, consider these reflections:

- Review a life event that has troubled you. See if you can accept it as something that happened, like it or not—and as truly just a part of a much larger and probably mainly positive whole.

◆ Consider an aspect of your body or personality that you don't like. Tell the truth to yourself about the extent to which you can change it and make a clear choice as to what you will actually do. Then see if you can accept whatever remains as just the way it is—and as only a small part of the much larger and generally positive whole that is you.

◆ Bring to mind a key person in your life. Have there been any ways that you've been trying to affect or change this person that are just not working? What limits to your influence here do you need to accept?

◆ Consider something you've wanted to happen but been frustrated about—perhaps a career shift, or a certain school working out for your child, or a sale to a new customer. Are the necessary supporting conditions truly present? If they are, then maybe stick with it and be patient. But if they are not present—if you're trying to grow roses in a parking lot—consider shifting your hopes and efforts in another direction.

37

Tend to the Causes

Let's say you want to have your own apple tree. So you go to a nursery and pick out a good sapling, bring it home, and plant it carefully with lots of fertilizer in rich soil. Then you water it regularly, pick the bugs off, and prune it. If you keep tending to your tree, in a few years it will likely give you lots of delicious apples.

But can you *make* it grow apples? Nope, you can't. All you can do is tend to the causes—but you can't control the results. No one can. The most powerful person in the world can't make a tree produce an apple.

Similarly, a teacher cannot make his students learn long division, a business owner can't make her employees invent new products, and you cannot make someone love you. All we can do is promote the causes of the results we want.

This truth has two implications, one tough-minded and another that's peaceful:

- You are responsible for the causes you *can* tend to. If you are not getting the results you want in your life, ask yourself: Am I truly doing everything I reasonably can to promote the causes of those results?

- You can relax attachment to results. When you understand that much of what determines whether they happen or not is out of your hands, you worry less about whether they'll happen, and you suffer less if they don't.

Paradoxically, focusing less on results and more on causes improves the odds of getting the results you want: you zero in on creating the factors that lead to success, and you aren't worn down by stressing over the outcome.

How

- Do what you can to lift your personal well-being. This is a *global* factor that will turbocharge all the other causes you tend to.

  So ask yourself: what makes the most difference to my well-being? It could be something that seems little; for me, a big factor is when I go to bed, since that determines whether I can wake up in time to meditate in the morning, which transforms my whole day. It could also mean dropping something that brings you down, like needless arguments with other people.

Pick *one* thing that will lift your well-being and focus on this for a while.

❧ Also consider a key area in your life where you are not getting the results you want, such as work, love, health, fun, or spirituality. In that area, identify one cause that will have big effects. For example, in a logjam, there's usually a "key log" that will free up the whole mess if you get *it* to move.

For example, if you want to lose weight, tend to the cause of exercise. If you want a mate, tend to the cause of meeting new "qualified prospects." If you want your kids to cooperate, tend to the cause of parental authority. If you want a better job, tend to the cause of an organized job search. If you want more peace of mind, tend to the cause of routinely relaxing your body.

❧ Tell the truth to yourself about causes and results: Are you pursuing the right causes of the results you're seeking? Or are you pulling hard on a rope (a cause) that's just not attached to the load you're trying to move (the result you want)?

Maybe you need to tend to other causes—perhaps ones at a deeper level, such as letting go of self-doubt or fear from childhood. Or perhaps the result you want is out of your power, and you just have to accept that.

❦ Let the results be what they are, learn from them, and then turn your attention back to causes. Don't get so caught up in your apples that you forget to water their tree!

38

Don't Be Alarmed

The nervous system has been evolving for about 600 million years. During all this time, creatures—worms, crabs, lizards, rats, monkeys, hominids, humans—that were real mellow, watching the sunlight on the leaves, getting all Zen, absorbed in inner peace . . . CHOMP got eaten because they didn't notice the shadow overhead or crackle of twigs nearby.

The ones that survived to pass on their genes were fearful and vigilant—and we are their great-great-grandchildren, bred to be afraid. Even though we've come a long way from the Serengeti, we're still quick to feel unsettled in any situation that seems the least bit threatening: not enough time to get through your e-mails, more news of a struggling economy, no call after two days from someone you've started dating, and so on.

Even if the situations you're in are reasonably good, there are other, innate sources of alarm rooted in our biology. Basically, to survive, animals—including us—must continually try to:

- ◄{ Separate themselves from the world
- ◄{ Stabilize many dynamic systems in the body, mind, relationships, and environment
- ◄{ Get rewards and avoid harms

But here's the problem: each of these strategies flies in the face of the facts of existence:

- ◄{ Everything is connected to everything else—so it's impossible to fundamentally separate self and world.
- ◄{ Everything changes—so it's impossible to keep things stable in the body, mind, relationships, or environment.
- ◄{ Rewards are fleeting, costly, or unobtainable, and some harms are inevitable—so it's impossible to hold onto pleasure forever and totally escape pain.

Alarms sound whenever one of these strategies runs into trouble—which is many times a day because of the contradictions between the nature of existence and what we must do to survive. Alarms below awareness create a background of unease, irritability, caution, and pessimism; the ones you're consciously aware of are emotionally and often physically uncomfortable—such as anxiety, anger, or pain.

Don't underestimate the amount of background alarm in your body and mind. It's hard-wired and relentless, inherent in the collision between the needs of life and the realities of existence.

While this alarmism has been a great strategy for keeping creatures alive to pass on their genes, it's not good for your health, well-being, relationships, or ambitions. Threat signals are usually way out of proportion to what is actually happening. They make you pull in your wings and play safe and small, and cling tighter to "us" and fear "them." At the level of groups and nations, our vulnerability to alarm makes us easy to manipulate with fear.

Yes, deal with real threats, real harms—but enough with all these false alarms!

How

Take a stand for yourself: "I'm tired of being needlessly afraid." Consider the price you've paid over the years due to false alarms: the running for cover, the muzzling of self-expression, the abandonment of important longings or aspirations.

Try to be more aware of the subtle sense of alarm, such as a tightening in your chest or face, a sinking feeling in your stomach, a sense of being off balance, or an increase in scanning or guardedness.

Then recognize that many alarm signals are actually not signals at all: they're just unpleasant *noise*, meaningless, like a car alarm that won't stop blapping. Obviously, deal with real alarms. But as for the ones that are exaggerated or entirely bogus, don't react to these alarms with alarm.

Accept that bad things sometimes happen, there are uncertainties, planes do occasionally crash, nice people get hit by drunk drivers. We just have to live with the fact that we can't dodge all the bullets. When you come to peace with this, you stop trying to control—out of alarm—the things you can't.

Keep helping your body feel less alarmed. I imagine my "inner iguana" lodged in the most ancient and fearful structures of the brainstem, and gently stroking its belly, soothing and settling it so it relaxes like a lizard on a warm rock. The same with my inner rat, or monkey, or caveman: continually softening and opening the body, breathing fully and letting go, sensing strength and resolve inside.

Alarms may clang, but your awareness and intentions are much larger—like the sky dwarfing clouds. In effect, alarms and fears are held in a space of fearlessness. You see this zig-zaggy, up-and-down world clearly—and you are at peace with it. Try to return to this open-hearted fearlessness again and again throughout your day.

39

Put Out Fires

In your heart, right now, you know if there are any vital matters that you're not dealing with: a harm or threat that's not being addressed, or a major lost opportunity. These are real alarms, and you need to listen to them.

For example, there could be unpaid bills on the verge of harming your credit score, a teenager who's increasingly disrespectful and defiant—or caught in the undertow of depressed mood—month after month without much exercise, a marriage that's unraveling thread by thread, abuse of alcohol or drugs, a co-worker who keeps undermining you, chronic overeating, or a nagging sense that there's something wrong with your health.

Quickly or slowly, "fires" like these will singe a life, and sometimes burn it to the ground.

If something's urgent—such as a clogged toilet, a letter from the IRS, a lump in an armpit—most people will get after it right away. But what if it's important-but-not-urgent—an issue or goal that you can always put off dealing with for one more day? It's easy to let these fires smolder—but in the end, they're the ones that usually cost you the most. You still know they're out there; they cast a shadow you can feel in your gut. And eventually their consequences always come home—sometimes during your last years, when you look back on your life and consider what you wish you'd done differently.

On the other hand, when you come to grips with important things, even if they're not urgent, that unease in the belly goes away. You feel good about yourself, doing what you can and making your life better.

How

Open to an intuition, a sense, of whatever you may have pushed to the back burner that truly needs attending. Consider your health, finances, relationships, well-being, and (if this is meaningful to you) spiritual life. Notice any reluctance to face significant unmet needs—it's normal to feel guilty or anxious about them—and see if you can release it.

Ask yourself: what gets in the way of you addressing important-but-not-urgent matters in a typical day? What do you finesse or manage each day but never solve once and for all? Or what do you keep postponing altogether?

What's not actually getting better no matter how much you hope it will?

Write down the name(s) of the important thing(s) you need to address. Tell a trusted person about this. Make it real for yourself that this issue *matters*. Face it. Keep facing it.

Bring to mind some of the many benefits that will come to you and others if you tackle this issue. Help them be vivid in your mind. See how your days will improve, how you'll sleep better, feel better, and love better. Open to your heart's longing for these benefits. Let the benefits call you, drawing you like honey does a bee.

Also bring to mind the short- and long-term costs to you and others of this issue continuing to smolder away. Be honest with yourself—willing to feel guilt, remorse, or shame in order to do the so honorable, so hard thing of looking squarely at these costs.

Feeling the benefits, and feeling the costs, make a choice: Are you going to put out this fire? Or wait another day?

When you choose to confront this issue, open to feeling good about that.

Then get to work. You don't need to have a complete plan to get started. Just know the first step or two—such as talking about the issue with a friend or therapist, gathering information (e.g., assessing a health concern), seeing a professional, doing one or more small positive actions each day, or getting structured support from others (e.g., a buddy to exercise with, a regular AA meeting). If you're stuck, you don't need a more perfect plan; you need to take imperfect action. The breakthrough will come when you *commit* to addressing an issue and then *structure* ongoing support and action toward that end.

If you find yourself procrastinating or getting bogged down, imagine that you are looking back on your life as you near its end. From that perspective, what will you be glad that you did?

40
Dream Big Dreams

Everyone has dreams: goals, big plans, reasons for living, contributions to others. They include starting a family, changing careers, going to college, deepening the emotionally and sensually intimate aspects of a long-term relationship, writing a book, living a spiritual practice, making art, getting a stoplight installed at a dangerous intersection, losing thirty pounds and keeping it off, saving the whales, saving the world.

Many of these dreams are rooted in childhood visions of what's possible. When the young elements are peeled away, what remains is often still deeply true for a person.

What are your own longings of the heart?

They could be quite concrete—and still be big dreams. Like everybody in the family doing their share of housework. Or finding a job that takes less than an hour to drive to. Or coming to peace with your mother or your son. Or planting roses. Or carving out half an hour a day for yourself.

Or they could be more far-reaching or lofty. Such as reducing bullying in schools or carbon dumping in the atmosphere, or pursuing your own spiritual awakening.

If you truly open to this question—*What are the dreams that matter to me?*—don't worry, you won't get caught up in silly stuff, such as wanting to get super rich and famous. Instead, you'll hear your soul speaking—your essence, your core, your deepest inner wisdom.

It's worth listening to what it says.

And then worth looking for ways—practical ones, grounded in daily life, that move you forward one real step at a time—to bring your dreams to life.

How

Find a quiet time and place, and ask yourself what you long for. Also imagine younger versions of yourself, and ask them what their dreams are.

Try to be open to what comes up, rather than dismissing it as unrealistic, too late, "selfish," or foolish. Perhaps write it down, even just a few words, or tell someone. If you like, make a collage of pictures (and maybe words) that represent your dream(s). And remember that your dreams aren't set in stone; you can let them breathe and change and grow.

Make room for your dreams in your thoughts and actions. Be their friend. Feel what it would be like if they came true, and how that would be good for you and others.

Without getting bogged down in details or obstructions, give thought to what you could do, in realistic ways, to move toward the fulfillment of your dreams. Look for the small things you can implement and build on each day. Perhaps go further and write down a plan for yourself, with—gulp—dates on it. Don't be daunted by things getting more real.

Then take action. If it helps, tell the truth about and keep a record of your actions—like writing down how much time you spend each day exercising, talking lovingly with your mate, or simply curled up relaxing. Focus on the things that will make the most difference; put the big rocks in the bucket first.

Throughout, let your dream live *you*. Feel into the wholesome heart of a dream—how it comes from deep within, how it is healthy, how it will serve you and others. Give yourself over to your dream.

Let your dream be a friend to you.

41
Be Generous

Giving—to others, to the world, to oneself—is deep in our nature as human beings.

When our mammalian ancestors first appeared, about two hundred million years ago, their capacities for bonding, emotion, and generosity were extraordinary evolutionary breakthroughs. Unlike reptiles and fish, mammals and birds care for their young, pair bond (sometimes for life), and usually form complex social groups organized around various kinds of cooperation. This takes more smarts than, say, a fish laying a swarm of eggs and swimming away—so in proportion to body weight, mammals and birds have bigger brains than reptiles and fish do.

When primates came along about sixty million years ago, there was another jump in brain size based on the "reproductive advantages" (love that phrase) of social abilities. The primate species that are the most relational—that have the most complex communications, grooming, alpha/

beta hierarchies, and so on—have the largest cortex (in proportion to weight).

Then early hominids emerged, starting to make stone tools about 2.5 million years ago. Since then, the brain has tripled in size, and much of this new cortex is devoted to interpersonal skills such as language, empathy, attachment to family and friends, romance, cooperative planning, and altruism. As the brain enlarged, a longer childhood was required to allow for its growth after birth and to make good use of its wonderful new capabilities. This necessitated more help from fathers to keep children and their mothers alive during the uniquely long juvenile phase of a human life, and more help from "the village it takes to raise a child." The bonding and nurturing of primate mothers—in a word, their *giving*—gradually evolved into romantic love, fathers caring for their young, friendship, and the larger web of affiliations that join humans together. Additionally, our ancestors bred mainly within their own band; bands that were better at the give-and-take of relationships and teamwork out-competed other bands for scarce resources, so the genes that built more socially intelligent brains proliferated into the human genome. In sum, giving, broadly defined, both enabled and drove the evolution of the brain over millions of years.

Consequently, we swim in a sea of generosity—of many daily acts of consideration, reciprocity, benevolence, compassion, kindness, helpfulness, warmth, appreciation, respect, patience, forbearance, and contribution—but like those proverbial fish, often don't realize we're wet. Because of the brain's negativity bias, moments of not-giving—one's own resentments and selfishness, and the withholding and unkindness of others—pop out with blazing headlines. Plus modern economies can make it seem like giving and getting is largely about making money—but that part of life is just a tiny fraction of the original and still vast "generosity economy," with its circular flows of freely given, unmonetized goods and services.

When you express your giving nature, it feels good for you, benefits others, prompts them to be good to you in turn, and adds one more lovely thread to the great tapestry of human generosity.

How

Take care of yourself. Don't give in ways that harm you or others (e.g., offering a blind eye to someone's alcoholism). Keep refueling yourself; it's easier to give when your own cup runneth over—or at least you're not running on empty.

Prime the pump of generosity. Be aware of things you are grateful for or glad about. Bring to mind a sense of already being full, so that you'll not feel deprived or emptied out if you give a little more.

Notice that giving is natural for you. You don't need to be a saint to be a giving person. Generosity comes in many forms, including heart, time, self-control, service, food, and money. From this perspective, consider how much you already give each day. Open to feeling good about yourself as a giver.

Give your full attention. Stay present with others minute after minute, staying with their topic or agenda. You may not like what they say, but you could still offer a receptive ear. (Especially important with a child or mate.) Then, when it's your turn, the other person will likely feel better about you taking the microphone.

Offer nonreactivity. Much of the time, interactions, relationships, and life altogether would go better if we did not add our comments, advice, or emotional reactions to a situation. Not-doing is sometimes the best gift.

Be helpful. For example, volunteer for a school, give money to a good cause, or increase your own housework or child care if your partner is doing more than you.

Do your own practice. One of your best contributions to others is to raise your own level of well-being and functioning. Whatever your practice is or could grow to be, do it with a whole heart, as a daily offering to whatever you hold sacred, to your family and friends, and to the widening world.

part five:

Be at Peace

42
Notice You're
All Right Right Now

To keep our ancestors alive, the brain evolved an ongoing internal trickle of unease. This little whisper of worry keeps you scanning your inner and outer worlds for signs of trouble.

This background of unsettledness and watchfulness is so automatic that you can forget it's there. So see if you can tune in to a tension, guarding, or bracing in your body. Or a vigilance about your environment or other people. Or a block against *completely* relaxing, letting down, letting go. Try to walk through an office or store that you know is safe without a molecule of wariness: it's really hard. Or try to sit at home for five minutes straight while feeling undefended, soft in your body, utterly comfortable in the moment as it is, at peace: this is impossible for most people.

The brain's default setting of apprehensiveness is a great way to keep a monkey looking over its shoulder for something about to pounce. But it's a crummy way to live. It wears down well-being, feeds anxiety and depression, and makes people play small in life.

And it's based on a lie.

In effect, that uneasiness in the background is continually whispering in your mental "ear": You're not safe, you're surrounded by threats, you can never afford to lower your guard.

But take a close look at *this* moment, right now. Probably, you are basically all right: no one is attacking you, you are not drowning, no bombs are falling, there is no crisis. It's not perfect, but you're okay.

By "right now," I mean *this* moment. When we go into the future, we worry and plan. When we go into the past, we resent and regret. Threads of fear are woven into the mental tapestries of past and future. Look again at the thin slice of time that is the *present*. In this moment: Are you basically okay? Is breathing okay? Is the heart beating? Is the mind working? The answers are almost certainly yes.

In daily life, it's possible to access this fundamental sense of all-rightness even while getting things done. You're not ignoring real threats or issues, or pretending that everything is perfect. It's not. But in the middle of everything, you can usually see that you're actually all right right now.

How?

Several times a day, notice that you're basically all right.

You may want more money or love, or simply ketchup for your French fries. Or want less pain, heartache, or rush hour traffic. All very reasonable. But meanwhile, underneath all the to-ing and fro-ing, you are okay. Underneath your desires and activities is an aliveness and an awareness that is doing fine this second.

There you are fixing dinner; notice that *"I'm all right right now,"* and perhaps say that softly in your mind. Or you're driving: *I'm all right right now.* Or you're talking with someone: *I'm all right right now.* Or doing e-mails or putting a child to bed: *I'm all right right now.*

Notice that, while feeling all right right now, you can still get things done and deal with problems. The fear that bad things will happen if you let yourself feel okay is unfounded; let this sink in. You do not need to fear feeling all right!

Sometimes you're really *not* all right. Maybe something terrible has happened, or your body is very disturbed, or your mind is very upset. Do what you can at these times to ride out the storm. But as soon as possible, notice that the core of your being is okay, like the quiet place fifty feet underwater, beneath a hurricane howling above the sea.

Noticing that you're actually all right right now is not laying a positive attitude over your life like a pretty veil. Instead, you are knowing a simple but profound fact: *In this moment I am all right.* You are sensing the truth in your body, deeper than fear, that it is breathing and living and okay. You are recognizing that your mind is functioning fine no matter how nutty and not-fine the contents swirling through it are.

Settling into this basic sense of okayness is a powerful way to build well-being and resources in your brain and being. You're taking a stand for the truth—and against the lies murmured by Mother Nature.

43

Honor Your Temperament

As hominids and early humans evolved over several million years while living in small bands, they developed a range of temperaments, with cautious, focused "turtles" at one end and adventurous, impulsive "jackrabbits" at the other end, with "tweeners" in the middle. Those bands that had a mixture of turtles, tweeners, and jackrabbits could adapt to changing conditions and outcompete bands that had just one type of temperament—the way a basketball team with nimble guards plus big forwards would beat teams with only guards or only forwards.

For similar reasons, we also evolved diversity in other aspects of temperament, including:

- Sociability—Some people are really extroverted, some are really introverted, and many are in the middle. In a general sense, with lots of exceptions in the details, extroverts are fed by social contact and drained by isolation; introverts are the opposite.

◄ Emotional inclinations—The ancient Greek model of the four personality types—sanguine (cheerful), choleric (prone to irritation), melancholic (tends to sadness), and phlegmatic (hard to move emotionally)—has at least a grain of truth to it.

Temperamental characteristics are innate, hard-wired into your DNA and thus your brain. Of course, they're just some of the tiles that make up the mosaic you are. Plus they're only *tendencies* whose expression is shaped by other parts of you (e.g., intelligence, warmheartedness), life experiences, and conscious intention. For example, I'm introverted but also love deep conversations (a typical therapist); so after a day of being with people, I get refueled by some time alone: reading, going for a run, and the like. Similarly, a person with a bit of a blue streak (i.e., melancholic) can internalize a soothing, encouraging sense of being cared about by others. Temperament is not destiny.

Different temperaments are a good fit with certain environments (e.g., situations, tasks, people) and not such a good fit with other ones. For instance, a sensitive infant would do well with an easygoing parent who is well-supported by his or her partner, but not so well with a single parent who is worn out and irritable; a jackrabbity first-grader will usually flourish in an experiential learning setting that's like a big pasture with firm fences, but will likely get many little corrections—which are stressful and dispiriting—in a classroom that's tightly controlled with lots of fine-motor table work; in a couple, things will go better if they find ways to give an introvert (like me) enough "cave" time and an extrovert (like my wife) enough connection, but worse if they don't.

When the fit between your temperament and an environment is not good, it's hard to function at your best—whether it was in school as a kid, or in an intimate relationship or at work today. Additionally, it's natural to feel at some level that there must be something wrong/weak/dumb/missing about you—which gets reinforced by any messages from the environment that, yep, the problem is with *you*, not it.

For example, a high degree of jackrabbititis now has its very own diagnosis—attention deficit/hyperactivity disorder (ADHD)—even though being jackrabbity has been wonderfully adaptive throughout most of the time humans and our hominid ancestors have lived on this planet. Further, people who are naturally wistful get told to cheer up and stop being mopey, introverts get told to go out and meet people, and turtles get told to stop being such sissies and jump into the deep end of the pool. This repeated sense that there's something not-right, not-optimal about oneself gradually sinks in and wears on a person's confidence, mood, and sense of worth.

But really, there's nothing wrong at all! We should each *honor* our temperament: accept it, see the things that are great about it, look for situations and relationships that play to its strengths, and take care of it when it's challenged (e.g., help a turtlish child get ready for anxiety-provoking transitions). In other words, work with nature, not against it.

How

Get a clear sense of your temperament. For example, compared to others of your age and gender, are you relatively:

- Distractible, impulsive, and stimulation-seeking? Or highly focused, judicious, and cautious?

- Interested in lots of social contact? Or in just a few good friends and considerable alone time?

- Cheerful, melancholic, easily irritated, or placid?

(It's fine to be in the middle of the range for these characteristics; then that would be what your temperament is.)

Think back on your childhood: did your temperament and your environments collide with each other significantly, leading either to criticism of you or simply a frustration inside that you couldn't be more successful academically or socially? As you consider this question, be kind to yourself. Remember that in childhood, it's the job of parents and teachers—who have many more options than kids do—to adapt environments as much as is possible and reasonable to the temperament of the child. Then consider the fit between you as an adult and your environments.

What are the strengths of your temperament? For example, people who are quick to anger are often quick to see injustice; children who are anxious are usually very conscientious; introverts have rich inner lives. What inclinations in your nature have been longing for more expression? Then consider the sorts of environments—such as occupations, romantic partners, settings, or schedules—that would support and draw on the strengths of your temperament. What could you do that's appropriate and skillful to nudge your current environments to play more to your strengths—or to get yourself into more suitable environments?

What are the needs or vulnerabilities in your temperament? For example, a spirited person needs a good deal of stimulation or life starts feeling like a thin soup; an extrovert needs a job with lots of interaction; a melancholic person is susceptible to feeling let down. Consider how you could address your needs and protect your vulnerabilities. For instance, if you're somewhat anxious by nature (I'd put myself in that boat), it's especially important to do what you can to create structure, predictability, and trust in your home and work.

Throughout these reflections, know that any issues have probably not been located in you or in your environments, but in the *fit* between you and them. Regarding yourself, have compassion for any stress or pain you may have experienced; appreciate the endurance and strength you've had in the times when you were the proverbial square peg in a round hole; challenge the expectations and other beliefs you've developed in collisions with your environments, such as a sense of inadequacy. Regarding your environments, consider them more as impersonal forces that may have been not good for you in some ways—while probably being suitable for at least some people—than as something inherently wrong or bad; consider if any forgiveness would be helpful to you here.

Last, appreciate the fact that no one has a perfect temperament. We're all pretty funky variations on the basic human model. Being able to see the humor in your temperament softens its edges and eases your interactions. For example, once as I was doing therapy, I squared my pad of paper to the edges of a small table. With a smile, my client teased me by reaching over to nudge the pad so it was now askew. We both laughed at my OCD-ish tendencies, which I'd disclosed in talking about her own. And then I squared the pad again because it bugged me so much!

44

Love Your Inner Child

As long as you've lived, your experiences have sifted down in your psyche, forming layers like the bands of colored rock in the Grand Canyon. The most fundamental layers were laid down in your childhood, when your brain was most impressionable.

Because of experience-dependent neuroplasticity, the things you felt, wanted, or believed as a child have been woven into your nervous system. For example, crying as an infant until someone came, joy at beginning to walk, fun with friends, feeling bad about yourself when scolded about schoolwork, power struggles with parents, wanting your body to be bigger/smaller/different in high school, wondering if anyone will like the real you, the bittersweet excitement of leaving home—whatever your own childhood was, experiences like these have sunk in to you and travel with you every day wherever you go.

Taken as a whole, these residues make up your inner child—which is not a silly cliché, but actually a large-scale system embedded in your brain that continually and powerfully influences your mood, sense of worth, expectations, and reactions. This child inside is at the core of who you are.

If you are embarrassed, ashamed, critical, controlling, squelching, pushy, or angry about this child, that will affect how you feel and how you act. Therefore, accepting the child parts within you, guiding them gently, and soaking your inner kid in cherishing nurturance will heal and feed the deepest layers of your psyche.

This inner child stuff can get conceptual, superficial, or merely sentimental. Instead, bring it down to the bone. Most childhoods are rocky, one way or another. As a kid, you probably felt hurt, were disappointed, felt like a loser, wanted recognition and love you didn't get, shelved some big dreams, and made decisions about yourself and life with the "logic" of a child. This is real. It had real effects. *And* you have a real chance today to be the strong, wise, and loving friend, coach, and yes, parent that you've always longed for.

How

Open to feeling cared *about* by someone. Next, move to feeling caring *toward* a friend, family member, or pet. Marinate in this sense of interest, support, and nurturance; let it fill your heart and mind. Then, staying grounded in the experience of caring, shift the target of this caring to *yourself*, especially yourself as a child.

Now, reflect back on your childhood as a whole, starting with your earliest memories. Stay with your *experience* of it, not the story line about it. What did it feel like to be a young child? To be in grade school? In high school? What were your happiest times? And most upsetting? What went well for you in your childhood—and badly? When did you feel really understood and supported—and not? What in you flourished in childhood—and what got bruised or wounded? What sort of kid were you—especially deep down? When did the best parts of you come out? What's become of them?

As much as you can, try to hold a sense of caring toward yourself while you engage these questions. Stay with your actual experience as a child, not critiquing it or justifying it, and definitely not shaming yourself for it. The vulnerable child inside everyone usually expects rejection, so it's afraid to show its teary, sniffly, snotty, whiny, needy, frightened, or angry face. Please don't push this child away. It wants to show itself but is afraid to. Make it safe for it to show itself to *you*.

Look for ways to bring the child inside you out to play. For example, my friend Leslie told me about moving to Wyoming and wandering in its extraordinary wilderness like a big kid, not trying to accomplish anything, feeling free and delighted. Take different routes to work; pick up (or return to) gardening, crafts, art, music, or a sport; quit being so darned serious and significant (this one's for me, too); goof off; play with your own kids; make messes; ask your inner child what he or she really wants to do. Don't be so constrained by routines and presumed limitations; remember what it felt like to be a kid on the first day of summer vacation; in the same way, the whole rest of your life stretches out before you: have fun with it!

Accept that you will never have a better childhood. Yes, assert yourself skillfully to get appropriate caring in your relationships. But also know the hard truth that it's on you, no one else, to be the main advocate, cheerleader, protector, and nurturer of the child inside—and the adult that kid has become. Keep both of them close to your heart.

45

Don't Throw Darts

Some physical and mental pain is inevitable. I remember being six and slipping on an icy sidewalk in Illinois and landing hard on my tailbone: ouch! Much later, in my fifties, when my mother passed away, there was a different kind of pain. To survive physically, you need a body that tells you it hurts when it's ill or injured. To flourish psychologically and in your relationships, you need a mind that sends different signals of distress—such as loneliness, anger, or fear—if you're rejected, mistreated, or threatened.

To use a metaphor from the Buddha, the unavoidable pains of life are its "first darts." But then we add insult to injury with our *reactions* to these darts. For example, you could react to a headache with anxiety that it might mean a brain tumor, or to being rejected in love with harsh self-criticism.

Further, it's common to have upsetting reactions when nothing bad has actually happened. For instance, you're flying in an airplane and everything's fine, but you're worried about it crashing. Or you go out on a date and it's fun, but then he/she doesn't call for a day and you feel let down.

Most absurdly, sometimes we react negatively to *positive* events. Perhaps someone complimented you, and you had feelings of unworthiness; or you've been offered an opportunity at work, and you obsess about whether you can handle it; or someone makes a bid for a deeper friendship, and you worry about being disappointing.

All these reactions are "second darts"—the ones we throw ourselves. They include overreacting to little things, holding grudges, justifying yourself, drowning in guilt after you've learned the lesson, dwelling on things long past, losing perspective, worrying about stuff you can't control, and mentally rehashing conversations.

Second darts vastly outnumber first darts. There you are, on the dartboard of life, bleeding mainly from self-inflicted wounds.

There are enough darts in life without adding your own!

How

Accept the inevitability of first darts. They hurt, but pain is the price of living. Try not to get offended by pain—as if it's an affront—or embarrassed about it, as if it's a personal failing.

When pain does come, hold it in a large space of awareness. In a traditional metaphor, imagine pouring a big spoon of salt into a cup of water and then drinking it: yuck. Next, imagine stirring that spoonful into a big bowl of clean water and drinking a cup: not so bad now. It's the same amount of salt—the same amount of physical or emotional pain—but now held and diluted in a larger context. Be aware of awareness: it's like the sky—pain passes through it like storm clouds, never tainting or harming awareness itself. See if you can let the pain be without reacting to it; this is a key aspect of an unconditional inner peace.

Observe second darts. They're often easier to see when others toss these darts at themselves—and then consider how you throw them at yourself. Gradually bring your recognition of second darts into the present moment, so you can see the inclination to throw them arise—and then catch them if possible before you stab yourself one more time.

A second dart will often trigger a cascade of mental reactions, like one boulder rolling down a mountainside setting off others in a chain reaction. To stop the landslide, start by relaxing your body as best you can. This will activate the calming, soothing parasympathetic wing of your nervous system and put the brakes on the fight-or-flight sympathetic wing.

Next, try to see more aspects of the situation that's troubled you, and more of your life these days altogether—especially the parts that are going fine. Because of the negativity bias, the brain narrows down and fixates on what's wrong, so you have to nudge it to widen its view to what's right. The bird's-eye, big picture view also deactivates the midline neural networks that do second-dart ruminating, and stimulates circuits on the side of your brain that can let things be as they are without reacting to them.

Don't put more logs on the fire. Don't look for more reasons to worry, criticize yourself, or feel mistreated. Don't get mad at yourself for getting mad at yourself!

When you throw second darts, you are the person you hurt most. The suffering—mild to severe—in second darts is truly unnecessary. As the saying goes, pain is inevitable, but suffering is optional.

46

Relax Anxiety
about Imperfection

"Imperfections" are all around, and they include: messes, dirty clothes, weeds, snarled traffic, rain during a picnic, wine stains on carpet; injury, illness, disability, pain; problems, issues, obstructions, losses—including with others; objects that are chipped, frayed, broken; mistakes, errors; confusion, lack of clarity; war, famine, poverty, oppression, injustice.

In a nutshell, an imperfection—as I mean it here—is a departure from a reasonable ideal or standard (e.g., dog poop on your shoe is not ideal, nor is the hunger that afflicts one in six people worldwide). These departures-from-ideal have costs, and it's reasonable to do what you can about them.

But we usually don't leave it at that: we get *anxious*— uneasy, nervous, troubled, stressed—about imperfection itself, rather than recognizing it as a normal, unavoidable, and widespread aspect of life. Instead of dealing with conditions as they are—weeds, injuries, conflicts with others—and just handling them, we get caught up in worrying about what they mean, grumbling, feeling deflated, becoming opinionated and judgmental, blaming ourselves and others, and feeling woe-is-me and yet again disappointed/mistreated/wronged.

These reactions to imperfection are major second darts (as described in the previous chapter). They make you feel a lot worse than you need to, create issues with others, and make it harder to take skillful action.

Here's the alternative: let the broken cup be a broken cup without adding judgment, resistance, blaming, or worry to it.

How

Make appropriate efforts to improve things, but realize the impossibility of perfecting anything; even the most sophisticated technology cannot produce a *perfectly* flat table. You just can't perfect your personality, thoughts, or behavior; trying to do so is like trying to polish Jell-O. Nor can you perfect others or the world. Open to this fact: you cannot perfectly protect your loved ones, or eliminate all of your own health risks, or prevent people from doing stupid things. At first this opening could feel poignant or sad, but then you'll likely feel a breath of fresh air, a freedom, and a surge of energy to do the things you *can* now that you're not undermined by the hopelessness of making anything perfect.

We need standards and ideals—from the strike zone in baseball to the aspirations in the world's sacred teachings—but we also need to hold these lightly. Otherwise, they'll take on a life of their own in your mind, like petty tyrants barking orders: "You *must* do this, it's *bad* to do that." Watch out for righteousness, for self-important moralizing insistence on your own view of how you, others, and the world should operate. Know if you have tendencies toward perfectionism; I do, and I've got to be careful about them or I become a difficult person to live with or work for, as well as unhappy inside.

Further, many things transcend fixed standards. For example, could there ever be such a thing as a perfect rose or a perfect child? In these cases, anxiety about imperfection is absurd—which applies to trying to perfect your body, career, relationships, family, business, or spiritual practice. Nurture these, help them blossom, but give up on perfecting them.

Most fundamentally, all conditions, no matter how imperfect, are perfectly what they are: the bed is perfectly unmade, the milk is perfectly spilt. I don't mean morally or pragmatically "perfect"—as if it would be just perfect to tear a shirt or start a war—but that all conditions are utterly, thoroughly themselves. In this sense, whatever is the case—from dirty diapers and everyday hassles to cancer and plane crashes—is the result in this instant of the perfect unfolding of the entire universe. Try to see that unfolding as a vast, objective process in which our personal wishes are as consequential for it as a patch of foam is for the Pacific Ocean. In this light, perfection and imperfection vanish as meaningful distinctions. There are only things in their own right, in and of themselves, without our labels of good or bad, beautiful or ugly, perfect or not. Then there is no anxiety about imperfection; there is only simplicity, directness, engagement—and peace.

47
Respond, Don't React

To simplify the explanation of a complex journey, your brain evolved in three stages:

- Reptile, fish—Brainstem, focused on *avoiding* harm

- Mammal, bird—Limbic system, focused on *approaching* rewards

- Human—Cortex, focused on *attaching* to "us"

Whether a person is a psychopathic criminal or a saint, these three systems—avoiding, approaching, attaching—are always at work. The key is whether they're at work in a good way—one that promotes happiness and benefit for yourself and others—or a bad one that leads to suffering and harm.

What's happening in your brain when these systems are functioning in a good way—when you're feeling fine, or even "in the zone," self-actualizing, or spiritually blossoming? The answer is important, because then you can deliberately stimulate and thus gradually strengthen the neural networks that underpin these good states of mind.

When you are not rattled by life—in other words, when you're feeling safe, fulfilled, and loved—your brain's avoiding system is *calm* (in a word), the approaching system is *contented*, and the attaching system is *caring*. This is the *responsive* mode of the brain, which delights, soothes, and refuels you. It's your home base, the resting state of your brain, which is real good news.

Now here's the bad news: we also evolved hair-trigger mechanisms that activate the fight-or-flight *reactive* mode of the brain and drive us from home when we're stressed, whether from the snarl of a leopard a million years ago or a frown across a dinner table today. When you feel even subtly threatened, the avoiding system shifts gears into *hatred* (to use a strong, traditional word that encompasses the full range of fear and anger); when you're at all frustrated or dissatisfied, the approaching system tips into *greed* (ranging from longing to intense obsession or addiction); and when you feel even mildly rejected or devalued, the attaching system moves into *heartache* (from soft hurt to awful feelings of abandonment, worthlessness, or loneliness).

The reactive mode was a great way to keep our ancestors alive in the wild, and it's useful today in urgent situations. But it's lousy for long-term health and happiness. Each time your brain lights up its reactive mode—each time you feel pressured, worried, irritated, disappointed, let down, left out, or blue—this triggers the same stress machinery that evolved to escape charging lions or lethal aggression from other primates or humans.

Most reactive mode activations—pushing you off home base—are mild to moderate. But they're frequent and relentless in the lives of most people, leading to a kind of inner homelessness that can become the new normal. Besides feeling crummy, this is bad for your physical health, since chronic stress leads to a weakened immune system, disturbed digestion, dysregulated hormones, and increased risk of heart attack or stroke. Stress wears on your mental health as well, bringing: pessimism, blue mood, and depression; heightened anxiety and irritability; "learned helplessness"; hunkering down, playing it safe, dreaming smaller dreams; clutching tighter to "us" and fearing and even exploiting or attacking "them."

So—let's come home.

How

This book is full of practices for calm, contentment, and caring—and there are lots of other good methods in *Buddha's Brain* and in the writings and teachings of many people. So I'm not going to focus here on any particular way to activate the responsive mode of your brain. The key point is to make it a *priority* to feel good, to look for every-day opportunities for peacefulness, happiness, and love, and to take all the little moments you can to marinate in well-being.

Because here's more good news: Each time you rest in your brain's responsive mode, it gets easier to come home to it again. That's because "neurons that fire together, wire together": stimulating the neural substrates of calm, contentment, and caring *strengthens* them. This also makes it harder to be driven from home; it's like lengthening the keel of your mental sailboat so that no matter how hard the winds of life blow, you stay upright, not capsized, and keep on heading toward the lighthouse of your dreams.

What's wonderful about this is that the *ends* of the journey of life—being peaceful, happy, and loved/loving— become the *means* of getting there. In effect—in a traditional phrase—you are taking the fruit as the path. Instead of having to scratch and claw your way up the mountain top, you come home to the meadow that is the natural state of your brain—nourishing, expanding, and beautifying it every minute you spend there. For as they say in Tibet, "if you take care of the minutes, the years will take care of themselves."

48
Don't Take It Personally

Here's an updated parable from the ancient Taoist teacher Chuang-Tzu: Imagine that you are floating in a canoe on a slow-moving river, having a Sunday picnic with a friend. Suddenly there is a loud thump on the side of the canoe, and it rolls over. You come up sputtering, and what do you see? Somebody has snuck up on your canoe, flipped it over for a joke, and is laughing at you. How do you feel?

Okay. Now imagine the exact same situation again: the picnic in a canoe, loud thump, dumped into the river, coming up sputtering, and what do you see? A large submerged log has drifted downstream and bumped into your canoe. This time, how do you feel?

The facts are the same in each case: cold and wet, picnic ruined. But when you think you've been targeted *personally*, you probably feel worse. The thing is, most of what bumps into us in life—including emotional reactions from others, traffic jams, illness, or mistreatment at work—is like an impersonal log put in motion by ten thousand causes upstream.

Say a friend is surprisingly critical toward you. It hurts, for sure, and you'll want to address the situation, from talking about it with the friend to disengaging from the relationship.

But also consider what may have caused that person to bump into you, such as misinterpretations of your actions; health problems, pain, worries or anger about things unrelated to you; temperament, personality, childhood experiences; the effects of culture, economy, or world events; and causes back upstream in time, like how his or her parents were raised.

Recognize the humbling yet wonderful truth: most of the time, we are bit players in other people's dramas.

When you look at things this way, you naturally get calmer, put situations in context, and don't get so caught up in me-myself-and-I. Then you feel better, plus more clearheaded about what to do.

How

To begin with, have compassion for yourself. Getting smacked by a log is a drag. Also take appropriate action. Keep an eye out for logs heading your way, try to reduce their impact, and repair your "boat"—relationship, health, finances, career—as best you can. And maybe think about finding a new river!

Additionally:

- ❧ Notice when you start to take something personally. Be mindful of what that feels like—and also what it feels like to relax the sense of being personally targeted.

- ❧ Be careful about making assumptions about the intentions of others. Maybe they didn't do it "on purpose." Or maybe there was one not-so-good purpose aimed at you that was mixed up with a dozen other purposes.

- ❧ Reflect on some of the ten thousand causes upstream. Ask yourself: What else could be in play here? What's going on inside the other person's mind and life? What's the bigger picture?

- ❧ Beware getting caught up in your "case" about other people, driven by an inner prosecutor that keeps pounding on all the ways they're wrong, spoke badly, acted unfairly, picked on you, really really harmed you, made you suffer, etc., etc. It's good to see others clearly, and there's a place for moral judgment—but case-making is a kind of obsessing that makes you feel worse and more likely to overreact and create an even bigger problem.

- ❧ Try to have compassion for the other people. They're probably not all that happy, either. Your compassion for them will not weaken you or let them off the moral hook; actually, it will make you feel better.

⚜ If you like, explore relaxing the sense of self—of *I* and *me* and *mine*—in general. For example, notice the difference between "there are sounds" and "I am hearing," or between "there are thoughts" and "I am thinking." Observe how the sense of self ebbs and flows, typically increasing when there are problems to solve and decreasing as you experience calm and well-being. This fluidity of "me" in the mind correlates with dynamic and fleeting activations in the brain; self-related thoughts are constructed all over the brain, tumbling and jostling with other thoughts, unrelated to self, in the neural substrates of the stream of consciousness (Gilliham and Farah 2005; Legrand and Ruby 2009). Appreciate that "I" is more of a process than an ability: a "selfing." Enjoy the ease and openness that emerge as the sense of self recedes.

And—really soak up the sense of strength and peacefulness that comes from taking life less personally.

49
Feel Safer

Consider these two mistakes:

1. You think there's a tiger in the bushes, but actually there isn't one.

2. You think there's no tiger in the bushes, but actually one is about to pounce.

Most of us make the first mistake much more often than the second one, for several reasons:

- Evolution has given us an anxious brain. In order to survive and pass on genes, it's better to make the first mistake a thousand times rather than make the second mistake even once; the cost of the first mistake is fear for no reason, but the cost of the second mistake could be death.

- This general tendency in the human brain is exacerbated by temperament—some people are naturally more anxious than others—and by life experiences (e.g., growing up in a dangerous neighborhood, experiencing trauma).

- Saturated with media, news about murders, disasters, economic turmoil, and horrible things happening to other people sifts into your mind— even though your own local situation is probably much less dangerous.

- In ways that have been repeated throughout history, political groups try to gain or hold onto power by exaggerating apparent threats.

In effect, most of us have a kind of paper tiger paranoia.

Certainly, it's important to recognize the real tigers in life, which come in many shapes and sizes: perhaps an impending layoff at work, a cough that won't go away, a teenager growing pot in the attic, a friend or coworker who keeps letting you down, or the health risks of smoking cigarettes. Try to notice any tendencies to overlook or minimize tigers, and do what you can about the ones that are real.

Meanwhile, try to recognize the ways that you—like most people—routinely overestimate threats while underestimating the resources inside you and around you. In effect, *most of us feel much less safe than we actually are.* The unfortunate results include unpleasant feelings of worry and anxiety; not hunkering down and reaching as high and wide as one might; stress-related illnesses; less capacity to be patient or generous with others; and a greater tendency to be snappish or angry (the engine of most aggression is fear). It's not good to feel like it's always Threat Level Orange!

Instead, feel as safe as you reasonably can.

How?

Some people get understandably nervous about feeling safer—since that's when you lower your guard, and things can really smack you. If this applies to you, adapt the suggestions here to your own needs, go at your own pace, and perhaps talk with a friend or counselor.

Further, there is no perfect safety in this life. Each of us will face disease, old age, and death, as well as lesser but still painful experiences. And many of us must deal with unsafe conditions in the community, workplace, or home.

This said, consider in your heart of hearts whether you deserve to feel safer: whether you are more braced against life, more guarded, more cautious, more anxious, more frozen, more appeasing, more rigid, or more prickly than you truly need to be.

If the answer is yes, here are some ways to help yourself feel safer, so that a growing internal sense of calm and confidence will increasingly match the true reality of the people and settings around you:

- Bring to mind the sense of being with someone who cares about you.

- Recall a time you felt strong.

- Recognize that you are in a protected setting.

- Mentally list some of the resources inside and around you that you could draw on to deal with what life throws you.

- Take a few breaths with l-o-n-g exhalations, and relax.

- All the while, keep helping yourself feel more sheltered, more supported, more capable, and safer. And less vigilant, tense, or fearful.

- Become more aware of what it's like to feel safer, and let those good feelings sink in, so you can remember them in your body and find your way back to them in the future.

You can practice with the methods above in general ways, such as in the morning plus several times a day if you tend to be fearful. Also try them in specific, unsettling situations, like before speaking up in a meeting, driving in traffic, getting on an airplane, or working through a sticky issue with your partner. Being on your own side, *help* yourself feel at least a little safer, and maybe a lot. Then see what happens. And take it in, again and again, if in fact, as they usually do, things turn out all right.

And there is really no tiger in the bushes after all.

50

Fill the Hole in Your Heart

As we grow up and then move through adulthood, we all have normal needs for safety, fulfillment, and love. For example, children need to feel secure, adolescents need a growing sense of autonomy, and young adults need to feel attractive and worthy of romantic love. When these needs are met by various "supplies"—such as the caring of a parent, the trust of a teacher, the love of a mate—the positive experiences that result then sink in to implicit memory to become resources for well-being, self-regulation, resilience, self-worth, and skillful action. This is how healthy psychological development is supposed to work.

But it doesn't always go this way, does it? In the lives of most people (me included)—even without any kind of significant mistreatment, trauma, or abuse—the incoming stream of supplies has sometimes been a thin soup: perhaps your parents were busy caring for a sick sibling or preoccupied with their own needs and conflicts, or you moved a lot as a kid and had a hard time connecting with peers, or high school was more than the usual social nightmare, or potential lovers were uninterested, or jobs have been frustrating and dispiriting, or . . . in other words, a typical life.

The shortages in a thin soup leave *lacks*, deficits, in key internal resources. For example, I was a year or two younger than my classmates, which led to a shortage of inclusion and valuing from them, which in turn led to a lack of confidence and sense of worth in groups that persisted into adulthood. The absence of good things naturally has consequences.

And so does the presence of bad ones. When blows land—when there is loss, mistreatment, rejection, abandonment, misfortune, or trauma—they leave *wounds*. Sometimes these heal fully, usually due to a rich soup of supplies. But often they don't, leaving pockets of unresolved emotional pain like pus beneath a scab, while also affecting a person's functioning like a lifelong limp from a broken ankle that never fully mended.

A lack or a wound will leave "a hole in your heart"—which gets even deeper when the two exacerbate each other. For example, I vividly recall the time a popular girl in high school really put me down; it was a minor blow in its own right, but my years of social isolation had left me with no shields or shock absorbers to buffer its impact, which was to make me feel awful about myself for a long time afterward.

So what can you do about your own lacks and wounds? You've got them; we all do. Life alone can be healing: time passes, you put more distance each year between yourself and the train wreck of your early childhood, seventh grade, first great love, last job, last marriage, or whatever, and you move on to a better place. But this essentially passive process of being carried by life is often not enough for a real healing: it's too slow, or it doesn't reach down deep enough, or key ingredients are missing.

Then you need to *actively* fill the hole in your heart.

How

It's fundamentally simple: you *take in good experiences* (chapter 2) that are specifically aimed at your own lacks and wounds. It's like being a sailor with scurvy: you need vitamin C—not vitamin E—for what ails you. For example, I felt both protected and independent as a child, so experiences of safety and autonomy as an adult—while valuable in their own right—did not address my issue: I needed the particular healing balm of experiences of inclusion and respect in groups.

Consequently, it's important to know what your own vitamin C is (and sometimes a person needs more than one kind). Perhaps you already know, but if not, here are some questions to help you find out: When your lacks or wounds developed, what would have made all the difference in the world? What do you long for today? What conditions help you feel truly happy—and bring out the best in you? What sort of experiences feed and soothe a deep hunger inside?

More specifically, here's a summary of some healing experiences—"vitamins"—targeted for particular lacks and wounds, organized in terms of the three motivational systems in your brain:

	Lack or Wound	**Vitamin**
Avoiding Harms	Weakness, helplessness	Strength, efficacy
	Alarm, anxiety	Safety, security
	Resentment, anger	Compassion for oneself and others
Approaching Rewards	Frustration, disappointment	Satisfaction, fulfillment
	Sadness, discontentment, "blues"	Gladness, gratitude
Attaching to "Us"	Not seen, rejected, left out	Attunement, inclusion
	Inadequacy, shame	Recognition, acknowledgement
	Abandonment, feeling unloved	Friendship, love

Once you have some clarity about the psychological vitamins you need, the rest is straightforward:

- Look for these vitamins in your life; also do what you can to create or increase them. For example, I keep my eyes open for opportunities to feel liked and appreciated in groups, plus I prod myself to join groups to create those opportunities.

- The vitamin you need is an *experience*, not an event. The point of situations in which you are protected, successful, or appreciated is to *feel* safe, fulfilled, and worthy. This is hopeful, because it gives you many ways to evoke key experiences. For example, if feeling that you matter to others is what will fill the hole in your heart, you could: look for signs that others wish you well, whether it's the smile of someone making you a sandwich in a deli, the encouragement of a coworker, or a lover's hug; think about the many people in your life today or in your past who like and appreciate you; ask your partner to be affectionate (and be open to hearing what would help him or her to do this); try to develop more relationships with people who are by nature warm and supportive.

- Be willing to get a slice of the pie if the alternative is no pie at all. For instance, if you finish a tough project at work, focus on the sense of accomplishment for everything you got done rather than on a few loose ends; if a friend is warm and loyal, open to feeling cared about even if what you really want is romantic love.

* Then, using the second and third steps of *taking in the good* (chapter 2), really savor the positive experience for ten or more seconds in a row while sensing that it is sinking down into you, giving you what you've always needed.

* Have confidence that every time you do this, you'll be wiring resources into your brain. When I started this practice myself, in my early twenties, the hole in my heart looked like the construction site for a skyscraper. But I just kept tossing a few bricks—a few experiences of feeling included—into that hole every day. One brick alone will make little difference, but brick after brick, day after day, year after year, you really can fill even a *very* big hole in your heart!

51
Let Go

I've done a lot of rock climbing, so I know firsthand the importance sometimes of *not* letting go! This applies to other things as well: keeping hold of a child's hand while crossing the street, staying true to your ethics in a tricky situation, or sustaining attention to your breath while meditating.

On the other hand, think of all the stuff—both physical and nonphysical—we cling to that creates problems for us and others: clutter in the home, "shoulds," rigid opinions, resentments, regrets, status, guilt, resistance to the facts on the ground, needing to be one-up with others, the past, people who are gone, bad habits, hopeless guests, unrewarding relationships, and so on.

Letting go can mean several things: releasing pain; dropping thoughts, words, and deeds that cause suffering and harm; yielding rather than breaking; surrendering to the way it is, like it or not; allowing each moment to pass away without trying to hold on to it; accepting the permanently impermanent nature of existence; and relaxing the sense of self and opening out into the wider world.

Living in this way is relaxing, decreases hassles and conflicts, reduces stress, improves mood and well-being, and grounds you in reality as it is. And it's a key element, if you like, of spiritual practice. To quote Ajahn Chah, a major Buddhist teacher who lived in Thailand:

If you let go a little, you will have a little happiness.

If you let go a lot, you will have a lot of happiness.

If you let go completely, you will be completely happy.

How

Appreciate the wisdom of letting go, and notice any resistance to it: perhaps it seems weak to you, foolish, or against the culture of your gender or personal background. For example, I remember talking with my friend John years ago about a woman he'd been pursuing who'd made it clear she wasn't interested, and he felt frustrated and hurt. I said maybe he should surrender and move on—to which John replied fiercely, "I don't *do* surrender." It took him a while to get past his belief that surrender—acceptance, letting go—meant you were wimping out. (All ended happily with us getting drunk together and him throwing up on my shoe—which *I* then had to surrender to!) It takes strength to let go, and fortitude, character, and insight. When you let go, you're like a supple and resilient willow tree that bends before the storm, still here in the morning—rather than a stiff oak that ends up broken and toppled over.

Be aware of the letting go that happens naturally all day long such as, releasing objects from your hands, hanging up the phone, pushing send on an e-mail, moving from one thought or feeling to another in your mind, saying bye to a friend, shifting plans, using the bathroom, changing a TV channel, or emptying the trash. Notice that letting go is all right, that you keep on going, that it's necessary and beneficial. Become more comfortable with letting go.

Consciously let go of tension in your body. Exhale long and slowly, activating the relaxing parasympathetic nervous system. Let go of holding in your belly, shoulders, jaws, and eyes.

Clear out possessions you don't use or need. Let in how great it feels to finally have some room in your closet, drawers, or garage.

Pick a dumb idea you've held on to way too long—one for me would be that I have to do things perfectly or there'll be a disaster. Practice dropping this idea and replacing it with better ones (like for me: "Nobody is perfect and that's okay").

Pick a grievance, grudge, or resentment—and resolve to move on. This does not necessarily mean letting other people off the moral hook, just that you are letting yourself off the hot plate of staying upset about whatever happened. If feelings such as hurt still come up about the issue, be aware of them, be kind to yourself about them, and then gently encourage them out the door.

Letting go of painful emotions is a big subject, with lots of resources for you in books such as *Focusing*, by Eugene Gendlin, or *What We May Be*, by Piero Ferrucci. Here's a summary of methods I like: relax your body; imagine that the feelings are flowing out of you like water; vent in a letter you'll never send, or out loud someplace appropriate; get things off your chest with a good friend; take in positive feelings to soothe and gradually replace the painful ones.

In general, let things be pleasant without grasping after them; let things be unpleasant without resisting them; let things be neutral without prodding them to get pleasant. Letting go undoes the craving and clinging that lead to suffering and harm.

Let go of who you used to be. Let yourself learn, grow, and therefore change.

Let go of each moment as it disappears beneath your feet. It's gone as soon as you're aware of it, like a snowflake melting as soon as you see its shape. You can afford to abide as letting go because of the miracle—which no scientist fully understands—that the next moment continually emerges as the previous one vanishes, all within the infinitely tiny duration of Now.

52
Love

We all want to *receive* love. But maybe it comes in a form you don't want—perhaps someone offers romantic love but that's not what you're looking for—or it doesn't come at all. Then there is heartache and helplessness; you can't make others love you if they won't.

Definitely, do what you can to get the love you need. But the practice here is about *expressing* love, distinct from receiving it. When you focus on the love you give rather than the love you get, then you're at cause rather than at effect; you're the cue ball, not the eight ball—which supports your sense of efficacy and confidence, as well as your mood. And it's enlightened self-interest: the best way to get love is to give it; even if it's still not returned, your love will likely improve the relationship, and help calm any troubled waters.

Sometimes people worry that being loving will make them vulnerable or drained. But actually, you can see in

216

your own experience that love itself doesn't do this: it protects and nurtures you when you give it. While you're loving, don't you feel uplifted and stronger?

That's because love is deep in human nature, literally woven into our DNA. As our ancestors evolved, the seeds of love in primates and hominids—such as mother-child attachment, pair bonding, communication skills, and teamwork—aided survival, so the genes that promoted these characteristics were passed on. A positive cycle developed: As "the village it takes to raise a child" evolved and grew stronger, the period of vulnerable childhood could become longer, so the brain evolved to become larger in order to make use of that longer childhood—and thereby developed more capacities for love. The brain has roughly tripled in size since hominids began making stone tools about 2.5 million years ago, and much of this new neural real estate is devoted to love and related capabilities.

We need to give love to be healthy and whole. If you bottle up your love, you bottle up your whole being. Love is like water: it needs to flow; otherwise, it backs up on itself and gets stagnant and smelly. Look at the faces of some people who are very loving: they're beautiful, aren't they? Being loving heals old wounds inside and opens untapped reservoirs of energy and talent. It's also a profound path of awakening, playing a central role in all of the world's major religious traditions.

The world *needs* your love. Those you live with and work with need it, plus your family and friends, people near and far, and this whole battered planet. Never

underestimate the ripples spreading out from just one loving word, thought, or deed!

How

Love is as natural as breathing, yet like the breath, it can
get constricted. Sometimes you may need to release it,
strengthen it, and help it flow more freely with methods
like these:

- Bring to mind the sense of being with people
  who care about you, and then open to *feeling*
  cared about. Let this feeling fill you, warming
  your heart, softening your face. Sink into this
  experience. It's okay if opposite thoughts arise
  (e.g., rejection); observe them for a moment, and
  then return to feeling cared about—which will
  warm up the neural circuits of being loving
  yourself.

- Sense into the area around your heart, and think
  of things that evoke heartfelt feelings, such as
  gratitude, compassion, or kindness. To bring
  harmony to the tiny changes in the interval
  between heartbeats, breathe so that your inhala-
  tions and exhalations are about the same length,
  since inhaling speeds up the heart rate and
  exhaling slows it down. The heart has more than
  a metaphorical link to love; the cardiovascular
  and nervous systems lace together in your body

like lovers' fingers, and practices like these will nurture wholehearted well-being in you and greater warmth for others.

- ❦ Strengthen these loving feelings with soft thoughts toward others, such as *I wish you well. May you not be in pain. May you be at peace. May you live with ease.* If you feel upset with someone, you can include these reactions in your awareness while also extending loving thoughts like *I'm angry with you and won't let you hurt me again—and I still hope you find true happiness, and I still wish you well.*

There is a notion that being intentional about love makes it false or at least second-rate. But actually, loving at will is doubly loving: the love you find is authentic, and the effort to call it forth is deeply caring.

To love is to have *courage*, whose root meaning comes from the word "heart." I've been in a lot of hairy situations in the mountains, yet I was a lot more scared just before I told my first real girlfriend that I loved her. It takes courage to give love that may not be returned, to love while knowing you'll inevitably be separated one day from everything you love, to go all in with love and hold nothing back.

Sometimes I ask myself, *Am I brave enough to love?* Each day gives me, and gives you, many chances to love.

If you choose just one thing from this book of practices, let it be love.

References

Baumeister, R., E. Bratlavsky, C. Finkenauer, and K. Vohs. 2001. Bad is stronger than good. *Review of General Psychology* 5:323-370.

Berridge, K. C. and T. E. Robinson. 1998. What is the role of dopamine in reward: hedonic impact, reward learning, or incentive salience? Brain Research Reviews 28:309-369.

Davidson, R. J. 2004. Well-being and affective style: Neural substrates and biobehavioural correlates. *Philosophical Transactions of the Royal Society* 359:1395–1411.

Dusek, J. A., H. H. Out, A. L. Wohlhueter, M. Bhasin, L. F. Zerbini, M. G. Joseph, H. Benson, and T. A. Libermann. 2008. Genomic counter-stress changes induced by the relaxation response. *PLoS ONE* 3:e2576.

Farb, N. A. S., Z. V. Segal, H. Mayberg, J. Bean, D. McKeon, Z. Fatima, and A. Anderson. 2007. Attending to the present: Mindfulness meditation reveals distinct neural modes of self-reference. *Social Cognitive and Affective Neuroscience* 2:313–322.

Gillihan, S. J. and M. J. Farah. 2005. Is self special? A critical review of evidence from experimental psychology and cognitive neuroscience. *Psychological Bulletin*, 131:76-97.

Goetz, J. L., D. Keltner, and E. Simon-Thomas. 2010. Compassion: An evolutionary analysis and empirical review. *Psychological Bulletin* 136:351-374.

Gottman, J. 1995. *Why Marriages Succeed or Fail: And How You Can Make Yours Last.* New York: Simon and Schuster.

Gu, Y., J. W. Nieves, Y. Stern, J. A. Luchsinger, and N. Scarmeas. 2010. Food combination and Alzheimer disease risk: A protective diet. *Archives of Neurology* 67:699-706.

Guerrero-Beltran, C. E., M. Calderon-Oliver, J. Pedraza-Chaverri, and Y. I. Chirino. 2010. Protective effect of sulforaphane against oxidative stress: Recent advances. *Experimental and Toxicologic Pathology.* December 1. Epub ahead of print.

James, W. 1890. *The Principles of Psychology* (vol. 1). New York: Henry Holt.

Kabat-Zinn, J. 2003. Mindfulness-Based Interventions in Context: Past, Present, and Future. *Clinical Psychology: Science and Practice* 10: 144-156.

Kabat-Zinn, J., Lipworth, L., and Burney, R. 1985. The clinical use of mindfulness meditation for the self-regulation of chronic pain. *Journal of Behavioral Medicine* 8:163-190.

Krikorian, R., M. D. Shidler, T. A. Nash, W. Kalt, M. R. Vinqvist-Tymchuk, B. Shukitt-Hale, and J. A. Joseph. 2010. Blueberry supplementation improves memory in older adults. *Journal of Agriculture and Food Chemistry* 58:3996-4000.

Kristal-Boneh, E., M. Raifel, P. Froom, and J. Ribak. 1995. Heart rate variability in health and disease. *Scandinavian Journal of Work, Environment, and Health* 21:85–95.

Lazar, S., C. Kerr, R. Wasserman, J. Gray, D. Greve, M. Treadway, M. McGarvey, B. Quinn, J. Dusek, H. Benson, S. Rauch, C.

Moore, and B. Fischl. 2005. Meditation experience is associated with increased cortical thickness. *NeuroReport* 16:1893–1897.

Leary, M., E. Tate, C. Adams, A. Allen, and J. Hancock. 2007. Self-compassion and reactions to unpleasant self-relevant events: The implications of treating oneself kindly. *Journal of Personality* 92:887–904.

Legrand, D. and P. Ruby. 2009. What is self-specific? Theoretical investigation and critical review of neuroimaging results. *Psychological Review* 116:252-282.

Maguire, E., D. Gadian, I. Johnsrude, C. Good, J. Ashburner, R. Frackowiak, and C. Frith. 2000. Navigation-related structural change in the hippocampi of taxi drivers. *Proceedings of the National Academy of Sciences* 97:4398–4403.

Maier, S. F. and L. R. Watkins. 1998. Cytokines for psychologists: Implications of bidirectional immune-to-brain communication for understanding behavior, mood, and cognition. *Psychological Review* 105:83-107.

McCullough, M. E., S. D. Kilpatrick, R. A. Emmons, and D. B. Larson. 2001. Is gratitude a moral affect? *Psychological Bulletin* 127:249-266.

Neff, K. D. 2009. Self-Compassion. In M. R. Leary and R. H. Hoyle, eds., *Handbook of Individual Differences in Social Behavior* (pp. 561-573). New York: Guilford Press.

Niedenthal, P. 2007. Embodying emotion. *Science* 316:1002.

Nimitphong, H. and M. F. Holick. 2011. Vitamin D, neurocognitive functioning and immunocompetence. *Current Opinion in Clinical Nutrition and Metabolic Care* 14:7-14.

Pecina, S, K. S. Smith, and K. C. Berridge. 2006. Hedonic hot spots in the brain. *The Neuroscientist* 12:500-511.

Rondanelli, M., A. Giacosa, A. Opizzi, C. Pelucchi, C. La Vecchia, G. Montorfano, M. Negroni, B. Berra, P. Politi, and A. M.

Rizzo. 2010. Effect of omega-3 fatty acids supplementation on depressive symptoms and on health-related quality of life in the treatment of elderly women with depression: A double-blind, placebo-controlled, randomized clinical trial. *Journal of the American College of Nutrition* 29:55-64.

Rozin, P. and E. B. Royzman. 2001. Negativity bias, negativity dominance, and contagion. *Personality and Social Psychology Review* 5:296-320.

Schiepers, O. J. G., M. C. Wichers, and M. Maes. 2005. Cytokines and major depression. *Progress in Neuro-Pharmacology & Biological Psychiatry* 29:210-217.

Seligman, M. E. P. 1972. Learned helplessness. *Annual Review of Medicine* 23:407-412.

Skarupski, K. A., C. Tangney, H. Li, B. Ouyang, D. A. Evans, and M. C. Morris. 2010. Longitudinal association of vitamin B_6, folate, and vitamin B_{12} with depressive symptoms among older adults over time. *The American Journal of Clinical Nutrition* 92:330-335.

Stein, D. J., V. Ives-Deliperi, and K. G. F. Thomas. 2008. Psychobiology of mindfulness. *CNS Spectrum* 13:752-756.

 **Rick Hanson, PhD,** is a neuropsychologist and author of *Buddha's Brain*, which has been published in twenty languages. He is founder of the Wellspring Institute for Neuroscience and Contemplative Wisdom and an Affiliate of the Greater Good Science Center at the University of California, Berkeley. He has been invited to lecture at Oxford, Stanford, and Harvard, and teaches in meditation centers worldwide. He lives with his family in the greater San Francisco Bay Area. For many resources freely offered, visit www.rickhanson.net.

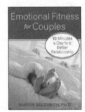